Frederick James Crowest

The Great Tone-Poets

Being short memoirs of the greater musical composers

Frederick James Crowest

The Great Tone-Poets

Being short memoirs of the greater musical composers

ISBN/EAN: 9783337084479

Printed in Europe, USA, Canada, Australia, Japan

Cover: Foto ©Thomas Meinert / pixelio.de

More available books at **www.hansebooks.com**

THE

GREAT TONE-POETS:

BEING

Short Memoirs of the Greater Musical Composers.

BY

F. CROWEST.

LONDON:
RICHARD BENTLEY AND SON,
Publishers in Ordinary to Her Majesty.
1874.

PREFACE.

Two years ago I was invited to contribute to the "Et Cetera" Magazine, a series of Articles on the great Composers, to be written in a style that would interest the general reader, as well as the musician. Some of this series duly appeared; and this would have been their first and last appearance, had I not, upon the decease of the Magazine, received many requests from teachers of music to complete and re-publish the series.

Those articles that have appeared in the Magazine have been revised, and in some parts re-written. New ones have been added; while to each biography has been affixed a table with the dates of the principal incidents in the composer's life, for the use of those engaged in examinations.

In the course of my task I have had recourse to, and made extracts from, many works, all of which I think I have acknowledged, but to the authors of which I here desire to express my indebtedness.

F. CROWEST.

November, 1874.

TO THE

REV. HARRY JONES, M.A.

RECTOR OF ST. GEORGE'S IN THE EAST,

AND FOR FIFTEEN YEARS

INCUMBENT OF ST. LUKE'S, BERWICK STREET,

THIS BOOK

is gratefully inscribed by

THE AUTHOR.

CONTENTS.

BACH. 1685—1750.

INTRODUCTION. Birth. Surroundings. Not a Prodigy. An Orphan. Under the Ohrdruff Organist. Avidity for Learning. A Coveted Treasure. Working by Moonlight. Alone in the World. A Chorister at Lüneburg. Listening to Reinken. Trudging to Zell. Without Funds. A Slice of Luck. Violinist in Court Band. Organist at Arnstadt Church. Vivaldi's Concertos. Progress in Organ-playing. Before the Consistory. Organist at Mühlhausen. The Terms of his Appointment. Court Organist and Conductor at Weimar. A Prodigious Organist. Pitted with Marchand. At Cöthen. Death of his Wife. Second Marriage. Before Reinken in Hamburg. An Embrace. Music Director at the Thomas-Schule, Leipzig. In Private Life. Before Frederick the Great. Music Parties at Home. Kindness to Young Aspirants. Harpsichord Knights. His Pupils. At the Keyboard. Trying Organs. His own Tuner. Bach in a Rage. His religion. His Works. Organ Preludes and Fugues. Organ Sonatas. The "Partite Diverse." The "Well-tempered Clavecin." The "French Suites." The "English Suites." The "Christmas Oratorio." Masses. The "Johannes-Passion." The "Matthäus-Passion." A Doubtful "Passion Music." Gloomy Times. Loss of Sight. The Last Work. A Transient Joy. Death from Fever. His Burial - - - 1

HANDEL. 1685—1759.

Introduction. Birth and Parentage. Early Signs of Talent. George to be a Lawyer. Musical Cravings Checked. Secret Music. Visit to his Brother. In the Private Chapel. An Irresistible Temptation. The Duke of Saxe-Weissenfel. Under Zackau. A Wonderful Pupil. A Young Composer. A Stir in Berlin. At Hamburg. Violinist in the Opera Orchestra. An Unexpected Conductor. Duel with Matthison. "Almira." In Italy. Enthusiastic Reception. Chapel-master to the Duke of Brunswick. "Rinaldo." Queen Anne. The "Utrecht." Music. Settled in London. George I. The "Water-music" Ruse. "The Passion" Oratorio. The Duke of Chandos and his Chapel. The "Chandos Anthems." The Royal Academy of Music. "Esther." "Acis and Galatea." The "Harmonious Blacksmith." Break-up of the Italian Opera Company. Handel turns *Impressario*. The Haymarket House. Failure of Numerous Operas. Sacred Music instead. Opera Abandoned, from Ill-health and Bankruptcy. Organ Concertos. "Saul." "Israel in Egypt." A Failure. "Ode on St. Cecilia's Day." "L'Allegro, Il Penseroso." An Ungrateful Public. Off for Dublin. Interviewed at Chester. Singing at "Soite." Reception in Dublin. First Performance of the "Messiah." The Ladies and their Hoops. The "Messiah." "Samson." Its first Performance. The "Dettingen" Music. "Joseph." "Belshazzar." "Hercules." "Deborah." The "Occasional" Oratorio. "Judas Maccabæus." "Joshua." "Solomon." "Theodoro." Handel's Favourite Piece. "Jephtha." Total Blindness. A Pitiful Sight. Lingering on. A last charitable Performance. Death - - - - - - 32

GLÜCK. 1714—1787.

Introduction. Birth. Poor parents. Early instruction in music. Loses his father. A wandering minstrel. Generous friends. Studying in earnest. In Italy. Under Martini. "Artaxerxes," his first opera. "Ipermnestra." "Demetrio." Lord Middlesex and Glück. Glück in London. "La Caduta del Giganti" at the Haymarket. Unsuccessful works. Packing up. In Vienna. Invited to Róme. More operas. Florence and Calzabigi. Reformed opera. "Orfeo." "Alceste." A Knight of the Golden Spur. Visits Paris. "Iphigénie." A slovenly Orchestra. A successful performance. Marie Antoinette and her Court. Vestris and his *chacone*. A squabble at Sophie Arnould's. An abrupt ending. A French "Alcestis." Madame Dubarry and her clique. Piccini invited to Paris. Glück and Piccini wars. "Armida" and its composer's impressions of it. Piccini's "Armida" and its success. The feud fiercer. "Iphigenia in Tauris." Its success. Piccini's rival work. Iphigenia in Champagne. A drunken prima donna. "The Danaïdes" libretto refused. In retirement. Visits from the Nobility. Glück's Will. Afflicted with paralysis. Death - - - - - - - 80

HAYDN. 1732—1809.

Introduction. Birth. Parentage and Home. A Painter's Subject. A good Timeist. A praiseworthy Schoolmaster. Secured by Reuter. A Young Shaker. Beautiful Cherries. A pattern for Students. His first Mass. A Purchase. Studying under difficulties. His voice breaks. Circumstances. Turns lacky to old Porporo. A Street Serenade. Curtz, the Clown. "The Devil on Two Sticks." Fiction Music. Censured Music. A party at Count Mortzin's. Haydn and Prince Esterhazy. A scene at Eisenstadt. A pitiful Figure. Engaged by Prince Esterhazy. Daily habits. Madame Haydn and Mdlle. Boselli. Haydn at home. At work. A sketchbook. The "Seven Words." Death of Prince Esterhazy. P. P. Saloman. Engagement for London. A parting. Prophetic words. In London. At a civic dinner. At Dr. Herschel's. A worthy Mus. Doc. An obstinate Captain. The twelve grand Symphonies. A farewell concert. Profitable stay. Gumpendorff. "The Creation." Its First performance. Its Reception in Paris. "The Seasons." An opinion. A life's work ended. In retirement. Amusement. Sinking health. A kind act. Glimmering embers. Disturbed times. A brave old man. "God Preserve the Emperor." Death - - - - - - - 104

MOZART. 1756—1791.

Introduction. Birth. Early promise. A child composer. A young quartetist. Profitable children. First appearance in Vienna. At home with the Empress. A varied treasure-trove.

At the Court of St. James's. Early compositions. In Holland. At Vienna again. More compositions. An imperial commission. Journey to Italy. Matins at the Sistine Chapel. Defying injunctions. "La Finta Giardinera" at Munich. In search for a patron. Constance Weber. "Idomeneo." "Die Entführung." Marriage. Composer and librettist at loggerheads. A hasty promise and hazardous performance. Called to account. A Mozart score at Sotheby's. "Figaro." Its reception. At Count Thun's. The Prague beauties. "Don Giovanni." Bowls and work. Symphonies. Instrumentation of Handel's "Messiah." "Cosi fan Tutte." A last journey. At home. Redeeming a promise. Incessant work. Numerous compostions. "Die Zaüberflöte." An ungrateful wretch. A mysterious visit. "The Requiem." Presentiments. Illness. His last days. A death-bed quartet. Death and Burial - 139.

BEETHOVEN. 1770—1827.

Introduction. Birth. A wretched home. An inhuman father. Pfeiffer, his first teacher. New masters. Talent at eleven years of age. His position at seventeen. Mozart's prediction. Death of his mother. A distasteful occupation. The Breunings. Visit to Vienna. A pupil of Haydn's. A princely patron. At the Lichnowski Palace. Earliest compositions. First public appearance. Deafness. The "Eroica" Symphony. "Fidelio" produced. Its indifferent reception. His "matured period." The "Egmont" music. The C minor and "Pastorale" Symphonies. The Mass in C. A private hearing. New style of Church music. An abrupt parting. A concert for the Fatherland. Death of his brother Carl. New burdens. Lawsuit with the "Queen of Night." An ungrateful nephew. The "Eighth" Symphony. The Mass in D major. The "Choral" Symphony. A journey to the Asylum for his nephew. An unkind brother. On a sick bed. Inflammation of the Lungs. Dropsy. A death-bed gathering. Beethoven's last moments. His death. Nature's requiem - 168.

SPOHR. 1784—1859.

Introduction. Birth and parentage. Natural talent. His first violin. Music in the kitchen. Under Dufour. In the Court orchestra at Brunswick. New Masters. Out in the world. Trudging from Hamburg. A ducal patron. First

Contents. xiii

artistic tour. Recognition under difficulties. Another tour. Director of ducal orchestra at Gotha. Marries Dorette Scheidler. Tour with his wife. "Alruna." Trip to Russia. Director of An der Wien Theatre. An unexpected patron. Von Tost as a house-furnisher. "Faust." "The Liberation" cantata. At Frankfort theatre. "Zemire and Azor." In London. A "Philharmonic" concert. D flat symphony. Concert at the Argyle Rooms. In Paris. Director of Court orchestra at Cassel. "Jessonda." "Der Berg Geist." "The Last Judgment." Its first performance in England. The C minor Symphony. "The Alchymist." The "Power of Sound" Symphony. Death of his Wife. "Calvary." Second Marriage. The "Historical Symphony." At the Norwich Festival. "Babylon" at Exeter Hall. "The Crusaders." A last look at Mendelssohn. The "Seasons" Symphony. In London. Guest of Dr. Farre. Pensioned from Cassel Orchestra. Unable to compose An Accident. Last public appearance. A Change. Slow decay. Death. - - - - - 190

WEBER. 1786–1826.

Introduction. Birth. In the track of the *troupe*. Food for the imagination. Early lessons. Budding genius. Youthful operas. A change. Vienna life. A gallant roysterer. An acquaintance of title. Under Vogler. Conductor of the Breslau Opera-house. Opposition. "Rubezahl." A close shave. Altered times. As private secretary. Imprisoned for debt. "Abu Hassan." A gratifying reception. A tour. "Sylvana" at Berlin. Music director at the Prague Theatre. Compositions. Caroline Brandt. Kapellmeister to the King of Saxony. Italian opposition. Marriage. The E flat Mass. The "Jubilee" Cantata and other works. "Preciosa." "Der Freischütz." Its reception. "Euryanthe." Beethoven and "Euryanthe." Inward disease. Exhausted. Offer from Charles Kemble. "Oberon." A sorrowful parting. A presentiment. At Sir George Smart's house. Covent Garden Theatre on the first night of "Oberon." The beginning of the end. An unsuccessful concert. A last letter. The evening before death. Weber's last words. Death. Home at last - - - - - - - 224

ROSSINI. 1792—1868.

Introduction. Birth. His parents. Their means of living. Rossini on the stage at seven years of age. His singing. A wandering horn-player. Under Tesei. The Countess Perticari. Under Mattei. A pattern student. A successful opera. The *donna* with but one good note. Numerous operas. "Tancredi." Its success. Malanotte and the "Aria del Rizi.". "L'Italiana in Algeria." Composing in bed. Lazy Rossini. "L'Aureliano in Palmira." Velluti and his singing. Barbaja. At the San Carlo. "Elizabetta." Rossini and the Sicilian's wife. "Il Barbiere di Siviglia." At work on the score. The first performance a *fiasco*. The effect on Rossini. Sigismundi and the "Otello" score. Mdlle. Colbran and Davide. "La Cenerentola." The air "Miei Rampolli." "La Gazza Ladra." Performed in London. Ebers and Lord Mount Edgcumbe. Smaller operas. "Mosè in Egitto." Its original *caste*. The prayer, "To Thee, Great Lord." Performed in London. "La Donna del Lago." A signal failure. Flight from Milan. Marries Mdlle. Colbran. "Zelmira" in Vienna. "Semiramide." Its first performance at the Fenice. In London. Presented to George IV. Auber on his pianoplaying. In Paris. Works for the Paris opera. "Guglielmo Tell." Its first representation. Fétis on its music. The overture. The original *caste*. An ended career. In retirement. The "Stabat Mater." The "Messe Solennelle." Illness and Death. His reforms in music - - - 256

SCHUBERT. 1797—1828.

Introduction. Birth. At his father's school. Signs of musical promise. An early acquaintance. A clever harpsichord player. Under Holzer. A chorister in the Imperial chapel. Early compositions, including "Hagar's Lament." A school assistant. A Mass in F, and other compositions. A prolific eriod. Various Masses. The "Mignon" songs. The "Songs from Ossian." The "Erl-King." The "Wanderer." The B flat and "tragic" Symphonies. Dramatic music. Schubert's inner life. Extracts from his diary. His appearance at twenty. At work. As a visitor. Favourite resorts and pastimes. Music master to Prince Esterhazy. In love with the prince's daughter. Unrequited love. Piano Sonatas. Overtures in the "Italian" style. The Sixth Symphony.

Contents. xv

His apartments. "Lazarus." Increasing fame. "Alfonso and Estrella." The B minor Symphony. Beethoven and Schubert. An interview. Beethoven and Schubert's music. Drinking to Death. "Rosamunde" music. Mr. Grove and Schubert's music. A labour of love. "Fierrabras." "Der Häusliche Krieg." The Müller-lieder. The A minor piano Sonata. Sad change in health. Causes. Extracts from diary. An Octet and three Quartets. The conductorship at the Kärnthnertor. A risky experiment. Two string Quartets. Trio in E flat. Recognition at last. Sowing the seeds of disease. The Seventh Symphony. The E flat Mass. "Miriam's Battle Song." Illness. Death and funeral. His works - - - - - - - - - 288

MENDELSSOHN. 1809—1847.

Introduction. Birth and circumstances. A loving teacher. A pleasant introduction. Mendelssohn at eleven years of age. Composer and conductor. A wonderful extemporist. A promising youth for the profession. The "Wedding of Camacho," and its scurvy treatment by the press. The "Midsummer Night's Dream" Overture. A student at the Berlin University. The "Calm Sea and Prosperous Voyage" Overture. Bach's "Matthew-Passion" revived. An old German theorist at home. Visits England. The guest of Moscheles. Successful *début* at the Philharmonic Concert. Tour in Scotland. His impressions. Visits Italy. An idol of society. The "Walpurgis Night" music. The "Reformation" and "Italian" symphonies. In Switzerland. Paris again. Once again in London. Espied at a Philharmonic rehearsal. At home in Berlin. Election for the Singakademie conductorship. Mendelssohn defeated. Made director of Düsseldorf Theatre. The "Lieder ohne Worte." At the Cologne Festival of 1835. A scene at the rehearsal. A charming memento of his visit. Conductor of the Gewandhaus Concerts. An unexpected bereavement. "St. Paul." Cecilia Renaud. "St. Paul" at Exeter Hall. Its composer in the gallery. "Lobgesang." The "Antigone" music. Another bereavement. Leipzig Conservatoire. Again in London. An unparalleled cadenza. Seeking repose. The "Elijah." Its first performance. A royal token. Overworked. Fanny Mendelssohn's death. Shattered health. Unfinished works. The "Night Song." Death and burial - - - - - - - - - 315

SCHUMANN. 1810—1856.

Introduction. Birth. Schumann the publisher. Robert at School. In the playground. First music lessons. Attempts at composition. Early tone-pictures. Death of his father. Designed for a lawyer. Studying for it. Sorry progress. The vacation at Leipzig. Excursion to Italy. Rudel, the guardian, and Robert's finances. Growing love for music. A successful *début*. Hatred for jurisprudence. A lovable letter. An unexpected request. Another profession. Under Wieck. A zealous student. An infernal machine. His hand crippled. Under Dorn for theory. A symptom of his malady. The "Neue Zeitschrift für Music." Its earliest contributors. A love affair. Clara Wieck. In Vienna. The "Storm-period" works. A transition. A Doctor of Philosophy. Marriage. Retirement and work. A year of song. Schumann and the "Futurists." The B flat Symphony. The D minor Symphony. The E flat major Quintet. "Paradise and the Peri." Visit to Russia. The "Music Journal" given up. The C major Symphony. The "Third Period." "Genevieve." The "Manfred" music. Its first performance in England. The "Faust" music. Director at Düsseldorf. Unfitness for the post. The E flat Symphony. The "Julius Cæsar" Overture. Numerous other works. Progress of his mental malady. Increasing symptoms. Attempted suicide. In the Endenich Asylum. Death - 347

THE GREAT TONE-POETS.

Bach.

However carefully we search among the great tone-poets, we fail to find another whose name, as a musical genius, excites the same feelings as that of Johann Sebastian Bach. For Bach has not yet become popular, and to but very few musical people does he appear in the light of a friend. The majority regard him with strong suspicion; they do not take to him; they have a kind of fear of approaching too near to him.

Why is this? First and foremost because they are not sufficiently acquainted with his music, and derive the opinions they express concerning it, more from hearsay than from any practical knowledge they have of it. Now, if this mode of judging poor Bach be allowed to continue, instead of being looked upon as a poet he will be regarded as a musical fiend, which certainly is not what the great master deserves.

If those who are interested in music would but hear his works frequently and judge for themselves, they would soon see how wrong an impression has gone abroad concerning them. Bach has been left too much to musicians and too little to the people, and till this is remedied the monstrous ideas held about him will never disappear. Go to Bach's works. They are difficult, but they contain forms, beauties, and an individuality of colouring not to be met with in any other composer.

Johann Sebastian Bach was born on the 21st of March, 1685, at Eisenbach, a pretty little town of Thuringia, where his father was Court organist. His childhood was spent amidst the lovely scenery surrounding his home, not far distant from the well-known Wartburg, where Luther so long lived and worked, and where years before the Minnesänger fought their celebrated battle of song.

Very little, however, is known of Sebastian's earliest years, beyond the fact that, unlike many other great composers, he gave no evidence of being an infant wonder, and that John Ambrosius Bach, his father, did not seek to make him one. But he had the benefit of growing up in an atmosphere, so to speak, of good music, and one that, besides, was deeply imbued with the fervour of religion—the religion Martin Luther had taught, which was then fast spreading throughout Germany, and was soon to find so glorious an exponent in Bach himself. Sebastian was not ten years old when he was left an orphan and dependent on his brother, John Christopher Bach, organist of Ohrdruff, to whom he owed his first lessons in singing and clavichord playing. His genius soon budded forth, and he mastered, with surprising ease, the exercises that were given him to study. Concerning his avidity for learning at this time, an interesting anecdote relates that Sebastian so soon played his exercises by heart, that his constant readiness for new ones became toilsome to his teacher, and this the pupil did not fail to observe. In his brother's possession was a book from which he himself studied, and which contained pieces by the most eminent clavichord composers of the day. These the ambitious Sebastian was bent upon securing, and plodding away at by himself. His request for the book, however, instead of being complied with, produced only a decisive "No!" Probably the young scholar felt hurt at this, but consoled himself with the thought of obtaining the coveted treasure surreptitiously, if he could not do so by fair means. It was locked up in a cupboard enclosed with rails, between which a small hand could pass, and Sebastian soon availed himself of an opportunity of abstracting it, replacing the book after having stealthily copied a small part of it. But this was slow work, for as he was allowed no candle, and could only work when unperceived by his brother in the evening, almost nothing was done but on moonlight nights; so that nearly six months elapsed before the laborious task was completed. Then, alas, "love's labour was lost;" the brother discovered what had been going on; demanded the copy which had cost the poor boy so much pains to obtain, and locked it up so safely that Sebastian saw it no more until after Johann Christopher's death.

This event restored to him the coveted score, but deprived him of his home and instructor, and left him at the age of fourteen alone in the wide world to shift for himself and to push his way in it as he best could. At this time he had a fine soprano voice, and advised perhaps, by some of his late brother's friends, or it may be, his own fear of want urging him on, he one day trudged off to Lüneburg in company with an old school-fellow named Eidman, and succeeded in obtaining a situation there as chorister in the choir of St. Michael's school. This opening contributed greatly to his advancement, for, besides continuing his musical studies, he received a fair education in the school, and had occasional opportunities afforded of hearing good and new music. These the ambitious boy failed not to grasp at, and even frequently to make the journey on foot to Hamburg, where, at St. Catherine's church, he could listen to the wonderful organ-playing of the famous Reinken. Sometimes he would jog on to Zell, a still greater distance, to hear the duke's prize band of French musicians, who played little besides French music in the French style. However, the band was a novelty in those parts, and Bach learned a great deal while listening to the performances.

A story is told of his having, on one of those journeys, made a longer stay at Hamburg than his funds allowed —which, probably, was not unfrequently the case, though without the same result as on this particular occasion—when, as he was tramping back to Lüneburg he stopped outside an inn on the road, attracted by such tempting odours from the kitchen as made him realize most keenly the disproportion between his money and his appetite. As he stood, probably working out in his mind some difficult mathematical problem of the relative value of pudding to pence, some one seems to have noticed him, and to have taken pity on his forlorn condition; for, hearing a window open, he looked up and saw two herrings' heads thrown out into the road. The boy picked them up, and to his great surprise, discovered a Danish ducat concealed in each. With this godsend he was able, not only to satisfy his craving appetite there and then, but to provide for a journey on some other day.

But the good times at the Lüneburg school came to an end. Sebastian lost his fine treble voice, and was of no further use in the choir. They, however, kept the orphan boy in the school till he was eighteen, at which age he secured a situation as violinist in the Duke of Saxe-Weimar's Court band. This appointment could not have been either very lucrative, or one that young Bach cared much for, as in the same year (1703) we find him exchanging it for that of organist to the new church at Arnstadt. This was more to his taste, for he much preferred organ-playing to fiddling, and there was also a fine new organ at Arnstadt, on which man had never yet played. But the duties were heavy, and the pay extremely light, a not unfrequent case with organists in the present day. He had to play on Sunday mornings from eight to ten o'clock, at the service on Mondays, and again on Thursdays from seven to nine; and for this he received the enormous salary of about nine pounds per annum in English money!

Duly installed in his post, he set to work at his own

improvement, and made diligent efforts to advance himself in his art. For this end he provided himself with the works of the greatest composers of his time, and for days and nights pored over their pages, taking note of their different styles, carefully observing the rules they followed, what they allowed, and what was avoided, till, aided by his wonderful talent, he acquired sufficient knowledge to set down his own ideas. A book that proved of much service to him was "Vivaldi's Concertos for the Violin." He had heard them much praised, and conceived the idea of arranging them for his clavichord, a task from which he learnt much, besides the advantage he derived from having the treasure, when once set, always within reach.

His organ-playing at this time began to excite much attention both far and near. Frequently his fancy carried him too far in playing the Church Service, and the congregation omitted to join in at the proper place. This brought upon him the censure of the elders of the church, and shortly after he was again summoned before the consistory, for extending a leave of absence of four weeks to more than three months, the whole of which he spent in the town of Lübeck, going daily to the church of St. Mary's, to hear the celebrated Dietrich Buxtehude's playing on the organ. This misdeed, and the "extraordinary variations" which he introduced into the chorales, made the elders very wroth; but Bach cared little for that. His sole aim was to improve the condition of church music; but this seemed impossible at Arnstadt, and he abided the time when he could effect his improvements elsewhere.

He had not to wait long. The organist of St. Blasius' church at Mühlhausen died, and the situation was offered to Bach, on the following terms, as the deeds of appointment show: "eighty-five guldens, three malters of corn, two clafters of wood, one of beech, and one of other wood, and six schock of small firewood, to be brought to his door." In less than a year, however, during which time Bach married, the St. Blasius' organistship was given up for that of Court organist at Weimar; a post which Duke Wilhelm Ernest had offered him.

Here was a sphere of work more to his liking, with a wider scope for the exercise of his art, and where he was surrounded with more intellectual and appreciative people. He remained at Weimar till the close of 1717, a period of nearly nine years, during the latter part of which, in recognition of the increasing greatness of Bach's reputation, the duke had elevated him to the post of conductor of the Court orchestra. In this capacity he had to compose the music for the band, and thus many of his earliest works were produced; on some of which his great fame rests.

As an organist and clavichord player, Bach's fame was at this time prodigious. One Jean Louis Marchand, a Frenchman, was then generally considered unrivalled for his wonderful playing, but those who knew Bach felt certain that he was the greater performer of the two. Marchand was a conceited fellow, and it is said that his pretentious manners had so disgusted the King of France that he banished him from his Court. After travelling from country to country, Marchand found a resting-place at Dresden, but here his offensive airs led Volumier, the director of the Dresden orchestra, to play off a practical joke on him. At one of the royal concerts, Marchand was to play some variations on a French air, his performance of which elicited great admiration and applause. But Bach also had been invited, and to please the king, Volumier brought him forward to play next. After a brief prelude, he took up the air that Marchand had just played, and extemporized twelve variations on the same theme, with such skill and grandeur, that Marchand's fine playing was quite eclipsed. Thereupon some angry words ensued, and Bach and Marchand were matched to play together on the following day, at the rooms of Field-Marshal Count Fleming. At the hour appointed Bach was there, and many of the Court, and connoisseurs too—but no Marchand appeared! An hour's waiting having failed to bring him, they sent to his lodgings, and discovered that he had taken the early morning express, and vanished from Dresden at break of day!

On Bach's return to Weimar, he was offered by a great *dilettante*, Prince Leopold of Anhalt-Cöthen, the appointment of chapel-master, which he accepted, much to the regret of those among whom he had for so long lived and worked. This new post he filled for nearly six years, when, on account of the insufficiency of the salary to meet the wants of his increasing family, he left Anhalt, and sought a livelihood elsewhere. The prince, however, was very kind to Bach; always took him with him on his journeys, and once or twice stood sponsor to his children. It was whilst he was away with the prince on one of these journeys that Bach lost his wife. He had left her quite well, but an unexpected illness carried her off, too suddenly for any news to reach him, even of her burial. Eighteen months after, he married again, and by this second marriage had thirteen children.

The first place towards which Bach turned his steps in search of a new situation was Hamburg, where the St. Jacobskirche organistship was vacant. But the appointment was not given to Bach, much to the surprise of all, except those who sold it. Erdmann Neumeister, the eloquent pastor of the church, took the matter up from the pulpit, and, in his next sermon, remarked, "If an angel had come down from heaven and played divinely, and wished to become organist, but had had no money, he might just as well have flown away again." While staying in this city, Bach met old Reinken, to whose wonderful playing he was so fond of listening when a boy. Reinken was verging on his hundredth year, and was filled with wonder and excitement when he heard Bach's playing. He took for his subject a theme that was a favourite with Reinken before he had grown too old to play,—the chorale, "An Wasserflüssen Babylon," and, for half-an-hour, improvised grand variations upon it. When Bach had finished, the veteran organist embraced him, exclaiming, "I thought this art had died out; now that I see it still lives, I can depart in peace."

Failing to obtain at Hamburg what he was in search of, Bach had to turn his face elsewhere. In this year (1723) Kuhnau, the director of the music at St. Thomas's School, Leipzig, died, and Bach was appointed in his stead. The duties were not light. He had to take his turn, every third week, at inspecting the schools; to teach the first class music; to arrange the music for four churches, the choirs of which were composed of the students of the Thomas-Schule; to attend funerals and superintend the singing of the chorales; to keep stock of the music and instruments in the school; and lastly, to play the grand organ in St. Thomas's church. The pay he received was about thirteen pounds per annum; another two pounds for wood and candles, interest on a legacy, amounting to three shillings and tenpence, a free lodging, and a fee of three shillings on the occasions of weddings, funerals, and the like. Bach held this post till the year of his death, a period of twenty-seven years. During this length of time he composed the chief of those great works which for a century and a half have so worthily perpetuated a name that will be more and more revered as these grand conceptions become more universally known.

Let us now glance at the private life and character of this marvellous man, when in the full vigour of life he settled down in the flourishing city of Leipzig.

If he was great as an artist, equally great was he as a man. He was an affectionate husband, a good father, and trusty friend. His modest and unassuming manners, his kindly and sympathetic disposition, his openheartedness and benevolence, made him beloved and esteemed wherever he went. Amongst his friends he numbered kings and princes, as well as men of humble rank. He was a man that never travelled; had he done so, he might have been richer and have made more friends than he did, or as some one says, "he might have gained the admiration of the whole world."

It was a long time before he could be induced to appear before Frederick the Great at Potsdam. After repeated invitations he at length undertook the journey, and one evening, just as the usual concert before supper was about to begin, a list of the day's arrivals was handed to the king. With his flute already in his hand— for this accomplished king always joined in the orchestra —he glanced down the list, and with much agitation turned to the assembled musicians and said, "Gentlemen, old Bach has come." He was immediately sent for to the palace, and introduced in his travelling dress, so great was the king's anxiety to see him. The concert that evening was given up, and the royal flute-player devoted himself to Bach. He led him through the palace apartments, and made him play on his Silbermann piano-fortes, of which he had collected no less than fifteen. The great master's playing amazed not only the king but the musicians who attended him. A masterly performance of a six-part fugue brought forth exclamations such as "There is only one Bach! only one Bach!" Anxious to hear his organ-playing, which he had heard so much praised, the king took him the following day to all the principal organs in Potsdam, and Bach's wonderful skill on this instrument increased the astonishment and admiration of his royal host. When Bach returned home, he sent the king a memento of this pleasant visit, in the shape of a musical offering, the principal theme of which had been supplied by Frederick himself.

Bach's humble apartments in the Thomas-Schule were always hospitably open to all lovers and connoisseurs of music; and frequently quartett parties were got together there. On these occasions the old man much enjoyed himself. He would take the viola part, and look well after the other strings besides. It afforded him pleasure also to accompany a song on the piano, or to give amusement by exhibiting his skill as a contrapuntist. If any who were present had brought new compositions—and not a few of these were brought by aspiring votaries for "Father Bach's" advice and criticism—he would amuse them by turning their trio into a quartett, or, sweeping away the top parts, would extemporize a totally different composition from the same bass. Then he would carefully look through the piece, and in the kindest manner point out its defects, or what was good in the score. Bach had many pupils, several of whom became eminent musicians. He might have had many more but that he was too conscientious, and would not take a pupil who had not, in his opinion, the ability to think musically.

A vigorous rule of his was that his pupils should

Bach. 15

compose entirely from the mind, and away from an instrument; and those who wished to do otherwise he used to ridicule as "Harpsichord Knights." Oh! that this were the case with all teachers and pupils. What an enormous decrease there would be in our music supply, and what a purer atmosphere we should then live and work in. How few of those who in the present day call themselves composers would deserve the name were they lodged, say in the Sahara Desert, or anywhere in fact where they could not get at an instrument, and had no other resources than pen, ink, and paper, and their genius! Then, again, if money and interest were thrown aside, and talent left to fight its own way, Art would certainly be better served; we should, with these eyesores removed, hear more of the truly-gifted musician than the charlatan, and be on the right road for men like grand old Bach, men who, if not as great, would at least work conscientiously as he did. Time tells an inevitable tale of the effusions of a musical quack; yet it is hard, in these civilized times, for a really gifted man, without money or interest to push him forward, to have no better consolation than that to sleep upon. But to return to Bach and his pupils.

He was equally as strict at the instrument as at composing. First, there was one position of the hand on the keyboard which he insisted upon, by which the fingers were always properly over the keys. Then there came months of five finger exercises to gain execution and touch. To make these the more interesting he would sometimes turn them into easy pieces, without at all losing their important purpose. Then he would compose for his pupils, pieces with turns, shakes, and other ornaments, after which he took them on to larger work, always classical, first playing the piece over, and leaving them with the command, "So it must sound."

Bach was a good judge of organs and organists, and was frequently sought for to act in this capacity. Forkel, in his life of him, says, "He could as little prevail upon himself to praise a bad instrument, as a bad organist. He was, therefore, very severe, but always just, in his trials of organs. As he was perfectly acquainted with the construction of the instrument, he could not be in any case deceived. The first thing he did was to draw out all the stops, and to play with the full organ. He used to say in jest, that he must first of all know, whether the instrument had good lungs. He then proceeded to examine the single parts. His justice to the organ-builders went so far, that, when he found the work really good, and the sum agreed upon too small, so that the builder would evidently have been a loser by his work, he endeavoured to induce those who had contracted for it, to make a suitable addition, which he, in fact, frequently obtained. After the examination was over, especially when the instrument had his approbation, he generally, to amuse himself and those present, showed his skill by performing on it, and thereby always proved anew, that he was really 'the prince of all players on the harpsichord and organ,' as he was once styled in a dedication."

There was one little thing he used to like to do himself, and that was, arranging the quill plectrums and tuning of his harpsichord, for he could find no one to do this to his satisfaction. He also tuned his own clavichord, and was so practised in the operation that it never cost him more than a quarter of an hour.

Notwithstanding his many amiable qualities, Bach had a hot and hasty temper, and this frequently led to amusing scenes. There is a story told of one Görner, a talented organist, who worked at one of Bach's churches, having struck a wrong chord at a rehearsal, whereupon the old man flew into such a passion that he tore off his wig and threw it at the unfortunate organist's head, thundering out, "You ought to have been a cobbler instead of an organist."

In religion, Bach was a zealous Lutheran, and not a so-called "pietist," as some have asserted. That religious atmosphere in which he grew up showed itself gloriously in his works, and in his life too. He passed a quiet and secluded existence in his home in Germany, where he dived into the study of his Bible and its sacred truths; and, satisfied with the faith into which he so deeply penetrated, he rose, and from time to time allowed his religious feelings to find vent in those grand inspirations, in which, as the talented Herr Pauer has it, "we find the glorification of Protestantism."

We turn from the composer to his works. Bach was a prolific writer. The long list of his works includes two hundred and thirty complete cantatas for solo, chorus, and orchestra; three complete sacred oratorios, "The Passions;" seven complete masses; twenty-one shorter church services, with Latin words; four complete funeral cantatas; eighteen cantatas for birthday and other congratulatory occasions; twenty-eight motets for double chorus; forty-eight preludes and fugues for the clavecin; numerous toccatas; six French suites for the clavecin; six shorter suites; thirty-nine long works for the organ; twenty-nine shorter pieces for the organ; six trios for organ, with pedal obligato; fifteen inventions in two parts; fifteen symphonies in three parts; six sonatas for the violoncello; six sonatas for violin, without bass; various concertos for one, two, three, and four harpsichords, or pianos; seven overtures for instruments; the four volumes of the "Clavier-Uebung;" the "Art of Fugue;" pieces for the flute; and a host of single pieces, far too numerous to be mentioned.

Among the instrumental music, we first find those grand and masterly works for his favourite instrument, which have tended so much to perpetuate his name—the preludes and fugues for the organ. The imposing character of these works, their dignified bearing over all other organ compositions, the skill and execution required to render them faithfully, stamp them as masterpieces which have never been approached by any master, and cause them to be the summit of the organist's art. In addition to these his other great organ works are the six sonatas or trios for two sets of keys and obligato pedal, which he composed while at Cöthen, for his son, William Friedmann, and which are works of especial beauty; and the preludes and variations on chorales, published under the title of "Partite Diverse." Of these latter Forkel says, "The number of them may amount to one hundred; at least, I myself possess above seventy, and know that here and there more of them exist. Nothing can be more dignified, sublime, and devout than these preludes."

With the pianoforte, Bach has for ever associated himself. The works he has composed for it may not suit the tastes and likings of young ladies of fashion and school-girls, and probably never will; but to the true amateur, to the student, and to the matured musician, these works are full of deliciously quaint forms, not again to be found in the whole stupendous *repertoire* of which the art boasts. To estimate their value would be impossible. Musician after musician, student after student, have worked day and night at them. Beethoven, Mozart, Haydn, and numerous others profited by them. They are the sure road along which all must travel ere they can attain to eminence or perfection in the art. The great Schumann advised all young musicians to make "Bach their daily bread;" and this is advice which not only the "young musician," but the highest in the art, might act upon profitably to the end of their lives. There is no fathoming Bach. A lifetime would not suffice to unearth all he has left, and to understand it thoroughly. This, however, should never deter the lover of music from making an early acquaintance with the great master; and to those who would do so, here is the advice of one far more capable of giving it than the present writer. Herr Pauer says, "I would advise all students to begin with the six small preludes, and afterwards to take the inventions for two parts. When the mechanical difficulties of these delicious little duets have been conquered, the fifteen symphonies for three parts may be attempted. The six French suites should come next, and after these the six duet sonatas for clavecin and violin, or those for clavecin and flute may be taken. Next, I should recommend the six great English suites, and the charming partitas, the Italian concerto, the different toccatas. Only after such preparations should the student begin the forty-eight preludes and fugues called 'The Well-tempered Clavecin.' But great enjoyment can also be derived from playing the organ works in the form of a duet for two performers on one instrument."

The work, "Das Wohltemperirte Klavier," to which Herr Pauer refers, is in two volumes, each containing twenty-four preludes and fugues in all the major and minor keys. The first volume was written during his five years' appointment at Cöthen, and probably on one of the journeys which his princely patron was in the habit of taking him, when, in an out-of-the-way place, with no musical instrument within reach, he resorted to the sketching of these pieces for a pastime. The second volume was composed in 1740, when the Thomas-Schule cantor was fast growing venerable.

Of this work Forkel does not omit to speak, and says, "The second part consists, from the beginning to the end, entirely of masterpieces. In the first part, on the other hand, there are still some preludes [and fugues, which bear marks of the immaturity of early youth, and have probably been retained by the author only to have the number of four-and-twenty complete. But even here the author corrected, in course of time, whatever was capable of amendment. Whole passages are either thrown out, or otherwise turned, so that in the latter copies there are very few pieces left which can be reproached as imperfect. Among these few I reckon the fugues in A minor, G major and G minor, C major, F major and F minor, &c.; the rest are all excellent, and some of them in such a degree as not to be inferior to those in the second part. Even this second part, which was originally the more perfect, received in the course of time great improvements, as may be seen by comparing old and new copies. In general, both parts of this work contain a treasure of art, which cannot be found anywhere but in Germany."

The six French suites are a collection of allemandes, courants, and other little pieces, with a nice light and pleasing melody to each which renders them very attractive.

The English suites are after the same style, but are longer pieces, and derive their different title from the fact of their being composed for an English nobleman. Some of the pieces, especially in the fifth and sixth suites, are perfect in their beauty. Of the whole work a talented German artist writes thus: "Bach was the first who embodied artistic feeling in this kind of casual form; he displayed so much of original invention, both of melody and harmony, in the 'Suites Anglaises,' that the brightness and animation, as well as the admirable keeping and dignity of these pieces, will always cause them to be regarded as models of style."

The works which have been referred to; the "Chromatic Fantasia," so full of ingenuity and wonderful modulations; and the "Fifteen Inventions" for the cultivation both of taste and skill, as their original title proves—"A faithful guide to show lovers of the pianoforte, a clear method of playing two and three parts correctly, and also how to obtain good inventions and to carry them out properly; but above all to acquire a cantabile style of playing, and a good foretaste of composition"—and the pieces for one and several pianofortes, are the finest of his works for this instrument.

Bach's other instrumental music cannot here be dwelt upon. We must pass on to the vocal.

For that religion to which he was so devotedly attached, Bach composed a vast quantity of music. The two hundred and thirty cantatas are the remains of a series of about three hundred and eighty, which he composed while he held his appointment at Leipzig, for every Sunday and festival for five successive years. Previous to this, the motets and cantatas were chosen without any regard to their colouring and connection with the other portion of the service; but Bach made it his business to acquaint himself with the preachers' texts, and the whole bearing of the day's service, choosing the theme for his cantata accordingly.

The most general form of these cantatas was, first a grand orchestral introduction, after which followed a fine and impressive chorus, succeeded by recitatives, airs, or duets, the whole concluding with a chorale, in which all joined. Their great beauty consists in the canto fermo, that is, the melody of the chorale, being discernible, though delicately and skilfully varied, throughout the whole composition. The orchestral accompaniments are remarkably fine, and quite independent of the voices. Besides the organ, strings, flutes, hautboys, and trumpets are employed.

The motets are of a similar character to the cantatas, and contain a wealth of grand musical imagination. They are for one and two choruses, without a band accompaniment. These are the works which so pleased Mozart when he visited Leipzig, that out of his short stay he devoted some hours to studying all that he could find in the Thomas-Schule library, and came away deeply impressed and wondering.

The "Oratorium Tempore Nativitatis Christi," the original title of the work better known as Bach's "Christmas Oratorio," was composed in 1734, during the full height of its composer's maturity. It is of a much more florid and cheerful style than he usually wrote in, which can probably be accounted for from the fact that a good deal of its music is borrowed from "The Choice of Hercules," and a drama he composed for the Queen of Poland, and is, therefore, not so religious and severe in character. The work is apparently in six parts, the first three of which, it is said, were intended to be performed on Christmas and two following days, the fourth on the Circumcision, the fifth on the following Sunday, and the sixth on the Epiphany.

Zealous Lutheran as he was, Bach did not withhold his talent from the Roman Church, but composed many small pieces and masses for them. The most notable is the High Mass in B minor, which has not unfitly been described as a "Gothic Cathedral in music," so solemn and majestic a composition is it. It is a work steeped deeply with religious fervour and feeling, and it would perhaps be difficult to readily find a mass to surpass it in this respect.

Lastly, we turn to Bach's most glorious conceptions—the "Passion" oratorios.

Originally, it is said, there were five of these "Passionmusik," but only three are now known, the St. Matthew, St. John, and one of doubtful authenticity, according to St. Luke. On the two former we offer a few remarks.

The "Johannes-Passion," meaning that according to

St. John's Gospel, is the earliest work of the two, and was probably composed during Bach's first years of residence at Leipzig. It is said to have been four times performed during its author's lifetime.

Compared with the "Matthäus-Passion," it is a more simple work, and in many respects less interesting, though it should not be forgotten that, had the "Matthäus-Passion" not cast its shadow over this smaller work, it would never have been thought of as a "study," but rather jealously cherished and esteemed as a masterpiece. Now, however, we can afford to look at it in this light if we like, though probably most people will be content to drop this comparison, and instead, seek to acquaint themselves with all the numberless beauties contained in each work, and to dwell upon the sublimity of such a genius as could twice so wonderfully idealize the same significant subject, as to give to the world two works, both of which, after more than a hundred and fifty years, maintain their place among the finest examples Art possesses in the oratorio form.

Many are the especial beauties in the "Johannes-Passion." Among the songs, there is one for the treble, "I follow Thee also," rendered strikingly beautiful by its soft organ and flute accompaniments. "Dissolve, O my heart," is another attractive soprano song. For the tenor also there occurs a fine melody immediately after

the passage where Peter goes forth to weep bitterly—
"Ah! my soul, ah!" it commences, and a song brimming with tender expression and feeling is poured out. "Consider, O my soul," is a fine study for a bass voice, as is also the solo part in the chorus, "Jesus, Thou who knowest death."

The choruses are simply masterly, and full of all that is characteristic of Bach. If there are any that attention should be especially drawn to, they are first the one which so fittingly and grandly opens the work, "Lord, our Redeemer," then the "Crucify," and that fine chorus at the end, "Rest here in peace," of so devout and peaceful a character, as to excite within us all the emotions of the holy occasion it refers to.

Originally the "Johannes-Passion" commenced with the chorale, "O man, thy heavy sin lament," now to be found at the end of the first part of the "Matthäus-Passion." We have to thank Mr. Barnby for the pleasure derived from this fine work. That talented musician first introduced it to an English audience at the Hanover Square Rooms on the 23rd of March, 1872.

On the merits of the "Matthäus-Passion" little need be said, for, thanks to the exertions of such musicians as Sir Sterndale Bennett and Mr. Barnby, there are few interested in music who have not already become acquainted with the many beauties contained in it. A few features, however, must not be left unrecorded.

Among the songs more attractive and beautiful than others, must be named the delicious soprano aria, "Break and die," than which nothing could be more exquisite, and that aria marked *largo patetico*, "For love my Saviour suffered," also for a soprano. For another voice may be mentioned the solo, "Have mercy upon me, O Lord," which, with its elaborate violin accompaniment, is of more beauty and fervency than words could ever express.

The tenor and bass voices have not been forgotten, for there are treasures for both these, which it would be impossible to extol too highly.

The choruses are extremely fine throughout; but of these a few stand out above the others, as for instance that grand opening one, "Come, ye daughters," for a double choir; one beginning, "My Saviour, Jesus, now is taken," with its wonderful and effective change of time for the thrilling thunder and lightning ending; one of half a bar only, where the excited rabble reject their Messiah, and shout at the top of their voices, "Barabbas!" and "In tears of grief," which so effectively closes this great conception of a still greater subject.

Another salient beauty in this work, and one not to be found in the "Johannes-Passion," is the soft and heavenly music which accompanies all that Jesus speaks, and, as it were, surrounds the divine Being with a halo of glory, separating Him from the other personages.

The first performance of the "Matthäus-Passion" was in St. Thomas's Church, Leipzig, at Vespers on Good Friday, 1729, when the composer himself conducted. It was divided into two distinct parts on this occasion, between which was preached a midnight sermon. A few more times it was heard, but when the good old cantor went down to his grave, the work was heard no more of for exactly a hundred years. From this long rest and oblivion, Mendelssohn rescued it, and superintended the performance of it in Germany. It was long after this, however, before it was introduced into England, and then our gifted countryman, (Sir) Sterndale Bennett, was to the fore in so good a work. This was on March 23rd, 1858, when his Royal Highness, the late Prince Consort, who took a great interest in the work, honoured the performance at St. Martin's Hall with his presence. Since that time the work has been frequently produced under the direction of Mr. Barnby, to whose continued exertions the increasing popularity of Bach's masterpiece is mainly due.

Bach's latter days were gloomy and dark. The hard work of his long life was telling upon him, and those once-young eyes had been too often strained since the nights when his ardour led him to copying music by moonlight. Now they began to fail him. Gradually becoming weaker and more painful, the old man submitted to two operations by an oculist. Both failed, and he completely lost his sight. Surrounded with darkness, and with his health gradually failing, he lingered for six months, when he seemed to be getting better. During this period he dictated his last work—the chorale, "When my last hour is close at hand."

A few mornings before his death his eyes were so much better, that he could bear the light; but, alas! it was only a transient joy—a last look on the beautiful earth. A few hours more, and a violent fever had overtaken him, which neither loving friends nor skilled physicians could cope with, and to which he quietly succumbed at a quarter-past eight on the evening of the 28th July, 1750.

Two days afterwards he was buried in St. John's churchyard, at Leipzig. No stone, no cross, marked his resting-place, and the world was told no more than that "A man, aged sixty-five, Johann Sebastian Bach, Musical Director and Singing Master of St. Thomas's School, was carried to his grave in the hearse."

Principal Incidents in the Life of Bach.

Born at Eisenbach, March 21st	1685
First Lessons from his Brother	1693
Organist to Arnstadt Church	1703
Court Organist at Weimar	1708
Sudden Death of his First Wife	1720
Director of the Thomas-Schule at Leipzig	1723

Bach.

Volume I. of the " Well-tempered Clavecin " written 1725
The " Johannes-Passion " finished 1729
The " Matthäus-Passion " finished 1729
The " Christmas Oratorio " composed . . . 1734
The " Passacagli " for Organ written . . . 1736
Volume II. of the " Well-tempered Clavecin" completed 1740
" Die Kunst der Fuge " written 1749
Died at Leipzig, 28th July 1750

Handel.

OF all those glorious names inscribed on the roll of master-musicians, not one perhaps is more revered, or is more familiar to the English people, either by his name or his works, than that of the great man who has immortalized his name with most of the grand narratives of Holy Writ, by wedding to them such sublime music as the reading and study of these sacred writings inspired within him. Nearly two hundred years have rolled by since he penned his heavenly melodies, and yet they always come to our ears as fresh and as welcome as spring flowers. What a preacher and poet! What thousands of hearts must have been turned by his tone-preaching! Where is the prelate who can move our souls as they are moved by Handel's "Messiah?"

George Friedrich Handel was born on the 23rd February, 1685, at Halle in Saxony, in which town his

Handel.

father was then practising as a surgeon. Hardly had the child had time to look around him before the sage doctor had decided that he should be brought up to the profession of a lawyer. He had, however, been moulded for something else. Let us see which eventually prevailed—Nature, or the grave old doctor of Halle.

At a very early age the child manifested such unmistakable signs of musical genius that his father, among others, could not fail to observe them. This talent for music he was determined to repress, that it might not interfere with the studies designed for George as a lawyer. He would not allow him to be taken to any place of entertainment lest he should hear music, while he forbade him to touch any musical instrument, and to make sure of being obeyed, Dr. Handel banished every musical instrument from his house. However, all his efforts to stifle the flame of genius in the boy were useless. By the help of his mother, who perhaps rather fostered little George's talent than otherwise, an old clavichord was secreted in a garret in their house, and to this he resorted when all had retired to rest, or whenever his father was away and he could practise unseen and unheard.

Thus did his inward craving for music lead him to evade his father's strict injunctions; and, with such a desire as this, joined to his wonderful talent and his indomitable perseverance, it is not surprising that in a very short time he became a skilful and surprising extempore player of the clavichord, notwithstanding he was but seven years old.

About this time an incident occurred which decided the future career of little George.

One day his father was about to pay a visit to the Court of the Duke of Saxe-Weissenfels, to see his son, who was in the duke's service. George begged hard that he might be allowed to go with him to see his brother, but the doctor refused, and it was not till he discovered that he was following the carriage that the father yielded to the little fellow's entreaties, and at length took him up into it.

They had not been many days at the Court before George caught the sounds of the organ in the chapel, and from that time he could not rest till he had touched its keys. He soon found an opportunity of doing so. One morning, when the service was over, he stole up to the organ unobserved, and could not resist the temptation of playing upon it. The duke, happening to be near, noticed the unusual style of the playing, and caused inquiries to be made as to who was the performer. "It is my little brother," replied the page. The duke, of course, was astonished, and sent both for the child-organist and his father. He was not long in fathoming the old doctor's mind on the subject of his son's talent, but after a great deal of persuasion, he succeeded in inducing Dr. Handel to give up the law scheme, and allow George to follow the calling for which Nature had so eminently fitted him.

On their return home, therefore, our young genius was placed under the tuition of Frederich Zackau, the organist of the cathedral at Halle.

He was now able to follow up with enthusiasm, and without any fear of angry opposition, the studies he loved so much. He proved a most diligent and extraordinary pupil, and soon mastered all that Zackau could teach him—composing at the early age of nine years motets and other pieces, which were sung in the cathedral. So surprising was the progress he made, that at the end of two or three years the conscientious master confessed that his pupil knew more than he did himself, and recommended him to go to Berlin, there to study other models.

In the year 1696 young Handel arrived in Berlin, and being but eleven years old, and possessed of such astonishing gifts, he caused no small stir among the composers and organists there. Chief among these were Bononcini and Attilio, whose acquaintance Handel soon made. No sooner had the former heard him play than he became envious of him, and ever after opposed him. Attilio, on the other hand, accepted the young stranger as he deserved, taking an interest in him, and praising him to all whom he met. Often, too, he would sit for hours and listen with delight to his younger brother-artist as he improvised on the harpsichord.

The fame of young Handel soon spread through Berlin, even to the king's chamber. The elector evinced so favourable a disposition towards the youthful wonder, that he proposed to become his patron and to send him to Italy, to finish his musical education. This offer was communicated to Handel's father, but he did not entertain it, and excused himself on the ground that he wished his son to be with him in his latter days, at the same time re-calling the boy to Halle.

Not very long after his return, Handel had the misfortune to lose his father, and had to bestir himself to provide for his own living. With this purpose in view, he set out for Hamburg in the year 1703.

On his arrival, he succeeded in obtaining an appointment in the Opera House orchestra as a violinist. Here his remarkable talent did not remain long undiscovered. One day, the harpsichord-player being absent, the orchestra found itself in a fix. Handel, however, sat down to the instrument, and to the surprise of every one, performed on it in such a style as they had never before heard.

This surprising leap from an insignificant post in the orchestra to that of temporary conductor, created much envious and jealous feeling among his associates in the orchestra, and one of them, named Mattheson, got so enraged with him that it terminated in their engaging in a duel outside the Opera House. Fortunately, neither of the combatants was hurt, though Handel had a narrow escape, as Mattheson's sword was only stayed from piercing his adversary, by its coming in contact with a button or something he carried under his coat, some say a music score, which broke the sword to pieces, and probably saved his life. After this affair of honour, the combatants became firm friends.

During his sojourn in Hamburg, Handel produced his first dramatic work, "Almira; or, the Vicissitudes of Royalty." It was first performed on the 8th January, 1705, at the German Opera House, where it was played for thirty consecutive nights with unbounded applause.

In the next month "Almira" was succeeded by "Nero," after which two others quickly appeared—"Florinda" and "Daphne"—all proving most successful, and spreading his fame far and wide through Germany.

In Hamburg Handel remained for about three years, during which time he accumulated sufficient means to enable him to pay a visit to Italy in the early part of the year 1706.

The first city to which he directed his steps was Florence, where he wrote and produced his opera, "Roderigo." This work gained for him great repute and favour among the Florentines, while the Grand Duke Giovanni de Medici showed his appreciation of it by presenting the composer with a service of plate and a purse containing one hundred sequins (fifty pounds), besides entertaining him at the palace before he left the city.

From Florence he moved on to Venice, where he was most enthusiastically received by the excited Venetians, and such musicians as Scarlatti, Gasperini, Corelli, and others. For the Venetians he produced his "Agrippina," an opera which brought him fresh laurels. For thirty consecutive representations the theatre was crammed, and resounded with deafening cries of "Long live the dear Saxon."

Handel then proceeded to the Eternal city, where he found the whole populace waiting to do him homage. Cardinal Ottoboni, a great *dilettante* and a noble and generous man, was one of the foremost of those who showed their esteem for young Handel. He constantly entertained the gifted musician during his visit, and made great rejoicings in his honour, of which Handel showed his appreciation by composing for the cardinal a short oratorio, "La Resurrezione," which was performed at one of his churches in Rome. "Il Trionfo del Tempo" (The Triumph of Time) was also written during his stay at Rome, and was executed by the cardinal's private band at one of their weekly concerts.

Naples was the next city visited by the composer; and for the Neapolitans he wrote his pastoral play, "Aci, Galatea, e Polifemo" (which must not be confounded with the English "Acis" composed in 1721 for the Duke of Chandos), and some smaller works. This play just suited the taste of the ardent Neapolitans. It contains airs of the most graceful and delicate nature, and is full of warmth and tenderness, like the soft and balmy air which its composer was inhaling in this lovely climate. Would that we could hear these works now, instead of some of the trash introduced into our programmes! Had the illustrious composer not overshadowed them by other brilliant conceptions, these efforts of his youth would long ere this have been rescued from oblivion.

With this city Handel completed his visit to the land of Art. In the year 1709 he began his homeward journey, no doubt greatly benefited by his residence among the Italians—indeed, such a visit at this period of his artistic life could not fail to be other than beneficial to him, when, with the severe and strict style of composition which he had acquired at the feet of Zackau and his other German masters, the youthful yet profound musician felt, that to become universal he must combine the grace and loveliness which characterizes the Italian school.

Passing through Hanover on his way to Halle, Handel came across the Elector of Brunswick, who was so taken with him that he immediately offered him the post of chapel-master, with a most liberal stipend. This offer Handel accepted, but, after paying a visit to his aged mother and his old music-master, Zackau, visited England before settling down in his new home.

He arrived in London in the winter of the year 1710, and was soon engaged by Aaron Hill, the manager of the Haymarket Opera House, to compose music for "Rinaldo and Armida," a work founded on Tasso's "Gerusalemme Liberata."

Its first representation took place on the 24th February, 1711, and proved an immense success. The cavatinas, "Cara sposa" and "Lascia che io pianga," were especial favourites, and soon became popular melodies, and were hummed everywhere. The music was published in various forms for the harpsichord, and some idea may be formed of the merits of this opera when it is known that Walsh, the music-publisher, made something like a thousand pounds by it.

Not long after the production of "Rinaldo," Handel had to think of returning to his new post. It was, however, with the greatest regret that the English people parted with their now favourite composer. Before leaving he had an interview with Queen Anne, who made him several valuable presents, and expressed the regret felt by the Court at losing him, at the same time making him promise to return to England as soon as the elector would allow him.

Arrived in Hanover, he found the elector anxiously awaiting him, and for a time he settled down to his new duties, besides composing various small cantatas and some chamber-duets for the Princess Caroline; but his brilliant reception and triumphs in London, and, moreover, his promise to Queen Anne, were ever present to his mind, and ere long he once more obtained leave to visit England, where he arrived early in the year 1712.

He found the whole nation ready to welcome him, and before he had been in London many days he brought out an ode for the queen's birthday, and was commissioned to compose a Te Deum and Jubilate for the occasion of a national thanksgiving in St. Paul's Cathedral for the Peace of Utrecht.

The result of his labours was the production of the interesting work known as the "Utrecht Te Deum" and "Jubilate." They were performed in the cathedral, with full band and organ, before a vast assemblage, including the queen, her ministers, and Court, together with the noblest in birth and genius in the land. Handel was organist on this occasion, and his wonderful playing, in which he had no equal, together with the band and chorus, made such music as had never before been heard in England. His work gained for him the admiration of all who heard it, as well as a pension of two hundred pounds a year from the queen.

Handel now found himself the idol of the people, sought after by the highest and noblest in the land, receiving invitations and engagements far more numerous than he could ever fulfil; and with such a field as this before him, he was in no great hurry to return to Hanover, which he seems to have regarded as too small a sphere for his talents. But the day of retribution for this ingratitude was not far distant.

Not very long after he had the misfortune to lose his royal patroness, Queen Anne, and with this came his day of reckoning for the neglect of his duties at Hanover. His old master, the elector, succeeded to the throne of England as George I., so that Mr. Handel was in a fix, and had to get out of it as best he could.

To do so he trusted to his divine art, and composed the twenty-five concerted pieces known as the "Water Music." Hearing from his friend Kilmanseck that the king and his party were about to make a trip along the Thames, he contrived to get this music performed in one of the boats following that of the king. The *ruse* succeeded perfectly; and eventually Handel regained the favour of his old master, who generously marked the occasion by adding a pension of two hundred pounds a year to that bestowed on him by Queen Anne.

Nearly the whole of 1716 was passed at the residence of Lord Burlington, in Piccadilly, where he did little more than direct the concerts, which this nobleman was in the habit of giving, and composing a few small pieces which were performed at them.

The next year Handel visited Hanover, where he wrote an oratorio, entitled "The Passion," after Brocke's poem, "The Sufferings and Death of Jesus Christ for the Sins of the World," and had it performed in Hamburg.

This is truly a grand conception, and contains no less than fifty-five pieces allotted to the chief characters— Jesus, Peter, James, and John, Judas, Pilate, and Caiaphas, with the Virgin Mary and three other Marys and a chorus. Some of the airs in this unknown work are said to be of "incomparable grandeur, and full of grief."

After a stay in Hanover of about a year, he returned to England, where he met the Duke of Chandos, who engaged him to act as chapel-master at the chapel he had erected near his residence at Cannons. No doubt the "Grand Duke," as he was styled, was as munificent in this offer as in everything else. He had erected for himself a magnificent palace, at a cost of £230,000. Near to it was his chapel, furnished like the churches of Italy, where "he was wont to go daily with true Christian humility, attended by his Swiss Guards." On Sundays the road was thronged by those who went, some on foot and others in their conveyances, to worship at the "Grand Duke's" chapel, where Mr. Handel played the organ.

For these services he composed much church music, the most notable of which is that known as the "Chandos Te Deums and Anthems." In these the great master appears to be training and preparing himself for a new sphere of composition. With their grand choruses, interspersed with solos exquisitely accompanied, these anthems seem each to form a miniature oratorio—a study in which the great genius is feeling his way to those far grander conceptions which followed this period, and in which he stands unrivalled.

For two years little occurred to interrupt his enjoyment of the pleasures Cannons afforded. He continued to com-

Handel. 45

pose for and conduct the services at the beautiful chapel; and, notwithstanding the shocks which the duke's fortune thrice received, we do not hear that the pleasant discussions which Gay and the satirical Pope, the witty Arbuthnot and Mr. Addison, joined in with Handel and the duke, lost any of their briskness.

In the year 1720, the assistance of Handel was sought to get together a cast of Italian singers, and to direct the "New Italian Opera," which a body of English noblemen had determined to try to revive in London. Handel was engaged, and soon got together a splendid troupe, including the celebrated songstress, Margarita Durastanti; and as a paper of the time has it, "Signor Senesino, the famous Italian eunuch, has arrived, and 'tis said that the company allows him two thousand guineas for the season."

The new society, under the title of the Royal Academy of Music, began its first season in the Haymarket house on April 2nd, 1720, and enjoyed unprecedented success. Among the earliest operas presented was a new effusion by the talented conductor, entitled "Radamistus." This work took the house by storm. Many persons fainted on account of the heat and closeness of the house, and hundreds were turned back at the doors.

In this flourishing state we must leave the new venture for the present.

This same year Handel's first English oratorio, "Esther," was written for his ducal master, and for which he was paid one thousand pounds. After being performed two or three times at Cannons, it was laid aside, and did not appear till some time later.

Following this came "Acis and Galatea," also written for the Duke of Chandos, in which Handel had recourse to much of the music in the Italian serenata, "Aci, Galatea, e Polifemo;" and it is to this, probably, and the similarity of their names, that the two compositions are erroneously supposed to be one and the same work. The words of the English "Acis" are, for the major part, by the poet Gay, but others of the frequenters of Cannons seem also to have contributed to it. Pope and Hughes each wrote some verses, and Dryden was applied to for the "Help, Galatea! help!"

The "Suites de pièces pour le clavecin," composed for his favourite pupil, the Princess Anne, also came to light about this time. In this collection we find that exquisite little piece, universally known under the title of the "Harmonious Blacksmith."

Nearly every one perhaps knows the anecdote associated with this delicious bit of music; but for the benefit of those who do not, it may be related.

One day, as Handel was making his way to the chapel at Cannons, he was overtaken by a shower of rain, which compelled him to seek shelter in the shop of a blacksmith, whom he knew as being the parish clerk. While there, he caught the melody which the blacksmith was humming while at his work, and to which every stroke of his hammer on the anvil made an agreeable bass. On returning home, the great musician, it is said, made out of it the piece referred to.

This anecdote, however, is open to doubt. Many say that the melody is by one Wagenseil, and that Handel graced it with variations, and added it to his "Suites de pièces," without acknowledging its source. Strange though it may appear, this is by no means improbable, for as a plagiarist there are grave imputations against Handel.

During this time the Opera House in the Haymarket had continued to flourish; but, alas! a cloud soon appeared.

The successful "Radamistus" was followed by "Muzio Scœvola," which for some reason or other was composed conjointly by Handel, Bononcini, and Attilio; and it was this untimely move on the part of the directors which eventually led to the dissolution and break up of the concern.

Bononcini and Attilio had been invited over to compose for the new society, and it is not to be supposed that they had quite forgotten their first meeting with

Handel in Berlin. The spirit of party was already perceptible in the ranks of the noblemen directors, and "Muzio Scœvola" did not lessen it. It brought the rivals into competition with each other, and Handel carried off the palm. His part of the opera was voted the best, by all but Bononcini and his admirers, and thus the spirit of party ran higher than before. It was long the talk of the town, and gave birth to Swift's epigram—

> "Some say that Signor Bononcini,
> Compared to Handel, is a ninny;
> While others say, that to him, Handel
> Is hardly fit to hold a candle.
> Strange that such difference should be
> 'Twixt tweedledum and tweedledee."

However, the crash did not come yet. Those who held the reins held them cleverly, and the rivals continued to compose for the society up to the year 1729, when dire discord took possession of this temple of harmony.

After "Muzio Scœvola," Handel produced his opera of "Floridante."

This was followed in 1723 by "Otho," the flower of his dramatic compositions. Burney says of this work, "that it would be difficult to find in it a single piece, vocal or instrumental, which had not been a favourite with the public;" while of one of its songs, "Affani del pensier," a contemporary of Handel's remarked, "That great bear was certainly inspired when he wrote that song."

"Giulio Cesare" followed immediately upon "Otho;" then came "Flavius," celebrated for the "Doni Pace" —the first scenic quintet ever composed.

In 1725 appeared "Rodelinda," in which the celebrated prima donna Cuzzoni was so successful, that the costume which she wore in the part was adopted by the ladies of the period, and "for a year the dress seemed a national uniform for youth and beauty."

"Scipio" and "Alexander" were produced in 1726; they were followed by "Admetus," and in 1728 by "Ptolemy," the last opera Handel wrote before the collapse of the Academy. It was performed only seven times, for the Opera House was now all but deserted, and its subscribers had migrated to Rich's Theatre, in Lincoln's Inn Fields, where Gay's "Beggar's Opera" was playing with "terrible success;" for it was more suited to the immoral tastes and tendencies of the time than the opera performances in the Haymarket; and, do what they would, the Academy could not attract the attention of the lewdly-inclined public and the indifferent subscribers. Threats were held out to the latter "that proper measures will be taken to oblige them to pay what is due;" but all to no purpose, for the divided body of directors became more vehement than ever against each other. Disagreements sprang up, till at length, overcome by their own differences, and their £50,000 capital being exhausted, the Royal Academy of Music dissolved, and closed its doors on June 1st, 1728.

A new phase now presents itself in Handel's career. Notwithstanding the disastrous failures he had so lately witnessed, in 1729 he turned *impressario*, and opened the Haymarket Theatre. After bargaining with Heidegger for the house, he started on a journey to Italy to get together his company. In this he was most successful, for he obtained there a splendid body of singers—excepting his bass, who came from Hamburg, "there being none worth engaging in Italy"—and on the 2nd December, 1729, the Opera House was again opened with a new opera by its manager, entitled, "Lothario," and a caste of the most eminent artists to support it. Alas! "Lothario" fell flat; and a series of failures commenced which ended in Handel's losing both health and fortune, and being compelled at last to turn his back on Italian opera. In spite of its attractions, "Lothario" was withdrawn after ten performances; it was followed by "Parthenope," which enjoyed a yet shorter reign, though it is one of the finest of Handel's dramatic inspirations. For the performances for the next few months some of Handel's older productions were resorted to with the addition of "new scenes and cloathes." But this was of no avail; the merciless public were as indifferent to the "new scenes and cloathes" as to the old; and once more the persevering *impressario* racked his brain for something new wherewith to win their attention and support.

This opera was "Porus," but it was only a last glimmer before Italian opera died out—being played for fourteen consecutive times, the latter ones to almost empty houses.

For the next season (1732) it was necessary to find some novelty for the dainty public, and "Œtius" was produced; but no—they would not listen to it; and after five representations it was found advisable to try "Sosarme," and then "Orlando," both of which failed in their mission. Sick and tired of these long-continued reverses, Handel was compelled to try some other kind of entertainment, and it was this step which finally led to the production of those grand masterpieces which he afterwards composed.

On the 19th April, 1732, there appeared an announcement to the effect that the sacred story of "Esther" would be performed in the Haymarket Theatre on the 2nd May following. This was the experiment Handel had now determined to try, for Bernard Gates had been performing it with his choir at the Chapel Royal, St.

James's, and it had caused a great stir. Handel therefore brought it out for the first time since it was laid aside at the Cannons' mansion twelve years back. At its first performance in the Haymarket the members of the Royal Family were present. It proved a splendid triumph, and gained for him the long-desired favour of the public.

The success attending the revival of "Esther" led him, no doubt, to think of his "Acis;" and on the 5th June we find it announced that "Acis and Galatea,' with several additions, will be performed by a great number of the best voices and instruments. There will be no acting on the stage, but the scene will represent in a picturesque manner a rural prospect, with rocks, groves, fountains, and grottoes, amongst which will be disposed a chorus of nymphs and shepherds."

On the day announced "Acis" appeared, together with the "nymphs and shepherds," "rocks and grottoes," and was equally as successful as "Esther" had been. But the novelty-seeking public could not be expected to listen long to the same thing; so in the year 1733 Handel gave his subscribers another work of the same stamp, under the title of "Deborah." This was first performed under royal patronage on March 17th, with "the house fitted up and illuminated in a new and particular manner." "Deborah" received "vast applause," and served to carry the enterprising manager safely through the season.

After this Handel visited Oxford, and there brought out his "Athalia," which was also received "with vast applause before an audience of 3,700 persons." It proved very successful, too, in a pecuniary sense, and in acknowledgment of its merits he was offered the degree of Doctor of Music. But this honour he declined in the following graceful terms: "Vat the divil I trow mein money away for dat which de blockhead wish? I no want." Soon after this he started for the Continent, whence he returned with a new company of singers, and on the 30th October, 1733, opened the Haymarket house for another season.

"Semiramis," "Cajus Fabricius," and "Arbaces," were successfully given; then followed "Ariadne," which, Hawkins says, "is of a not very elevated style, and is calculated to please the vulgar;" and "Parnasse in Festa," which was the last novelty that Handel produced before the expiration of his lease of the theatre.

No sooner did this occur than he commenced operations in Lincoln's Inn Fields Theatre, but finding it unsuited for his purpose, Handel moved into the new Covent Garden Theatre. "Pastor Fido," "Terpsichore," and other works were given there. For the latter part of the season of 1735 another novelty, "Alcina," was provided for the public.

The great composer now received an invitation to set music to Dryden's "Alexander's Feast." This superb and masterly composition was soon completed, and of its first performance a journal of the time says : "There never was upon the like occasion so numerous and splendid an audience at any theatre in London, there being at least thirteen hundred persons present, and it is judged that the receipts of the house could not amount to less than four hundred and fifty pounds." This success did not last long. The public again became indifferent, and Handel was compelled to produce at very short intervals "Arminius," "Giustino," "Dido," and "Berenice." None of these succeeded, and "Berenice" had seen but four representations when Handel, with all his funds exhausted, a bankrupt, and his health seriously shattered by the strain it had received, was forced to close the Opera House. Suffering from an attack of paralysis, he was taken to Aix-la-Chapelle.

From this town he soon returned "greatly recovered in health," and the first commission he received was from the new director of the Haymarket Theatre, which had been reopened during his absence abroad. "Faramondo" was the result; but this work was performed only five times, when it was followed by "Xerxes," which suffered a similar fate. With the public in this state of indifference, the new director thought it advisable to close the theatre, and once more Handel was free from the troubles of Italian opera.

He did not remain idle, but at once set to work with prodigious activity, and after producing the famous Organ Concertos, he put his pen to the first of that series of colossal works which he continued to the year of his death.

In these works the great genius adopts the oratorio form of composition, and the examples of this form of writing which he has left us, have gained for him the same pre-eminence in oratorio composition as Mozart holds with the opera, or Beethoven and Haydn with the symphony. In them, too, can be seen, far more clearly than in his operas, the enormous extent of his learning, his vast perceptive powers, and the extraordinary ingenuity which he brings to bear upon his art. This is especially discernible in the grand and massive choruses which move so pompously through these works. The resources of counterpoint are taxed to their very utmost. As we listen we are filled with admiration for the musician, whilst we perceive with what subtle skill subject is followed by subject in response, and succeeded by the counter-subject and its many digressions, winding about in the most intricate manner, like so many threads being woven into one grand whole. Then, again, his heavenly melodies! What hope fills us as "I know that my Redeemer liveth" falls on our ears, or the "Comfort ye my people!" and what shall be said of such airs as "He was despised," "How beautiful are the feet," Jonathan's air in "Saul," "Sin not, O King," and many others?

"Saul" was the first of the immortal masterpieces of this, Handel's greatest, creative period. It was begun on the 3rd July, 1738, and completed on the 27th September following. With this novelty in his hands he took the King's Theatre in the Haymarket, and on the 16th January, 1739, opened it for the performance of oratorios twice a week.

In due time appeared the announcement that "the theatre will be opened with a new oratorio, composed by Mr. Handel, called 'Saul.' The pit and boxes will be put together. The gallery will be opened at 4, and the pit and boxes at 5. To begin at 6 o'clock."

The first performance of "Saul" proved most successful, and it was frequently repeated before the season closed.

Of all the now unheard compositions of Handel, this one in particular deserves to be rescued and laid before the public. The "Messiah" and "Judas Maccabæus" are given over and over again as each season comes

Handel. 57

round, and occasionally we get "Israel in Egypt;" but if conductors wait till the public get tired of these, the unknown works of Handel will never be properly and fairly heard. Moreover, this tardiness to present new works claims attention on other grounds. For whatever effect the production of untried works might have on the pockets of the promoters of our concerts, one thing is certain, that their not being produced has a most prejudicial effect on our musical progress, which is robbed by it of that impetus that the production of unknown works necessarily imparts; while it spares our soloists the necessity of studying new airs, and deprives the orchestras, as well as the amateur element of which the choruses of the musical societies are formed, the opportunity of reading and enjoying new music, with the beauties of which they are, perhaps, totally unacquainted. Many of the orchestra and chorus of these societies could not give their respective parts of "Judas" or the "Messiah" from memory. Are our choral societies, then, to go on like revolving machines, with no variation but that which the turning out of these three oratorios affords? We trust not; but hope that ere long they will add to the pleasure which is already derived from Handel's oratorios, by bringing to light more of these unknown masterpieces.

The oratorio of "Saul" is certainly one of Handel's

finest conceptions, and is replete with music of the most tender and beautiful nature. The overture is remarkable for its exquisite grace and beauty, and the minuetto, the last of its four movements, is especially fine. Immediately following it is the majestic chorus, "How excellent Thy name," the Israelites song of triumph for the victory over Goliath and the Philistines, to the exulting themes of which they again return after having recounted the victory of their youthful deliverer, David; but this time their shouts of rejoicing are rendered more triumphant than before by the spirited "Hallelujah" which they add to their song of praise. In some graceful airs that follow, the shepherd-boy David is introduced to King Saul, who gives him his daughter's hand; while in the midst of the ceremony distant music is heard, and the silver-toned bells fill the air with their undulating sounds, nearer and nearer approaching. The news of the great Goliath's defeat has rapidly spread over the hills of Judah, and the daughters of Israel have come out to meet the conqueror. Soon the symphony is over, and their clear voices, in merry time, ring out the song, "Welcome, welcome, mighty King!" On hearing David's praises sung, Saul is filled with envy, and an evil spirit takes possession of him. Jonathan now breaks in with his fine recitative, "Imprudent women," and soon is heard

Handel. 59

in the alto air, "O Lord, whose mercies," David's heartfelt prayer for Saul. He lifts his harp, and with soothing music seeks to allay Saul's moody madness; but Jonathan proclaims, "'Tis all in vain, his fury still continues," and David is compelled to flee. Jonathan is charged to destroy David, but in the most pathetic tone cries, "No, no, cruel father, no. Against the world, my best, my dearest friend I must defend." "Hast thou obeyed my orders?" cries Saul; but no, "Alas!" sings Jonathan; and then follows perhaps the most sublime melody in the oratorio, "Sin not, O King." This appeases Saul, and in the recitative which follows, David receives the assurance of safety, and accepts the hand of Saul's daughter, Michal. She sings of her lover in the delicate melody of "O fairest of ten thousand fair," and she in her turn is lauded by her lover, in the "O lovely maid," till they both unite in the melodious harmony of

> "How well in thee does Heaven at last
> Compensate all my sorrows past."

But no sooner does Saul return to his palace than the evil spirit again takes possession of him, and while David is sitting in his house he is aroused by the cry of Michal, "Fly, fly, for death is near." The messenger Doeg seeks David. "Alive or dead, he must be brought to Saul." Michal cares little for such threats, and sings, "No, no, let the guilty tremble," as Doeg pursues his search. David, however, is nowhere to be found, and the messenger is compelled to return from his fruitless errand. The mad king then seeks the assistance of the witch of Endor. Soon he reaches her abode, and is greeted with the witch's words, "With me, what wouldst thou?" "Bring up Samuel," cries Saul; and in the infernal music which follows is heard the witch's cry to the "infernal spirits." The apparition of Samuel arises, and in the bass solo, "Why hast thou forced me from the realms of peace?" again foretells his fate, for sparing the king of the Amalekites.

This treatment of Saul's interview at Endor is one of the most masterly pieces that Handel ever wrote, and is truly a marvellous conception.

Now is the prophecy of Samuel fulfilled. Israel has gone out to battle with the Philistines. The fight is long and fierce, and the valleys are steeped with the blood of the slain. Israel is overcome and put to flight, and both Saul and Jonathan are killed. The panting Amalekite then tells his tale, "Impious wretch. Fall on him, smite him, let him die!" cries David.

"Since thy own mouth hath testified
By thee the Lord's Anointed died."

The Dead March is then heard, the grave and mournful tones of which are familiar to all. No dirge is complete without this march; and who is there whose bosom has not heaved for the loss of some loved one, as the piercing tones fell on the ear? No matter how unexpectedly heard, or how busily engaged we may be, the first sounds of the muffled drums and the wailing harmonies instantly arrest us, sending a thrill of sadness through the soul, and causing a feeling of gloomy depression, which is not dispelled till the last solemn tones have long died away. In a short fugal chorus, Israel then mourns for Saul and Jonathan, and David declaims, "O, let it not in Gath be heard." After the short chorus, "Eagles were not so swift as they," David resumes his song in the pathetic air, "In sweetest harmony they lived." Abner, the captain of the host, then appears with the encouraging words,

"Ye men of Judah, weep no more."

The strength of Israel revives; the mighty hosts arise, and yearn for revenge; the one universal cry is, "Gird on thy sword—pursue—pursue," and as this grandest chorus in the oratorio speeds on in its course, increasing in intensity as the fugue enters, we easily realize the numberless mass of armed men fast pressing on across the Judæan hills, hastening to avenge themselves for the blood of Saul and Jonathan.

"Israel in Egypt" was the next work which the immortal genius produced. It was begun on October 1st, 1738, and in the short space of twenty-seven days this enormous work, containing no less than twenty-eight colossal choruses, four recitatives, and three duets, was completed!

Of all Handel's oratorios the "Israel" is certainly the finest, if not the most popular one. It abounds with music which he never excelled in any of his works, and in one or two cases never equalled; nor has he been less masterly in his appeal to our emotions by the wonderful analogous music which is to be found in this oratorio. What other than a feeling of depression takes possession of us as the themes of the double chorus, "And the children of Israel sighed," gradually creep over each other? How sublime, too, the effect produced by the mournful sigh of Israel, murmured out by the second chorus, as if bowed down by the heavy burden which the first chorus is piling upon them in the severe contrapuntal treatment of the theme allotted to them, till at length their cry reaches heaven, and Moses is sent to them. Then follows Handel's wonderful treatment of the plagues of Egypt, in which we are introduced to some of the grandest effects ever produced through the agency of music, by him, or any other composer. "He turned their waters into blood" is the

Handel. 63

first of the plagues treated, and by his ingenious recourse to the chromatic scale, Handel has certainly succeeded in kindling within us a feeling of abhorrence. After "Their land brought forth frogs," in which to imitate the leaping of the frogs seems to be the composer's intent, we come upon the magnificent choruses, "He spake the word" and "He gave them hail." In the former, without disturbing its character as a chorus, we get the wonderful music of the buzzing and laboured humming of the great swarm of "all manner of flies;" and in the hailstone chorus the rattling of the hail, with the mingled fire and hail running along upon the ground, is almost visibly portrayed by the masterly orchestration. "He sent a thick darkness" forms, with the music wedded to it, another of those grand conceptions which make us cherish the name of this great tone-poet. No sooner is the second bar of its introduction sounded than the sensation of darkness is kindled within us, only to be more intensely felt when the analogous words are sung. Then follows the last and most dreadful of the plagues, "He smote all the firstborn," equally wonderfully treated. Israel's departure from the land of Egypt, and Egypt's rejoicing thereat, are contained in the grand choruses which follow, till we come to "I will sing unto the Lord," in which Israel triumphs for the overthrow of "the horse and his rider," one of the finest and boldest choruses ever written. "The Lord is a man of war," a duet for basses, is another of the salient beauties of this oratorio, and, as well as the tenor song, "The Enemy said," has never been equalled in any of his writings. Another massive chorus, "The people shall hear," followed by the lovely contralto air, "Thou shalt bring them in," and we come to the final chorus of this masterpiece, "Sing ye to the Lord," which after the first few bars is none other than "I will sing unto the Lord," the joyful and triumphant strains of which the great composer has thought fit to adopt to close his mighty work of twenty-seven days.

On the 4th April, 1739, "Israel in Egypt" was given to the world, and proved a signal failure! Indeed, so much so, that for the next performance, some days after, it was found necessary to announce that "the oratorio will be shortened and intermixed with songs." Alas! for the taste of a public which could not tolerate the "Israel" without a coating of Italian love-lays. However, we must not be hard upon the public, who managed to endure, with the cherished ballads tacked on to it, three performances of this sublime oratorio! But how was this? Handel, like many other great men, was far in advance of his age, and the tastes and tendencies of those who supported music in his time were not likely to lead them to listen to an oratorio Biblical in theme, while they could go to Lincoln's Inn Fields and enjoy the more congenial subject of "The Beggars' Opera." Moreover, the great composer had ceased to pander to the vicious taste of the degraded public; and in "Israel"—the chief cause of his unpoplarity—he had reached in the choruses the height of sublimity.

The year 1739 was a fruitful one. "Saul" was produced; "Israel in Egypt;" the music to Dryden's "Ode on St. Cecilia's Day;" and the twelve grand concertos for violin, tenor, violoncello, and harpsichord accompaniment.

Referring to the latter masterly pieces a paper of the time says, "These concertos were performed at the Theatre Royal in Lincoln's Inn Fields, and now are played in most public places with the greatest applause."

Early in the following year came his admirable rendering of Milton's "L'Allegro" and "Il Penseroso."

This ode is one of Handel's finest compositions, yet it did not please his audiences, notwithstanding that an enthusiastic poet of the day was moved on hearing it to write—

"If e'er Arion's music calm'd the floods,
And Orpheus ever drew the dancing woods,
Why do not British trees and forests throng
To hear the sweeter notes of Handel's song?
This does the falsehood of the fable prove,
Or seas and woods, when Handel harps, would move."

The refusal of this last new work decided Handel to seek another field for his labours. He was tired of the treatment he had been receiving in London, and accordingly the great and persevering composer turned his back upon the ungrateful English public and prepared for a journey to Ireland. Pressing invitations had been long pouring in both from the nobility and the various musical societies which performed his works. He therefore determined to pay them a visit, and early in November, 1741, Handel started for the journey to which Pope alludes in his "Dunciad" when he says—

> "But soon, ah ! soon, rebellion will commence,
> If music meanly borrows aid from sense.
> Strong in new arms, lo ! giant Handel stands,
> Like bold Briareus, with his hundred hands ;
> To stir, to rouse, to shake the soul, he comes,
> And Jove's own thunders follow Mars's drums.
> Arrest him, Empress, or you sleep no more—
> She heard, and drove him to the Hibernian shore."

On his way to Dublin, Handel made a stay at Chester, of which Burney says : " I was at the public school in the city, and very well remember seeing him smoke a pipe over a dish of coffee, at the Exchange coffee-house; for being extremely curious to see so extraordinary a man I watched him narrowly as long as he remained in Chester, which, on account of the wind being unfavourable for his embarking at Parkgate, was several days.

During this time he applied to Mr. Baker, the organist, my first music-master, to know whether there were any choirmen in the cathedral who could sing at sight, as he wished to prove some books that had been hastily transcribed, by trying the choruses which he intended to perform in Ireland. Mr. Baker mentioned some of the most likely singers. A time was fixed for this private rehearsal at the Golden Falcon, where Handel was quartered; but, alas! on trial of the chorus in the 'Messiah' 'And with His stripes we are healed,' poor Janson, after repeated attempts, failed so egregiously, that Handel, after swearing in four or five different languages, cried out in broken English, 'You schountrel, tit not you dell me dat you could sing at soite?' 'Yes, sir,' said the painter, 'but not at *first* sight.'"

On the 18th November, 1741, Handel arrived in Dublin, and repaired to his house in Abbey Street, where a sort of box-office was opened to receive subscriptions for his concerts.

On the night of the first concert, the Musichall in Fishamble Street was crowded to suffocation. One after another his works were unfolded before these vast audiences; and at the performances of his "Acis" and "L'Allegro," the crush was so great that the doors had to be closed, and a bill put up to the effect that "no more money could be taken." Handel had brought over with him his oratorio the "Messiah," and to that "generous and polite nation," as he calls the Irish people, had been reserved the first opportunity of passing judgment upon this sublimest of oratorios. To their honour be it recorded, the verdict was one of enthusiastic approval; and though nearly one hundred and fifty years, with its ravages and changes, have passed away since the audience which filled the Music-hall in Fishamble Street, Dublin, set that seal upon it, the "Messiah" is to this day the most popular of all oratorios.

On the 13th April, 1742, at mid-day, Neal's great music-hall was closely packed with an audience anxiously awaiting Handel's new oratorio. The chief singers on that occasion were Mrs. Cibber and Mrs. Avolio, the chorus being sustained by choristers from St. Patrick's and Christ's cathedrals; while the band, which, as Handel wrote, was "really excellent," was under the direction of Mr. Dubourg.

An anecdote is told of Mrs. Cibber having sung "He was despised," so pathetically, that a reverend gentleman in the boxes forgot himself so far as to audibly exclaim at the close, "Woman, for this be all thy sins forgiven." Another relates that, in compliance with the request that "the ladies who honour this performance will be pleased to come without their hoops," the fair sex for the

Handel. 69

most part actually did leave those articles at home on that occasion.

The success of the first performance was so great that the critics could not find words to express the exquisite delight it afforded. The proceeds for the charities amounted to four hundred pounds, and it was certainly the most brilliant event of Handel's life.

The "Messiah" was begun on the 22nd August, 1741, and completed on the 14th of the next month, so that this great masterpiece was composed in the marvellously short space of twenty-three days.

After the grave movement of the overture, with its startling chords, as if to arrest the attention for the divine history about to be told, there follows the sprightly fugal movement which concludes the overture, and then "Comfort ye my people" reaches our ears. What consolation it brings with it as the mighty Messiah assures His people that "their iniquity is pardoned." Soon hope revives, their hearts leap for joy, and with one consent they break forth with "The Glory of the Lord." But "Who may abide the day of His coming?" They are not prepared for the spotless King "like a refiner's fire." Their sins are great and numberless. Who shall cleanse them? He will Himself— "He shall purify" bursts out in gladsome tones. With the notes of the "Pastoral Symphony" Bethlehem and its associations are instantly before us. The shepherds' pipes have ceased, and they with their flocks are drawn together for the night on the hill-sides around Bethlehem. The beautiful blue sky is spangled with the brilliant lights of heaven; the great day luminary has gone down, and Night has slowly drawn her sombre mantle over its setting rays; the air is filled with the delicious odour of myrrh, aloes, and cassia, earth's incense rising to heaven—all is rest—

" All things are hush'd as Nature's self lay dead ;"

when lo! the blue firmament of heaven is suddenly brightened with the "Glory of the Lord," and the "Angel of the Lord" appears to the bewildered shepherds. "Fear not, I bring you good tidings," is the seraph's joyful message, and suddenly the whole heaven around is opened, and myriads of the heavenly host sing, "Glory to God in the highest, and on earth peace, good will toward men."

In the first part of this oratorio, the coming of the Saviour of mankind is treated; in the second and more important part the Life, Sufferings, and Resurrection of our Lord are set forth. It contains three of the finest choruses Handel ever wrote—" Behold the Lamb of God," "Lift up your heads," and the "Hallelujah," while the solos are exquisitely beautiful, abounding

Handel. 71

with tenderness and sympathy. Who is not moved as the plaintive air, " He was despised"—curiously enough written in the major key—or the tenor air, " Behold, and see if there be any sorrow," is poured into their ears? To the short chorus, no less noble than its larger brethren, "The Lord gave the Word," succeeds the going forth of the preachers, in that delicious soprano melody, " How beautiful are the feet;" the mighty extent of their mission is then revealed; one after another the parts roll on with their powerful cry, "Their sound is gone out into all lands." The Gospel for a time has to wage fierce war against the world, but ultimately the Word prevails, and " Hallelujah, for the Lord God Omnipotent reigneth," bursts forth from every tongue. The praise is loud and long;—" King of Kings, and Lord of Lords " is the reiterated strain, till the whole earth is awakened by the rejoicings, and joins with her tremendous voice in the cry, " Hallelujah! Hallelujah!"

The third part is devoted to the contemplation of "things that shall be hereafter"—death, resurrection, and life eternal. The pure melody, " I know that my Redeemer liveth," opens this part in the most befitting manner, and we come upon the fine bass solo, " The trumpet shall sound." " If God is for us " prepares us for the grand strains of the myriads of white-robed angels around the throne. " Worthy is the Lamb" is their continual cry, to which ascription there is but one response. Heaven and earth, sea and sky assent in the severe chorus which follows, the whole creation unites in the great "Amen."

Towards the latter part of the year 1742 Handel returned from his pleasant visit to Ireland, and on the 18th February, 1743, gave his new oratorio, "Samson," at the Theatre Royal, Covent Garden.

Beard, the famous English tenor, sang the part of Samson; yet the fashionable world would not listen to it, and to draw upon his audiences, gave tea and card parties whenever Handel announced a concert. "Samson" is a wonderful treatment of Milton's thrilling poem. Nearly the whole of the work is made up of airs and recitatives — the piercing lamentations of Samson and his followers,—the choruses being limited. Where they do occur, however, they bear the hand of the master; for instance, the chorus of the priests of Dagon, and "Round about the starry throne," or the double chorus, "Fixed in his everlasting seat," though short, are superbly written. Most of the solos are exquisite, some of Samson's songs being especially beautiful. "Why does the God of Israel sleep?" and "Your charms to ruin," are among these, while the treacherous Dalilah has some appropriate music allotted to her.

Handel. 73

This oratorio was immediately followed by the serenata "Semele," and the fine Te Deum and Anthem for the victory at Dettingen. They were sung in the presence of the king at St. James's Chapel, and were declared to be "so truly masterly and sublime, as well as new in their kind, that they proved this great genius to be not only inexhaustible, but likewise still rising to a higher degree of perfection."

For the Lent concerts of 1744, the oratorios of "Joseph," "Belshazzar," and "Hercules" were provided, but none of them were tolerated more than once or twice. However, Handel would not give up. A few months after he took the Haymarket Theatre, and among his other oratorios brought out "Deborah." But it was of no use. The clique against him was composed for the most part of those who supported music; and after struggling through a few performances, the noble man was compelled to close the house and declare himself a bankrupt.

The theatre closed, Handel sat himself down and wrote the "Occasional Oratorio."

This, notwithstanding much that has been said and written to the contrary, is certainly one of Handel's masterpieces, and deserves to be more frequently heard. The overture is exceedingly fine, and full of melodious music. "O Lord, how many are my foes," with its hautboy accompaniment, and that tender strain in the minor, "He has his mansion fixed on high," are of the highest order. "His sceptre is the rod of power," and "To God our strength," make two very energetic bass songs—the trumpet and hautboy accompaniment to the latter being most effective. Nor has the tenor voice been forgotten. "May balmy peace," and the delicate minor air, "When Israel, like the bounteous Nile," are two songs which none but a master could write.

"Judas Maccabæus" was brought out at Covent Garden on the 1st April, 1747, and the public smiled upon it! It was composed in honour of the return of the Duke of Cumberland from his recent victory at Culloden. With the Jews of the day it was a favourite, for it sets forth one of the most interesting episodes in their history.

"Mourn, ye afflicted," the cry, "Hear us, O Lord," as the Jews go forth to battle, and "We never will bow down," are its finest choruses; while "Arm, arm, ye brave," and "Sound an alarm," both in "Judas," are universally admired. Much has been said and written about the "repetition of sentiment" and "inferiority" of "Judas," but we can see no reason for this except that people *will* write what others have written before them. "Judas" has no other place but that in the first rank of Handel's oratorios.

Handel. 75

This same year has the merit of producing "Joshua," a work of but thirty days.

It possesses much that is graceful and masterly. "Ye sons of Israel," the opening chorus, is a noble conception, while of the "Glory to God," the matured musician, "Father Haydn," remarked that "he was perfectly certain that only one inspired author could or ever would pen so sublime a composition." "Hail, mighty Joshua," is also another truly Handelian chorus. Some of its melodies, too, are lovely. "Hark! 'tis the linnet," with its playful flute and violin accompaniment, and Joshua's song, "While Kedron's brook," are two of the finest.

"Solomon" was composed between the 5th May and 19th June, 1748, but was not performed till March, 1749, and then only twice. After this it was laid aside and heard no more of till Handel brought it out for the season of 1759. Such was the early fate of this great work.

The sparkling overture ended, we have instantly before us three magnificent and complicated choruses, such as Handel delighted to write; then follows the fine music between Solomon and Pharaoh's daughter. The duet, "Welcome as the dawn of day," and the air "With thee th' unsheltered moor I tread," both in this part, are two very pleasing pieces. The second part, opening with one of Handel's best and most intricate choruses, "See the censer curling rise," is devoted to that interesting episode in Solomon's reign, when the two women sought his judgment as to which should have the living child. All the music with which Handel has graced this scene is of the noblest quality. The true mother's touching air, "Can I see my infant gored," is simply sublime, and Zadoch's song, "See the tall palm," is a happy inspiration. The Queen of Sheba's visit to Solomon is treated in the third part, and here the mighty genius is as charmingly fresh as before. There is a good deal of recitative, but not a note too much, or it would not be there. "Every sight these eyes behold," and "Will the sun forget to streak," with its delicate flute obligato, are two chaste airs, which the Queen of Sheba has to sing.

The choruses—Handel's great *forte*—are rich in this part. Two of the finest are, "Shake the dome," and "Praise the Lord with harp and tongue," till, passing the pleasing duet, "Every joy that wisdom knows," we come upon that masterly piece of choral-writing which closes this magnificent oratorio, the double chorus, "The name of the wicked."

"Theodora" appeared on the 16th March, 1749, but was badly received,—so neglected was it that Burney relates that "Handel was glad to give orders for admission to any professors who did not perform. Two

Handel.

of these gentlemen having afterwards applied to Handel for an order to hear the 'Messiah,' he cried out, 'Oh, your sarvant, mein herren: you are tamnaple tainty—you would not co to 'Teodora'; tere was room enough to tance dere, when dat was perform.'

"This work was Handel's favourite; and he used to say that the chorus, 'He saw the lovely youth,' in 'Theodora,' was far beyond anything in the 'Messiah.'"

"Jephtha," his last oratorio, was produced in February, 1752, and under most painful circumstances. For a year Handel had had the score before him, and could not get through it. Again and again he seized his pen, yet only to lay it down again by reason of the dimness of his eyes. Poor Handel! his sight was fast going. Two operations were performed which partly relieved him, when his indomitable ardour led him to work on "Jephtha" again. He completed it. Alas! the last few pages of the score show too clearly the progress the fearful malady had made. Another unsuccessful operation, and darkness came over him. With immense grief he could cry—

> "O dark, dark, dark amid the blaze of noon,
> Irrevocably dark—total eclipse
> Without all hope of day!
> O first-created beam, and thou great Word,
> 'Let there be light, and light was over all;'
> Why am I thus bereaved Thy prime decree?
> The sun to me is dark."

The good Handel resigned himself to his sore affliction, and though he could no longer compose, he continued to give performances in aid of the Foundling Hospital and other charitable institutions, when he used to improvise upon the organ. On one of these occasions " Samson " was given, and when Beard, the singer, came to the pathetic air of the sightless hero, " Total Eclipse," the grand old master at the organ was seen to grow pale and tremble, and many of the audience were moved to tears as the blind musician was led forward to bow to their applause.

For a few years the great master lingered on, with the infirmities of age gradually creeping upon him. He was sensible that Death was not far off; but, at peace with God and man, he awaited its approach without dismay. His prayer was "that he might breathe his last on Good Friday, in hopes of meeting his good God, his sweet Lord and Saviour, on the day of His resurrection." This was granted.

On returning home from one of his charitable performances, a faintness came over him, and Dr. Warren, Handel's physician, had him carried to bed. From this bed he never rose again. Slowly he sank, and passed quietly and peacefully out of the world on Good Friday, April 14th, 1759, at the mature age of seventy-four years.

Handel.

His music has gone out into all lands, but in our midst—in the Poet's Corner of the old pile at Westminster—his mortal remains are peacefully resting, with sublime tone-waves ever hovering over them.

PRINCIPAL INCIDENTS IN THE LIFE OF HANDEL.

Born at Halle 23rd February	1685
First Opera " Almira" produced	1705
Visited Italy	1706
Settled in London	1712
"Esther" composed	1720
"Saul" first performed	1739
"Israel in Egypt" first performed	1739
The "Messiah" first performed	1742
"Sampson" composed	1743
"Judas Maccabæus" first performed	1747
Afflicted with blindness	1752
Died April 14th	1759

Gluck.

THOUGH Glück has left us fewer of his compositions than have most of the great masters, yet he has for ever associated his name with the opera, not alone by his superb works, but by the reforms also which, late in life, he effected in this branch of the art. " The regenerator of the opera," as he has been rightly and deservedly called, stepped upon the scene just in time to rescue opera from the state of degeneracy and decay into which it was sinking. Partly from the caprice and vanity of singers, and partly from a too prevailing spirit of concession among composers, all that had been grand and effective in Italian opera was being degraded into the tiresome and ridiculous. Glück's end and aim was, in his own words, "to restrict the art of music to its true object—that of aiding the effect of poetry by giving greater expression to the words and scenes; but, without interrupting the action of the plot, and without weakening the impression by needless ornamentation."

That he succeeded, most people agree. His works are powerful in their simplicity. They are strictly original, and are stamped with high and refined feeling; truth and naturalness being the abiding principles on which they are formed.

On the borders of Bohemia stands the small town of Weissenwangen, and here, on the 2nd July, 1714, Christopher Willibald Glück was born.

His parents were in anything but easy circumstances, and, notwithstanding the love for music which young Glück early manifested, they could afford no money for teachers. The boy was therefore sent to one of the common schools, and there, simultaneously with his A B C, he was taught the gamut, and the art of reading from music as well as from books—a course which might with advantage be adopted in English schools; we should then probably have more native talent to lavish our praise and our money upon, instead of having to send abroad for recipients of them. But Glück is our subject, not native talent.

Christopher was still young when he lost his father. He had been badly off before, but this misfortune made matters still worse. Gradually he was neglected, till ultimately the poor lad was left totally to his own exertions for a livelihood.

Fortunately, he had taken to studying the violoncello,

but with no better help than an old instruction-book afforded him. His talent and industry, however, had overcome many difficulties, and he had made sufficient progress to enable him to obtain an engagement with a company of wandering minstrels. His daily bread, if nothing more, was thus certain, though happily more than that came from his connection with the *troupe*.

From Prague the wandering musicians slowly wended their way to Vienna, and there Fortune smiled on the young Slavonian.

Glück's talent soon attracted attention; and, together with his forlorn condition, won the sympathy of a few generous hearts in Vienna, who not only provided him with proper sustenance, but also furnished him with means to continue his musical education. The grateful fellow made good use of this opportunity, and for a year or two completely gave himself up to the study of harmony and counterpoint.

At the age of twenty-four, Glück bade adieu to his many kind friends in the then German capital, and set out for Italy, for the purpose of completing his musical studies.

He took up his residence in Milan, where he had the good fortune to become acquainted with the celebrated theorist, Padre Martini.

Glück placed himself under his direction, and for

something like four years or more, found in him a worthy master and friend.

After this long term of diligent study, Glück felt that the time had arrived to give a work of his own to the world, and he then composed his first opera, "Artaxerxes."

This was given at the Milan Theatre in 1741, and met with much success.

The reception accorded to "Artaxerxes," tempted one of the Venice managers to try a work from the young composer's pen, and the following year Glück was busy upon "Clytemnestra" for this city.

Another genuine success attended his efforts here; the coffers of the theatre benefited largely, and the enterprising managers bargained for "Demetrio," which met with a no less favourable reception.

The next two years' work was divided alternately between Milan and Turin, for which cities he wrote five or six operas.

At the end of this time, Glück had made an immense impression throughout Italy. His fame, too, had spread to other countries, and tempting terms for operas flowed in from all directions.

The ears of Lord Middlesex were tickled by all he had heard of Glück, and he longed to get the young composer over to the King's Theatre in the Haymarket.

On the part of the English public, the noble manager made a liberal offer, which Glück could not resist. He arrived in London, in 1745, just as the rebellion in Scotland had broken out, and found the theatres closed, and the whole city in a state of suspicion and confusion.

But the opportunity of hearing Glück was not to be lost. Lord Middlesex appeared before the Government and implored them, for the great composer's sake, to re-open the theatre. His influence at last prevailed; and the house was soon as busy as ever.

"La Caduta del Giganti" (the Fall of the Giants), was composed expressly for Glück's introduction to the English public. It excited little interest, however; and the audiences seemed to care more for Mdlle. Violetta's dancing than for the demi-political opera.

In the following year "Artamene" was produced, but alas! it met with the same fate as its predecessor. Other operas were composed during the few years Glück remained in England, but none of them created any enthusiasm. It is said that the number of these unsuccessful works is between forty and fifty.

His visit to England was certainly not a success; though it should be remembered that he came at a time when a formidable rival, Handel, was here in the zenith of his popularity; honoured and courted, too, by fashionable society. Besides, people's minds were more occupied then with political events than with the progress of the Arts.

Disappointed at the reception accorded him, Glück quietly took his departure for Vienna. In this city he lived in retirement till the year 1754, when he was invited to Rome, where he produced "La Clemenza di Tito," "Antigone," and several others, all with more or less success. He was certainly high in the favour of the Italians at that time.

From Rome, Glück went to Florence, where he made the acquaintance of one with whom he was destined to play an important part. This was Ranieri di Calzabigi, a poet of a high order. Their first meeting left the two men sworn friends, bent on effecting a reform in Italian opera.

Glück soon after returned to Vienna, and in 1764 produced "Orfeo" as an example of reformed opera.

It was received with great favour, and was played twenty-eight times in succession, a long run in those days. Guadagni's splendid singing and acting made "Orfeo" quite the rage, so that ere long it was known all over Europe. At Paris and Parma it became an especial favourite. It was composed to celebrate the marriage of the Emperor Joseph the Second; and its original caste included the following august personages: the Archduchess Amelia, who played the part of Apollo; the Archduchesses Elizabeth, Josephine, and Charlotte—the Graces—and the Archduke Leopold, who presided at the harpsichord.

Our composer, then, was fifty years old, when in "Orfeo" he laid the foundation of his imperishable fame. This is undoubtedly the first of his operas in which we find him in that true vein, which, so late in life, he began to develop. Glück before "Orfeo" is nobody; and so well is this known, that it has been commonly said, "Glück never composed an opera till he was fifty." It contained most of the reforms, and the simplicity and purity he gradually developed, till that perfection of character was reached which we have in "Alceste" and "Iphigénie en Tauride." Five years intervened between "Orfeo" and "Alceste," though the difference in the two works would seem to imply more.

"Alceste," the second opera on the reformed plan, which simplified the music in favour of the poetry, was produced in Vienna in 1769. Calzabigi again supplied the text.

The first performance took place at the Burg Theatre. It is thus described by Sonnenfels: "I am in the land of miracles. A serious melodrama with natural voices, music without *solfège* or rather chirruping. Italian poetry without affectation and bombast. The Burg Theatre has been opened with this threefold wonder."

Glück. 87

The opera of "Alceste" was a long stride from "Orfeo," and explains his reforms more boldly. Glück dedicated it to the Grand Duke Leopold of Tuscany, and in a lengthy dedication set forth his views.

Starting with its libretto, Calzabigi set aside all flowery descriptions, surperfluous comparisons, and cold, formal maxims, for the language of the heart, powerful passions, striking situations, and an ever-varying drama.

Its music is thoroughly Glückish throughout. All the noble simplicity of style—which the dedication proves was his intention and aim—the avoidance of difficult passages at the cost of distinctness; the subserviency of the whole of the music to the poetry: the new style of overture which was to be a kind of programme music to the whole opera; all these, and many other new views, contained in this interesting dedication, are strongly exemplified throughout the work.

The reception it met with did not quite please Glück, although on and off it was performed on the Vienna stage for two or three years. Dr. Burney, when he visited Vienna in 1772, says, "It was still being performed, and," goes on the learned doctor, "it seemed to have impressed the lovers of music in the imperial capital with a partiality for that speciés of dramatic music, which was not likely be be soon removed. The critics, moreover, were not favourably disposed towards it, and in dedicating his next works, "Paride ed Elena," to the Duke of Braganza, Glück does not miss the opportunity of expressing his opinion of those gentlemen. In this dedicatory letter dated from Vienna, October 30th, 1773, Glück says, "The sole reason that induced me to publish my music of 'Alceste,' was the hope of finding successors, who, following the path already opened, and encouraged by the full suffrages of an enlightened public, should take courage to destroy the abuses introduced on the Italian stage, and bring it as far as possible to perfection. I bitterly feel that I have hitherto striven after this in vain. Pedants and critics, an infinite multitude, who form the greatest obstacle to the progress of the Fine Arts, loudly protested against a method which, were it actually to take root, would at once destroy all their pretensions to supremacy of judgment, and injure their sphere of influence. They thought themselves entitled to pronounce a verdict on 'Alceste' from some informal rehearsals, badly conducted, and even worse executed; the effect to be produced in a theatre being calculated from that in a room, with the same sagacity as in a certain city of Greece, where judgment was passed at the distance of a few feet, on statues originally intended to be erected on the most lofty columns. A fastidious ear perhaps found a vocal passage too harsh, or another too impassioned, or not sufficiently studied, forgetting that, in their proper places, such forcible expression and striking contrasts were absolutely required. One pedant took advantage of an evident oversight, or perhaps an error of the press, to condemn it as if it had been some irremediable sin against the mysteries of harmony; it was likewise decided in full conclave, that this style of music was barbarous and extravagant."

There were, however, better days in store for "Alceste." Despite the disparaging critics, it increased Glück's fame wondrously. The Parisians wished to see him, and to have a new work from the revolutionizer of Italian opera.

Attached to the French Embassy at Vienna was one Du Rollet, a bit of a poet. To him, Glück confided the offer made to him by the French Académie Royale, and his desire to visit the French capital. Du Rollet saw nothing but success in such a visit, and advised Glück to go, at the same time promising him a libretto from his own pen, to set for his *début*. Late in 1773, therefore, the Chevalier Glück, for he had lately been created a Knight of the papal order of the Golden Spur, set out, with Du Rollet's libretto, arranged from Racine's "Iphigénie en Tauride," under his arm, *en route* for Paris.

Arrived in Paris, Glück set to work to put "Iphigénie" upon the stage. This work had cost him nearly a year to write, besides a long and careful study of the French language, which Rousseau declared was radically unmusical. Glück had not as much difficulty with the language, however, as he had with his French musicians. He met a terribly slovenly and ignorant orchestra, all up in arms against the foreign music. But this was smoothed down by his patron and former pupil—the Dauphiness Marie Antoinette. The first performance took place on the 19th August, 1774, when it was found necessary for the police to take precautions against a disturbance. But "Iphigénie" proved an enormous success. Marie Antoinette herself gave the signal for applause, and the whole house followed her example. In some parts the house was in raptures, the military brandishing their swords in the general applause.

Sophie Arnould was the "Iphigenia," and thoroughly satisfied the composer in her *rôle*. Larrivée filled the part of Agamemnon, and for once it is said abstained from singing through his nose, so that the public were unable to say, as they generally did, when he had finished one of his fine airs, "That nose has really a magnificent voice!"

The French people were now in ecstasies with Glück.

They fêted him, and declared with enthusiasm that he had discovered the ancient music of the Greeks; that he was the only musician in Europe who knew how to express the real language of the passions; in short, that he was a little god of music.

Of its effect upon the Court, we have Marie Antoinette's own testimony in a letter to her sister.

"A glorious triumph, at last, my dear Christine," writes the amiable dauphiness. "On the 19th we had the first performance of Glück's 'Iphigénie.' I was quite enchanted with it, and nothing else is talked of. . . . All the world wish to see the piece, which is a good sign, and Glück seems well satisfied. I am sure you will rejoice as much as I do at this occurrence."

Following "Iphigénie," Glück brought out an adaptation in French, of his "Orpheus," which was not very successful, though "the ballet was very fine."

Edwards, in his "History of the Opera," relates that Glück and the celebrated Vestris had a grand squabble as to the introduction of dancing into "Orpheus." Vestris, Voltaire, and Frederick of Russia were the only three great men in Europe, according to the dancer's theory, and he would have his *chacone* in the opera somewhere.

"Write me the music of a *chacone*, Monsieur Glück," said the god of dancing.

"*A chacone!*" exclaimed the indignant composer. "Do you think the Greeks, whose manners we are endeavouring to depict, knew what a *chacone* was?"

"Did they not?" replied the astonished Vestris.

"Then they are much to be pitied."

Another squabble which took place between Glück and the Prince d'Hennin, is on record in connection with this opera.

The caprice of the interesting Sophie Arnould compelled Glück, as well as the orchestra, to go to her house for the rehearsals of "Orpheus." On one of these occasions, the prima donna was singing, and the orchestra in full swing, when suddenly the door opened and in marched the Prince d'Hennin. No notice was taken of his entrance, when suddenly the prince, addressing Sophie Arnould in the middle of her air, said, "I believe it is the custom in France to rise when any one enters the room, especially if it be a person of some importance."

Glück leaped from his seat with rage, rushed towards the intruder, and, with his eyes flashing fire, said to him, "The custom in Germany, sir, is to rise only for those whom we esteem." Turning to Arnould, he added, "I perceive, mademoiselle, that you are not mistress in your own house; I leave you, and shall never set foot here again;" then hurriedly replacing his antique head cap with his wig, and putting on his coat—for he always conducted in this free style—Glück made straight for the street.

Marie Antoinette was much annoyed when she heard of the treatment her favoured Glück had received, and insisted on the prince paying him a visit and making an apology for the insult.

In 1775 Glück produced a gala opera called " Cythère .assiegée," which found little favour; and, soon afterwards, an adaptation suitable for the French boards of his " Alceste."

This work roused the city once more to excitement. The theatre was crammed at every performance, and crowds of excited military and citizens were turned away from the doors. Marie Antoinette's favourite composer was again lauded to the skies, and his admirers declared there was no composer to compare with him.

Ever since his arrival there had been one powerful opponent at the French Court, in the general applause for Glück. This was Madame du Barry, the celebrated favourite of Louis XV., who, when Marie Antoinette had her pet composer, longed also to have hers.

Du Barry was an Italian by birth, and had no difficulty whatever in mustering a powerful Italian faction about her, bent upon open opposition to Glück and his theory.

Glück's praises had long enough rung in the ears of the imperious favourite, and "Alceste" brought things to a climax. She would have some one to represent Italian music, and forthwith applied to the Neapolitan ambassador to request Piccini to come to Paris.

Piccini's arrival was the signal for action. Madame du Barry rose up, and, assisted by Louis XV. himself, began to rally her forces. A powerful Italian party gathered round her, and first showed their strength and intentions by inducing the Grand Opera people to entrust to Piccini the composition of an opera, which they had previously agreed for with Glück.

A furious war broke out. All Paris joined in it, and bitter and fierce it was while it lasted. Politics, and everything but this battle royal, for the time, were forgotten. The press took up different sides; pamphlets appeared; poems, cruel satires, epigrams, and the like swamped the city, and in some of these the rival composers were attacked most unmercifully, though they took no active part in the affair. Piccini had come to Paris for little else than to secure the tempting payment held out to him, and Glück was in Germany when the feud broke out. However, the respective leaders kept things going very briskly, and so zealously in fact, that no door was opened to a stranger till the question was answered "Are you a Piccinist or a

Glückist?" It was the same in the cafés and in the streets: "Monsieur, êtes vous Picciniste ou Glückiste?" decided whether a meeting was to have a comfortable ending or not.

Amusing and many were the reports about Glück. The Piccinists declared he had got out of the way purposely; that he had no melody in him; that he was dried up and had nothing new to give France. But one evening in society these reports were dispelled.

"Do you know," said the Abbé Arnaud, one of Glück's warmest partisans, "that the chevalier is coming back to us with an 'Orlando' and an 'Armida' in his portfolio?"

"But Piccini is also at work upon an 'Orlando!'" replied a Piccinist.

"So much the better," replied the abbé, "for then we shall have an 'Orlando' and also an 'Orlandino.'"

In 1777 the Abbé Arnaud's words were realized so far as "Armida" was concerned, for Glück returned to Paris with this opera in his possession. As to the other, when he heard that Piccini was working on the same text, he burned all that he had already written; and, as he quaintly puts it in a letter, "perhaps, thereby, saved the public from hearing bad music."

"Armida" made its *début* at the Paris Grand Opera on September 23rd, 1777. It was at first just successful, a *succès d'estime*, and no more, though afterwards it blazed into immense popularity.

Many of the critics were down upon it after its first performance, and one spoke of it in most disparaging terms. He said that only the first act and part of the fifth were applauded, and the rest but coldly received. The whole opera, in his opinion, was too noisy, and the composer had taken a wrong view of Quinault's book.

Glück's opinion of "Armida" was very decided and exalted, as is evident from what he wrote and said about it.

He took great pains in composing it, and, when treating with the opera director, demanded a bill of conditions as to rehearsals, &c., without the fulfilment of which he declared he would keep "Armida" for his own pleasure, the music being written in a manner which would prevent its soon growing old.

In a letter to his friend Bailly du Rollet, the composer speaks just as highly of it. "I have put forth," he says, "all the little strength still left in me, in order to finish 'Armida.' I must confess that I should like to finish my career with it."

The Princesse de Lamballe's diary speaks of Glück and his work. From it we glean that "Glück composed his 'Armida' in order to make a flattering allusion to Marie Antoinette's beauty. I never saw her majesty display so much interest in any event as in the success of this piece. She really became quite a slave to 'Armida,' and had the unusual complaisance to hear every piece of Glück's before it was rehearsed in the theatre. Glück often told her that he always re-arranged his music according to the impression that it made on the queen."

Another entry relates that when one day the unfortunate princess was wishing him joy at the increasing success of his work, he exclaimed, "Ah, my dear princess, all I now want to raise me to the seventh heaven are two such beautiful heads as that of her majesty and your own."—"If you want only that," answered the princess, "we can be painted for you, Herr Glück."—"No, no, you do not understand me, I mean living heads; my actresses are very ugly, and Armida as well as her *confidante* ought to be very lovely."

One more extract, and then adieu to the entries which so fair a hand once penned. "Great as was the public success of 'Armida,' no one prized this work more highly than the composer himself. Glück was passionately enamoured of it; he said to the queen that the air of France had redoubled the powers of his musical genius, and the sight of her majesty had given such a wonderful impetus to his ideas that his compositions had become like herself, angelic and sublime."

7

The stir made by the new work, added only fuel to an already fierce fire, and this was doubly increased when Piccini appeared, and, with his completed commission for the opera house, achieved a most brilliant success.

Here was something for the Du Barry clique to harp upon, and about which there could be no two opinions—Piccini's "Orlando" had undoubtedly been more successful than Glück's "Armida."

The Glückists must therefore achieve a success which should surpass that of their rivals; and, accordingly, they besought Marie Antoinette to prevail on Glück to write another opera.

While this feud was going on, the direction of the opera house passed into the hands of one Devismes, who, as soon as he assumed command, conceived the plan of setting both Glück and Piccini to work upon the same subject—" Iphigenia in Tauris."

The effect of this step on the rival factions may be imagined. The Piccinists demanded that their "Iphigenia" should be produced first, and Devismes gave his word of honour to Piccini that it should be; telling him also that his opera would be put into rehearsal before Glück's.

Glück soon after completed his "Iphigenia," and handed it to Devismes, but Piccini, relying on this gentleman's honour, when he heard the news gave little heed to it, though he resolved to complete his own task as quickly as possible.

Going to the theatre, however, a few days afterwards with his " Iphigenia " completed, he was horror-struck to find that Glück's work was already in rehearsal!

He flew to Devismes's room, and entreated him to stay the rehearsals. But it was of no use; the manager was extremely sorry, and in despair, but he had received a command to produce Glück's work immediately, and he could do nothing but obey.

The rehearsals of Glück's " Iphigenia," therefore, went on, and on 18th May, 1779, the opera was first performed. Its success, the excitement it caused, and the impression made by the music, were marvellous.

All were now for Glück, Piccini included, upon whom it had such an impression that he declared that his own work should not be brought out.

Devismes, however, wished otherwise, and soon afterwards another "Iphigénie" stood on the same boards.

The first night made it evident there was little success for it; the public had drunk too deeply of Glück to be intoxicated with other music. The second night's performance came off, and with it a burlesque instead of an opera. No sooner had the curtain gone up than

Piccini discovered, much to his alarm, that something was wrong with his *prima donna*. Iphigenia was unable to stand upright; she rolled to all the compass points of the stage, repeated the words, stammered, hesitated, made faces at the pit and orchestra, till, finally, all were convinced that Mdlle. Laguerre was drunk! Although the king was present, the house was soon in an uproar of laughter; and some facetious individual sang out, "This is not 'Iphigenia in Tauris,' this is 'Iphigenia in Champagne.'"

For this serious misdemeanour *mademoiselle* was sent to prison for two days, after which she re-appeared and sang the part divinely.

This did not put an end to the musical war. Piccinists and Glückists went on with their strife as fiercely as ever; nor did it cease till Glück died, and Piccini had sought retirement at Passy.

In September of the following year Glück finished "Echo et Narcisse," and with this work determined to close his career.

Shortly after its production the libretto of "The Danaïdes" was offered him, but he declined it, saying, "I mean to write no more operas. I am old—I have finished my career; and, besides, the annoyances I lately met with in Paris about my opera 'Narcisse,' have for ever disgusted me. I write no more operas."

Glück.

There is little left to tell of Glück's life.

Worn out with the fatigue of seventy years' incessant work, the old man passed into retirement at Vienna, to enjoy the fruits of his long labours. He had grown rich; he had earned something like thirty thousand pounds. In his declining years he frequently received friendly visits from kings, and princes, and persons of distinction. Amongst others, the Emperor and Empress of Russia paid him a visit, and comforted the aged composer with assurances of the pleasure they had always derived from his music.

In 1786 he made his will. It is dated April 2nd, and runs thus:—"As nothing is more certain than death, nor more uncertain than the time of it, I, the undersigned, being in the full possession of all my faculties, give my last instructions as follows:—

" 1. I commend my soul to the infinite mercy of God; my body to be interred according to the rites of the Holy Catholic Church.

" 2. I bequeath the sum of twenty-five florins for fifty masses for my soul.

" 3. I bequeath to the poor-house one florin, to the General Hospital one florin, to the Bürger Hospital one florin, to the Normal School one florin—four florins in all.

" 4. Further, I bequeath to each of my domestics

still in my service at the time of my death one year's wages.

"5. I leave it entirely to the will and pleasure of my heir-general to give anything to my brothers and sisters.

"6. As the fundamental principle of every testament is the appointment of an heir, I hereby appoint my dear wife, M. Anna von Glück, née Bergin, as my sole and exclusive heir; and, that no doubts may arise as to whether the silver and other personal property be mine or my wife's, I hereby also declare all the silver and other valuables to be the sole property of my wife, and, consequently, not included in my previous bequests. Should, however, this my last will and testament not prove valid, I hope it may be considered legal as a codicil.

"Lastly, I appoint my highly-esteemed cousin, Joseph von Holbein, Royal Hofrath, executor to this my will; and I bequeath to him a snuff-box, as a remembrance.

"Signed, and witnessed, &c.,

"CHRISTOPH GLUCK."

Shortly after this act he was seized with a paralytic stroke, but still lingered on till the 15th November, 1787, when the "Michael Angelo of Music" passed into the spirit world.

Glück.

Principal Incidents in the Life of Gluck.

Born on the 2nd July	1714
Under Padre Martini in Italy	1738
First Opera, "Artaxerxes," produced	1741
Glück visited London	1745
"Orfeo" produced at Vienna	1764
"Alceste" first performed	1769
"Iphigénie" produced at Paris	1774
Glückists and Piccinists War	1777
"Armida" first performed in Paris	1777
"Iphigenia in Tauris" first performed	1779
"Echo et Narcisse" composed	1779
Struck with paralysis	1786
Died, 15th November	1787

Haydn.

FOREMOST among those master-musicians who have benefited Art by creating what may be termed a landmark in music, must be placed the familiar name of Haydn. Unfettered by the rules and trammels of any one school or master, he followed the bent of his own inclinations, formed his own conceptions of what was good and beautiful in music, and created a style eminently his own—one which established itself in his very first composition for strings, and to a great extent revolutionized instrumental music. In music for the chamber Haydn has never been equalled; while his "Creation," masses, or symphonies, would each alone have rendered his name immortal. The list of works composed by Haydn comprises upwards of eight hundred compositions, including one hundred and eighteen orchestral symphonies, eighty-three quartets for stringed instruments, twenty-four

Haydn. 105

operas, fourteen masses, and an immense number of smaller compositions.

The 31st March, 1732, was the memorable day that brought Francis Joseph Haydn into the world. This was at Rohrau, a small town not very far distant from Vienna.

His father was a poor wheelwright, and his mother, before her marriage, had been cook in the service of Count Harrach, the lord of the village of Rohrau. It was an humble, but a happy and peaceful home in which Haydn passed his childhood; though, as is the custom throughout Germany, even these poor people had their musical evenings.

Neither of Haydn's parents had received any musical education, but the father was fond of music, and, moreover, was gifted with a fair tenor voice. He could also play a little upon the harp, though he knew not a note of music; while the mother possessed a good store of simple airs, which she often sang to the harp accompaniment of her husband, and to that of their little boy also, who loved to stand in front of them scraping away with the nearest approach to a fiddle that he could command —two pieces of wood, one of which served as a violin, the other as a bow.

What a subject for a painter—the future great symphonist enjoying his music under these circumstances!

Thus busily engaged, he one day attracted the attention of his cousin Frank, a schoolmaster, who had come to pay the family a visit. He was well acquainted with music, and was so much astonished to see a boy of but six years old beating time with such precision, that he at once proposed to take little Joseph into his own house, and to teach him music. This was agreed to; and when the schoolmaster cousin returned home, he had in his charge the future composer of "The Creation."

Haydn received instruction in the violin and other instruments; and his marvellous aptness for music was soon spread about by those who visited the schoolhouse.

Two years passed thus, when Kapelle-meister Reüter chanced to find his way to the schoolhouse. He was in search of boys for the choir of the cathedral of St. Stephen at Vienna, and no sooner did the schoolmaster hear this than he proposed his young relative, Haydn. Reüter tried him at sight singing, and the precision and purity of tone with which he sang perfectly charmed the *maître de chapelle*. "But you do not shake," said Reüter. "How can you expect me to shake when my cousin cannot?" replied the boy. "Come here," said Reüter, "I will teach you;" and the kind musician took him between his knees, and succeeded in getting from him a perfect shake. For this, little Joseph was rewarded with a plate of fresh cherries, which the learned professor emptied into his coat pocket. Never did Haydn forget this; and in after-years he used to say that whenever he heard a shake, he always thought of those beautiful cherries.

Reüter returned to Vienna with his prize, and soon installed him in the choir of St. Stephen's, where, in addition to his school lessons, he received instruction from very good masters in singing and in playing the violin and piano. Here was music such as the boy's soul longed for; and from this period Haydn has said, that he did not recollect to have passed a single day without practising sixteen hours, and sometimes eighteen.

Let all young students who desire to accomplish anything bear this in mind, and take a lesson from the incessant application of this great genius to his studies; or from Handel, who wore the keys of his favourite harpsichord into the shape of the bowl of a spoon by his incessant practising upon them.

Thus early, music was Haydn's constant employment and enjoyment: for he seldom repaired to the playground after the services at St. Stephen's; or if he was persuaded to do so by his brother-choristers, as soon as he heard the organ he quickly deserted them, and returned to the church. Perhaps his mind was busy upon a composition which came to light while he still sang as a boy in the choir stalls of St. Stephen's. This was a mass, which, the little fellow having composed, laid before Reüter, the Kapelle-meister. Of course it was a pretty medley of unheard-of progressions and resolutions, which young Joseph had got together; and old Reüter honestly ridiculed it, telling him, that before he could ever succeed in composition it would be necessary for him to learn the rules of harmony and counterpoint. This rebuke accompanied the return of his score, and the young chorister was left to his own resources for the best means of acquiring the advised theoretical knowledge.

He was at a loss what to do—for Reüter did not give the chorister boys theory lessons, and Joseph was far too poor to be able to pay for them from other masters. However, in his travels about Vienna, he came across a second-hand book-shop, where he saw a copy of Fux's celebrated treatise on composition for sale. Of this he became the happy possessor, after which he took but little rest until he had completely overcome its obscure and intricate rules. Without fire, shivering with cold in his garret, and oppressed with sleep, he is said to have pursued his studies to a late hour of the night, by the side of a harpsichord out of repair and falling to pieces in all parts. Still, his love for music made him forget all this, and he has said that he was never more happy at any other period of his life. "Sitting at my old worm-eaten harpsichord," he says, "I envied no king upon his throne."

Three years flew by, and then came a sad trial for Haydn. In his sixteenth year his voice broke, and he was obliged to leave the cathedral choir. His music lessons ceased; he was thrown on the world, and was worse off than ever. However, he still had his cherished treatise and his old worm-eaten piano; and with these he passed nearly all his time in the cold and cheerless regions of the garret. What he gained by teaching paid for this sixth-story apartment, while one Fräulein Martinez supplied the young musician with food in return for piano and singing lessons.

Not long after this, Haydn managed to get introduced to a family in Vienna, where the celebrated Nicolo Porporo was a constant visitor, and, at all hazards, our young musician determined to obtain instruction from the great Italian artist, of whom he had heard so much. Accordingly, he turned lackey. Every day he rose early, beat the old man's coat, cleaned his shoes, and disposed in the best order his antique periwig. But old Porporo was sour beyond all that can be imagined. "Fool" and "blockhead" were the salutations Haydn at first received on entering his room in the morning; but gradually, observing the talent of his gratuitous servant, he softened down, and gave him some good advice and instruction, especially in singing.

Haydn made good progress with Porporo; so much so, that the old Italian engaged him to accompany on the piano, while he gave his singing lessons. Besides this, Haydn at this period held other appointments. Shortly after daybreak he had to be at the church of the Brothers of Mercy, where he conducted the music at a salary of sixty gulden (£6) a year. Thence he repaired to Count Haugwitz' chapel, to play the organ at the ten o'clock service; after which he went to Saint Stephen's, where he was then singing tenor.

Haydn was barely twenty years old when he produced his first opera.

One Bernadone Curtz was at that time performing in Vienna, and drew crowds to the Carinthia Theatre by his wit and humour as a clown. Moreover, he had a handsome wife, and Haydn and two friends found some fun in performing a newly-composed serenade under the clown's windows.

Down came Curtz, struck by the marked beauty and originality of the music.

"Who composed that?" he asked.

"I did," replied Haydn.

"What, you—at your age?"

"Yes!"

"Gad, this is droll; come upstairs."

Upstairs with the clown Haydn went, was introduced to the handsome wife, and descended with the "Devil on Two Sticks"—the libretto for his first opera.

Haydn took the poem home, set to work upon the music, and all went on smoothly until he came to the part of the storm, when a great obstacle presented itself. He had never yet seen the sea, much less a storm! How was he to describe by music that which he knew nothing about? Sorely puzzled, he sent for the clown, but alas! upon his calling, Haydn discovered that he, too, laboured under the same disadvantage. However, pacing up and down the room where Haydn was seated at the piano, the excited Curtz suddenly exclaimed: "Imagine a mountain rising, and then a valley sinking; and then another mountain, and then another valley; the mountains and the valleys follow one after the other, with rapidity; and at every moment alps and abysses succeed each other." It was of little avail—Haydn got no idea from this description. "Add thunder and lightning," said Curtz; "but particularly, represent distinctly these mountains and valleys." Haydn drew his fingers rapidly over the keyboard, then through the semitones, tried innumerable dissonant chords, passed from one end of the piano to the other, and yet

Curtz was dissatisfied. At last, losing his temper, Haydn dashed his hands upon the two extremes of the keys, exclaiming, " The devil take the tempest !" " That's it, that's it !" shrieked out the clown, springing upon his neck, and almost choking him. Thus Haydn got over the tempest-music in the " Devil on Two Sticks."

The opera was completed, and he received his pay for it—twenty-four sequins (£12). It had immense success, though it lasted only for a few days; for a nobleman of Vienna, perceiving that he was being ridiculed in it, brought an action against Curtz, and caused the opera to be prohibited. Haydn never forgot the trouble the storm music gave him, and many years afterwards as he thought of it when crossing the Straits of Dover in bad weather, he laughed during nearly the whole of the passage.

A year after his adventure under Curtz's windows, Haydn followed up the "Devil on Two Sticks" with six instrumental trios, which, from their great novelty, and the peculiar style and originality of the music, at once brought their composer into notice. They were strongly censured for their "dangerous innovations," and the musicians of Vienna reproached the composer for his "errors of counterpoint, heretical modulations, and too daring movements." However, they only fanned them into greater popularity by their jealous invectives. A similar reception was accorded to his first quartet, which appeared soon after these trios; but all that the pedantic composers could do or say was of little use, for the musical amateurs of Vienna soon learned the quartet by heart.

Haydn's sun was now rising. He continued to increase in popularity, and every new work gained for him fresh admirers, rendering the opposition of his enemies more and more futile. Thus passed two or three years; but, in 1758, when Haydn was twenty-six years old, a piece of good fortune came in his way.

At one of Count Mortzin's evening parties, there chanced to be present Prince Antony Esterhazy, and, on this particular occasion, the programme opened with a symphony by Haydn, which so delighted the princely amateur, that he entreated Count Mortzin to give up Haydn to him, and he would make him second leader in his private orchestra.

This was agreed to, but by some means the arrangement fell through, and would probably have been heard no more of, had not one Freidburg reminded Prince Esterhazy of the young rising musician. Two years afterwards, it is said, he formed the plan of setting Haydn to compose a symphony, to be performed on his birthday, at Eisenstädt, where the prince resided. Haydn executed it, and, the day of the ceremony having arrived, the prince, seated on his throne, and surrounded by his court, attended at the usual concert. Haydn's symphony was begun. Scarcely had the performers got to the middle of the first allegro, than the prince interrupted them, and asked who was the author of that fine composition?

"Haydn," replied Freidburg, at the same time making the poor dark fellow, trembling, come forward.

"What!" exclaimed he, "is it this Moor's music? Well, Moor, from henceforth you remain in my service. What is your name?"

"Joseph Haydn."

"Surely I remember that name: why, you are already engaged to me. How is it that I have not seen you before?"

Confused by the majesty which surrounded the prince, Haydn made no reply.

The prince continued, "Go, and dress yourself like a professor; do not let me see you any more in this trim —you cut a pitiful figure. Get a new coat, a wig and buckles, a collar, and red heels to your shoes; but I particularly desire that they may be of a good height, in order that your stature may correspond to your intelligence. You understand me; go your way, and everything will be given you."

Thus, when he was twenty-eight years old, Haydn

was placed at the head of the grand orchestra which this wealthy prince maintained. His duties consisted in composing for the orchestra and rehearsing for the performances, which took place four times every week in the Eisenstädt palace. This post he held for over thirty years, when the death of Prince Esterhazy caused him to vacate it.

From this time Haydn was fully occupied, and led a very regular life. He rose early in the morning, dressed himself very neatly, and then sat down at a small table by the side of his pianoforte, where the hour of dinner usually found him still seated. In the evening he went to the rehearsals or the opera, and sometimes he devoted a morning to hunting. Any other leisure time he had to spare, was passed among his friends or with Mdlle. Boselli, a charming singer attached to the service of the prince.

Here some mention must be made of an event which occurred about this time. Before Haydn entered Prince Esterhazy's service, he had married the daughter of one Keller, a barber, who, instead of turning out for "his wealth," soon became "an occasion of falling;" and, as a friend of Haydn's has it, "he found he had got a prude, who, besides her troublesome virtue, had a mania for priests and monks. The poor composer's house was continually filled with them, and the disturbance of a noisy conversation prevented him from pursuing his studies; and, further, in order to escape curtain lectures from his wife, he was under the necessity of supplying the convents of each of these good fathers, gratis, with masses and motets. To be teased into troublesome jobs by perpetual bickerings is a situation, of all others, the most irksome to men whose productions depend on the suggestions of their own minds. Poor Haydn sought consolation in the society of Mdlle. Boselli, and this step did not tend to augment his tranquillity at home. At length he separated from his wife, to whom he behaved, as far as regards pecuniary matters, with perfect honour."

After this, little occurred for many years to interrupt the daily routine at the palace, or that is worth recording; so a glimpse of Haydn at home and at work may not now be uninteresting.

In general, Haydn never sat himself down to composition unless he felt in a good disposition and humour for writing. Then he always found it necessary to have his hair put in the nicest order, and he dressed himself with a degree of magnificence as if he were going out on some state business. Frederic II. had sent him a diamond ring; and Haydn has said, that often, when he sat down to his piano, if he had forgotten to put on his ring, he could not summon a single idea. The paper, too, on which he composed must be the finest and whitest possible, or he could not get on. He wrote with so much neatness and care, that it is said the best copyist could not have surpassed him in the regularity and clearness of his characters.

After these preliminaries, Haydn began his work by noting down his principal idea or theme, and choosing the keys through which he wished to pass. Then he would imagine a little romance, which might guide him, and furnish him with musical sentiments and colours. Thus we get the titles, "The Fair Circassian," "The Hermit," "The Enamoured Schoolmaster," "The Poltroon," "The Voyage," and others, all of which served as guides while Haydn described and imagined them in music. All Haydn's symphonies are little histories told by sound, and can well be understood and better followed if the listener should happen to know the history or romance connected with the composition.

Another of his habits was this. Just as Leonardo da Vinci sketched in a little book which he always carried about him, the singular faces he met with, so Haydn carefully noted down the passages and ideas which came into his head. When he was in good spirits and happy, he hastened to his little table, and wrote subjects for airs and minuets. Did he feel himself disposed to tenderness and melancholy, he noted down themes for andantes and adagios; and afterwards in composing, when he wanted a passage of such a character, he had recourse to his magazine.

During the thirty years' solitude at Eisenstädt, Haydn wrote a vast number of compositions; and these gained for him throughout Europe an immense reputation, such as the unambitious kapell-meister, who wrote more for his prince than for the world, was quite unconscious of. It was during this period that he composed the music to the "Seven Words," for a religious service called the Entierro, or the Funeral of the Redeemer, which at that time it was the custom in Spain to celebrate with the greatest ceremony and pomp on Good Friday. A preacher explained, in succession, each of the seven words pronounced by Jesus from the cross, and the intervals left between each exposition were filled up by music worthy of the greatness of the subject.

The directors of this sacred spectacle caused an advertisement to be circulated, in which they offered a considerable reward to any composer who should supply seven grand symphonies, expressive of the sentiments which each of the seven words of the Saviour ought to inspire. Haydn alone made the attempt, and thus came this sublime music. In the year 1801 he added words to it, and brought it out as the oratorio of "The Seven

Words of the Saviour on the Cross." Of all his works Haydn is said to have preferred this oratorio.

The year 1790 brought with it great changes. Haydn's beloved patron died, leaving him a pension for life of a thousand florins. There was nothing now to keep him any longer in Germany. John Peter Salomon, who had already made repeated, but ineffectual, attempts to induce Haydn to come to London, hearing of Prince Esterhazy's decease, hastened to Eisenstädt, to tempt Haydn to appear at his "grand concerts." His terms were one hundred sequins (fifty pounds) for each concert, for which Haydn was to compose a new piece, if possible a symphony, and conduct the performance of it himself. Haydn accepted this offer, and at the age of sixty prepared for his first journey beyond the mountains around his home.

But there were many dear and beloved friends to part from. There was Mozart. "Oh, papa!" said Mozart, "you have had no training for the wide, wide world, and you speak too few languages." "My language," replied the papa, "is understood all over the world." Then there was Dr. Leopold Genzinger, physician to the Esterhazy family, with his charming wife, Frau v. Genzinger Albrechtsberger, besides many more to say farewell to.

The day fixed for Haydn's departure was the 15th

December, 1790. He spent the whole of it in the company of Mozart. He dined with him; and at the moment of their separation, with tears in his eyes, Mozart spoke those sadly prophetic words—"We shall now, no doubt, take our last farewell in this life." Haydn was deeply affected, interpreting those words as referring to himself, the old man; but scarcely had a year elapsed when he had to make the following entry in his diary: "Mozart died December 5th, 1791,'"—the younger was taken away. How Haydn loved Mozart! Many years afterwards, when in conversation Mozart was mentioned, Haydn burst into tears, but, recovering himself, he said, "Forgive me; I must ever, ever weep at the name of my Mozart."

After a rough passage across the Channel, Haydn arrived safely in London, and took lodgings at 18, Great Pulteney Street. "My arrival," he says, "caused a great sensation throughout the whole city, and I went the round of all the newspapers for three successive days. Every one seems anxious to know me. I have already dined out six times, and could be invited out every day if I chose; but I must in the first place consider my health, and in the next my work. Except the nobility, I admit no visitors till two o'clock in the afternoon, and at four o'clock I dine at home with Salomon. I have a neat, comfortable lodging, but very dear. My landlord is an Italian, and likewise a cook, who gives us four excellent dishes; we each pay one florin thirty kreutzers a day, exclusive of wine and beer, but everything is terribly dear here. . . . I wish I could fly for a time to Vienna, to have more peace to work; for the noise in the streets, and the cries of the common people selling their wares, are intolerable; but in order to be more quiet I intend to engage an apartment some little way out of town."

While here Haydn saw plenty of English life. He was invited to a civic feast at the "Geld Hall" (Guildhall), in company with the Lord Mayor and his wife, the Lord Chancellor, the Duke of "Lids" (Leeds), the Minister Pitt, and others. After dinner, dancing commenced; besides which, he says, "songs were shouted or toasts given amid the most crazy uproar of hurrahs and clinking of glasses. The effluvia from the lamps was most disagreeable."

The Prince of Wales (George IV.) invited him to his brother's country seat. Here he stayed two days, and had much music with the royal family. They made him sing, while the prince accompanied "very tolerably" on the violoncello; and Sir Joshua Reynolds also commenced his portrait, which was destined to hang in the prince's private sitting-room.

His diary also shows that on June 19th, 1792, he

visited Dr. Herschel, then the great astronomer, but previously an oboe player in the Prussian service during the Seven Years' War, and at one time organist at Bath. The great telescope, and the astronomer, too, astonished Haydn very much.

Another mark of honour was paid to Haydn while in London. The University of Oxford was anxious to bestow upon him the diploma of a Doctor of Music, but custom required that previously he should send to the University a specimen of composition. Accordingly Haydn addressed to the examiners an example of his musical learning, which, upon examination, turned out to be so composed that, whether read backwards or forwards, beginning at the top, the bottom, or the middle of the page, in short, in every possible way, it always presented an air and a correct accompaniment.

Of course he had a fair share of calls from admirers during his residence here. One of these was a gentleman of the navy, who one morning presented himself with the remark, "Mr. Haydn, I presume?" "Yes, sir," "Are you willing to compose me a march for the troops I have on board? I will give you thirty guineas; but I must have it done to-day, because I sail to-morrow for Calcutta."

Haydn agreed to do it. As soon as the captain was

gone he opened his pianoforte, and in a quarter of an hour the march was ready. Feeling some scruples at gaining so easily what appeared to him a considerable sum, he returned home early in the evening and wrote two other marches, intending, first, to give the captain his choice of them, and afterwards to make him a present of all three as a return for his liberality.

Early the next morning came the captain. "Well, where's my march?" "Here it is." "Will you just play it on the piano?" Haydn played it. The captain, without uttering a word, counted the thirty guineas out on the piano, took the march, and walked away.

Haydn ran after him to stop him: "I have written two others which are better; hear them, and then make your choice." "I like the first very well, and that is sufficient." "But hear them." The captain marched downstairs, and would hear nothing. Haydn pursued him, crying after him—" I make you a present of them." The captain, quickening his pace, replied, "I won't have them."—" But, at least, hear them."—" The devil should not make me hear them."

Haydn, piqued, immediately hastened to the Exchange, inquired what ship was on the point of sailing for the Indies, and the name of the commander. He then rolled up the two marches, enclosed a polite note, and sent the parcel on board to the captain. The obstinate fellow, suspecting that the musician was in pursuit of him, would not even open the note, and sent back the whole. Haydn tore the marches into a thousand pieces, and never forgot the captain as long as he lived.

Altogether Haydn passed about three years in London, during which time he wrote some of his most famous works. Among these are the twelve masterly symphonies (known as the "Twelve Grand Symphonies") which he composed for Salomon, and which created such a stir at the Haymarket house.

Haydn took the greatest pains with these compositions, feeling that in them he was upon his trial before a new and greatly expecting public. It is related that, referring to them, Salomon remarked, "You will never surpass these symphonies;" to which Haydn replied promptly, "I never mean to try,"—nor did he. They gained for him the most enthusiastic applause from the Haymarket audiences as well as from the critics of the day. "It is truly wonderful," writes one of them, "what sublime and august thoughts this master weaves into his works. Passages often occur which it is impossible to listen to without becoming excited; we are carried away by admiration, and are forced to applaud hand and mouth. The Frenchmen here cannot restrain their transport in soft adagios;

they will clap their hands in loud applause, and thus mar the effect. In every symphony of Haydn, the adagio or andante is sure to be repeated each time, after the most vehement encores. The worthy Haydn himself conducts on these occasions in the most modest manner. He is, indeed, a good-hearted, candid, honest man, esteemed and beloved by all."

On May 4th, 1795, Haydn took his farewell benefit concert at the Haymarket Theatre, and a note in his diary testifies how well he was received on this occasion. "This evening," he says, "I made four thousand florins. That is only to be done in England."

Pocketing this, and something like eight thousand more besides, which he had saved while here, he bade adieu to many kind friends, and shortly after set out for Germany.

He was soon safe again in Vienna, and, with the profits from his London engagements, he bought a small house and garden in the Faubourg Gumpendorff, in one of the quiet suburbs of Vienna; and, in this peaceful dwelling, the great master lived quietly and comfortably till the day of his death.

The visit to London was not without its effect upon the mind of Haydn. He had heard Handel's "Messiah" splendidly rendered by an orchestra of over a thousand performers at Westminster Abbey; and the effect of this sent him back to Germany with his mind stirred with the impulse to compose an oratorio.

The result was that great and glorious conception—"The Creation." No sooner was he settled in the quiet domicile at Gumpendorff, than he fell to work upon this masterpiece. This was late in 1795, and in the beginning of the year 1798 the oratorio was completed. Two years the old man took to rear this colossal musical structure; for, he said, "I spend much time over it, because I intend it to last a long time."

Haydn always led a very religious life. All his scores are inscribed at the commencement with the words, "*In nomine Domini*," or "*Soli Deo gloria;*" while at the conclusion of them is written "*Laus Deo;*" but "I was," he says, "never so pious as when engaged upon the 'Creation;' I fell on my knees daily, and prayed earnestly to God that He would grant me strength to carry out the work, and to praise Him worthily." It is said, too, that in composing, whenever he felt the ardour of his imagination decline, or was stopped by some insurmountable difficulty, he rose from his work, and resorted to prayer,—an expedient which, he said, never failed to revive him.

A few weeks after its completion, the "Creation" was first performed in the rooms of the Schwartzenberg Palace. "Who can describe the applause?" wrote an eye-witness. "The flower of the literary and musical society of Vienna were assembled in the room, which was well adapted to the purpose, and Haydn himself directed the orchestra. The most profound silence, the most scrupulous attention—a sentiment, I might almost say, of religious respect—were the dispositions when the first stroke of the bow was given. The general expectation was not disappointed. A long train of beauties, till that moment unknown, unfolded themselves before us: our minds, overcome with pleasure and admiration, experienced during two successive hours what they had rarely felt,—a happy existence, produced by desires, ever lively, ever renewed, and never disappointed."

Very soon after this first hearing, the score of the work was in the hands of Messrs. Breitkopf and Härtel, the music-publishers of Leipzig. In the letter accompanying it, Haydn says:—"As for myself, now an old man, I only wish and hope that the critics may not handle my 'Creation' with too great severity, and be too hard upon it. They may possibly find the musical orthography faulty in various passages, and perhaps other things also, which I have for so many years been accustomed to consider as minor parts; but the genuine connoisseurs will see the real cause as readily as I do, and willingly cast aside such stumbling-blocks. This, however, is entirely *inter nos;* or I might be accused of conceit and arrogance, from which, however, my heavenly Father has preserved me all my life."

The work very soon found its way round Germany, and Europe, too. Paris strove to surpass all other cities in doing homage to Haydn's masterpiece, and in the year 1800 a performance of it took place there. On this occasion the applause was deafening; and the *virtuosi* engaged in it, in their enthusiasm, and to show their veneration for Haydn, resolved to present him with a large gold medal, which was adorned on one side with a likeness of Haydn, and on the other with an upright lyre, over which was a burning flame in the midst of a circle of stars. On the medal was this inscription:—"Hommage à Haydn, par les Musiciens qui ont exécuté l'Oratorio de la 'Creation du Monde,' au Théâtre des Arts, l'an IX. de la République Française. MDCCC."

In England the "Creation" is, and probably ever will be, the most popular of all Haydn's works. For depth of feeling, solemnity, and suitability of character; for its powerful and complete grasp of the subject—in fact, for its whole bearing as an oratorio — the "Creation" holds a place among the finest examples which have ever been written in this form of composition.

The work opens with an overture representing chaos; and the singular music which the composer has put into, it is so eminently suited to the subject, that one cannot fail to recognize therein that awful state, when "the earth was without form and void, and darkness was upon the face of the deep." The strangely dull sounds which first break upon the ear, are soon followed by a few streams of melody rising above the confusion and indefiniteness of the enormous mass of chaos, to be instantly hurled to destruction by the vast and rude powers of nature, as they sweep madly on in their headlong fury. The clarinet and flutes each strive to extricate themselves from this tumultuous blending of noises. Gradually they succeed—their melodies begin to assume shape, and a disposition to order is heard and felt. The overture ends, but darkness and chaos still remain. Nor is this altered by the recitative, "In the beginning," which the angel Raphael delivers; nor even by the *sotto voce* chorus, which says, "The spirit of God moved upon the face of the waters," until it reaches that bar which describes the creation of light— "And there was light." Here, by his sudden and masterly recourse to the refulgent harmony of the major tonic of the key, Haydn has succeeded in producing one of the grandest effects of which the musical art can boast. It is marvellous. The sensation produced by this sudden transition from darkness to the brightest noonday light, has been rightly said to resemble "the effect of a thousand torches suddenly flashing light into a dark cavern."

In the magnificent soprano air and chorus, "The marv'llous work," the angels give praises for the work of the second day. Then follow two of the finest songs in the oratorio, "Rolling in foaming billows," and "With verdure clad," both dwelling upon, and beautifully illustrative of, the third day's work. This is no sooner ended than the countless angelic host uplift their harps and lyres, and, in the fine fugued chorus, "Awake the harp," the whole sacred vault of heaven resounds with their joyful proclamation in praise of the Creator.

A piece of placid symphony informs us that a new day's work is about to be begun. A soft, streamy note from the violins, rendered more prominent as the second violin steals in, at once suggests the rays of the rising sun; and, as the violas and 'cellos add their deeper colouring, the picture becomes more distinct and real. Instrument after instrument helps to expand the great mass of light rising before us, ever and ever increasing in intensity, till at last in all its dazzling brightness the great orb of day appears. The time changes to an *adagio*, and we instantly feel that it is night, with the moon silently advancing through the clouds; and this is confirmed, as Uriel, in a delicate snatch of melody, sings: "With softer beams and milder light, steps on the silver moon, through silent night." The remainder of the angel's song, with its rich orchestral accompaniment, describes the birth of the stars, and instantly after, these and the whole inhabitants of heaven ring out in joyful time, "The heavens are telling the glory of God;" one of the sublimest pieces of choral music that Haydn or any other master ever penned. This concludes the first, and perhaps the grandest part of the oratorio.

Part the second is devoted to the work of the fifth and sixth days, and contains some of the most beautifully descriptive music that this great master has written. Who does not enjoy the characteristic air, "On mighty pens," as it represents the creation of the birds—the swift and audacious eagle; the merry lark, soaring far in the sky; the tender dove, cooing to its mate; and the delightful notes of the nightingale's song? Or, who is there who does not admire the picturesqueness of the exquisite trio, "Most beautiful appear," with its "gently sloping hills," the "cheerful host of birds," the "thronged swarms of fish," and the "immense leviathan of the deep," as the double basses imitate the effect of the lashing of the tail of the great whale, as he "sports on the foaming wave?" Well has Haydn followed up all this with a grand tribute of homage—the colossal trio and chorus, "The Lord is great; His glory lasts for ever."

The creation of the beasts is next related in a masterly recitative for the bass. The lion first appears. "Cheerfully roaring stands the tawny lion," and his tremendous roar, imitated by the trombones and contra-fagotto, leaves a vivid impression on the hearers. The "flexible tiger," the "nimble stag," the "noble steed," the "host of insects," are all introduced, and wonderfully and faithfully depicted by the ingenious and varying treatment of the time and the appropriate colouring of the music which accompanies this splendid recitative. The tenor air, "In native worth," so full of all that is pure and dignified, announces the creation of man and the formation of Eve—"a woman fair, and graceful spouse;" both of whom are soon heard praising their Creator in the trio, "On Thee each living soul awaits." So ends the work of the "Creation;" and it is proclaimed in a fugued chorus of great power, "Achieved is the glorious work," which the new-born Creation sings.

The third part of this oratorio describes Adam and Eve in their abode of bliss before the Fall; continuing in their service of gratitude and praise, and holding pure and innocent converse with each other. Their guileless songs, "By thee with bliss," and "Of stars the fairest," rise up to heaven, and are there joined in by the angels, singing in chorus, "For ever blessed be His power;" "Resound the praise of God our Lord;" "Hail, bounteous Lord!" &c. In "Graceful consort," a charming duet, full of tenderness and affection, the emotions of the blissful pair find vent; but, alas! "Ye strive at more than granted is," recites Uriel, "and more desire to know than know ye should." The concluding chorus, "Sing to the Lord, ye voices all," is full of energy, and forms a worthy conclusion to this grand conception. The orchestration throughout is full and rich, except in the parts where a few bars are allotted to the solo voices; and where the instruments, being softened and thinned, give all the more prominence to the singular and beautiful effect which the composer has here produced. After the last of these effective passages, the whole of the voices and instruments combine and complete, in the most befitting and impressive manner, this sublime work of the "Creation."

There is one other work which must be glanced at before closing this sketch—viz., the "Four Seasons," founded on Thomson's poem, by Haydn's friend, Baron von Swietin. In 1801, while the musical world was yet stirred by the commotion which the "Creation" had caused, and while its melodies were fast travelling over Europe, Haydn completed and gave to the world, the grand idyllic oratorio of the "Seasons."

This work is divided into four parts—Spring, Summer, Autumn, and Winter, each of which is treated in the most natural and characteristic manner, the whole forming one grand picture of a year's rural life. In Spring is seen the impatient husbandman, driving to the plough his lusty steeds, sowing the seed, and praying for the refreshing rain to swell it. Soon, the dew-drops and lilies appear, the playful lambkins caper, the tuneful birds are heard, and all Nature awakens in the duet, "Spring her lovely charms unfolding."

In the spirited bass song, "From out the fold the shepherd drives," the summer day's work commences. 'Tis early morn, and, as the shepherd guides his flocks, he cannot refrain from resting awhile to watch the glory of the rising sun. Then, the oppression and exhaustion which overtake all nature as the summer's sun darts down his fierce noonday rays; the fearful storm which follows upon this intense heat; the freshness which pervades the air as the storm clears up, and the delightful evening which closes the day, are all brought vividly before us by the marvellously rich and descriptive orchestration that Haydn has wedded to the text. So descriptive, in fact, is the music, that the composer's intention might easily be perceived even were there no text to guide the listener.

The Autumn is, perhaps, yet more interesting than

the other parts of this beautiful picture. First, we have a hunting scene, with all its attendant merriment and jollity. In one of its finest choruses the stag is loosed. "He flies! he flies!" they shout, and the excited hunters burst off in hot pursuit. For a while they are lost, but in time their approach is heard; and this exciting and vigorous chorus concludes with the clamorous joy and huzzas of the triumphant sportsmen. Immediately there follows the vintage, beautifully represented by the music. "Joyful, joyful the liquor flows," sing the careless drinking party, as the bowls and tankards are freely filled. In the distance are heard the merry sounds of the fife, fiddle, and bagpipe, to which the young people are dancing. Soon they are joined by the joyous tipplers, and the revelling strains become more boisterous than before. " Brim the foaming cup; push it on; press it on; send it around," sing the excited vintners; and we leave them most energetically concluding this amusing chorus with the words, " All hail to the wine! All hail!"

Winter is the last division of this interesting work; and with masterly skill the great composer has shown us the cheerless and stormy outside world, in contrast to the snug and cheerful life inside the "trav'ller's" cot. A fine bass song—" In this, O vain, misguided man, the picture of thy life behold"—appeals strongly to the heart of every listener, besides preparing us for the grand double chorus, "Then comes the dawn," which concludes this grand musical Idyl, composed when Haydn was verging on threescore years and ten.

Of the merits of these two oratorios, Haydn has expressed himself thus:—"My 'Creation' will endure, and probably the 'Seasons' also." Again, on being warmly congratulated after the first performance of the "Seasons" Haydn remarked, "It is not the 'Creation;' there, angels sing; here, rustics."

Haydn did little more after this. "I have done," he said to a friend, after completing the "Seasons;" "my head is no longer what it was. Formerly, ideas came to me unsought; I am now obliged to seek for them, and for this I feel I am not formed." His two last quartets came to light in 1802; and a third, numbered 84, was begun, but this he was compelled to leave unfinished.

He withdrew to the quiet retirement of Gumpendorff, and employed his time in adding basses to ancient Scotch airs for a London bookseller. But his health showed signs of a speedy decline, and in 1805, his physician ordered him to discontinue even this occupation. Sorely did the old man feel this; and, unable longer to work, he was haunted with the fear that he should live to want money.

At this period he was much pleased when his friends

came to visit him; and would not fail to remind any negligent one by a card, upon which he wrote the words, "All my strength is gone; old and weak am I," set to an appropriate phrase of music out of his unfinished quartet. In his retirement he drew up his will; and six weeks before his death read it over to his servants and others who had dwelt around him, asking them, with his usual benevolence and goodness of heart, whether they were satisfied with its provisions or not. They were quite taken by surprise by this last act of kindness, and thanked him with tears in their eyes for so generously providing for them in time to come.

Gradually the grand old man became more and more feeble, but it was long before the embers of life died out. Probably they would have smouldered longer had not the intelligence of the outbreak of war exhausted the remnant of fire left. Haydn's love for his country lay deep. Long before, he had written its national melody, "God preserve the Emperor," the sounds of which he could now hear from the distant battle-field.

About the 12th of May the French army was within half a league of Haydn's little garden, and firing upon his beloved Vienna. Four shells fell close to his house, and his servants ran to him full of terror. Rousing himself from his chair, the old man asked with a dignified air, "Why this terror? Know that no disaster can come where Haydn is." A convulsive shivering came over him, and he spoke no more. His servants carried him to his couch, for he was too weak to walk, and there he lay for some days quite exhausted. But the booming cannon were not out of hearing. His loyalty warmed within him; and on May 26th he desired to be carried to his piano, when, with much emotion, and as loud as he was able, he thrice sang "God preserve the Emperor." A kind of stupor then came over him, from which he never recovered, and five days later—on the morning of the 31st May, 1809—the great Father of Symphony breathed his last.

PRINCIPAL INCIDENTS IN THE LIFE OF HAYDN.

Born at Rohrau, March 31st	1732
Joined St. Stephen's Choir, Vienna	1740
First Opera—"The Devil on Two Sticks," produced	1750
Conductor of Prince Esterhazy's Orchestra	1760
Visited London	1790
"The Creation," commenced	1795
"The Creation," first performed	1798
"The Seasons," composed	1801
The Last composition—A quartet	1802
Died, 31st May	1809

Mozart.

"O, MOZART! immortal Mozart! how many and what countless images of a brighter and better world hast thou stamped on our souls!" These were Schubert's lovely words, and how true they are. They breathe the sentiment of millions of souls, who feel that in Mozart's music the very angels seem to sing. How charming, how delicious the atmosphere every bar of it lifts us into! We feel out of the earth at times, so forcibly does it appeal to the higher emotions. No music is more beautiful than Mozart's, and but little so tranquillizing as the tones of this master of. song. It rivets the untutored ear as no other does; it softens, exalts, and inspires all that is best within the human heart. It makes us tender and loving; and besides, with its gay and sportive melodies it at times exhilarates our spirits in the happiest manner. It is for the young and old alike; and for this affinity to the human passions, Mozart's music will live, so long as there are emotions for it to charm and excite.

The 27th January, 1756, is a red-letter day in musical annals, for then Wolfgang Amadeus Mozart was born. Almost as soon as the little fellow could walk, his fondness for the sounds of the piano-forte was observed. He would always linger about the instrument while any one was playing, and when his father—himself a musician of the highest repute among those of his time—was giving his sister her lesson; or he would be busily engaged picking out the thirds and other pleasing concords, and otherwise gratifying his early musical tastes.

It was soon perceived that the family gift had been freely bestowed on little Woferl—as his parents called him—and when he was about four years old, his father gave him a few easy lessons. His progress made it apparent that he was no ordinary musical genius. In a very short time he could play easy minuets with wonderful correctness, and even at this early age he composed small pieces on the clavier, which his father noted down for him.

For some time the elder Mozart continued the simple and interesting lessons with increasing and surprising results. Wolfgang soon outpaced Maria in her pianoforte studies, besides continuing to increase in the wonderful aptitude for composing, which he had so early shown.

An interesting story is told of the infantine genius sitting down to write a concerto, when he was but six years old! Returning home one day with a friend, the father discovered Master Wolfgang busy with pens, ink, and paper.

"What are you doing there?" said Leopold.

"Writing a concerto for the clavier," replied Wolfgang.

"It must be something very brilliant; let us look at it."

"No, no! it is not ready yet," replied Wolfgang.

The father, however, persisted, and soon became possessed of the score, so blotted as to be scarcely readable. At the first glance the two friends laughed heartily at what appeared to be a rare medley of notes; but upon examination, the father perceived in it ideas far beyond his or his friend's expectations, and with evident signs of emotion, he handed to him the mental efforts of his baby-boy to inspect.

This unlooked-for source of joy led the father to turn his attention more fully to the education of his son; and to the clavier he soon added the violin. This addition to his studies was brought about by the following little incident. It happened that Wenzl, an excellent violinist, paid Leopold Mozart a visit for the purpose of trying over some new trios. Wenzl played the first violin, Schactner second, while the father played the viola. Little Wolfgang begged that he might be allowed to join in with a small fiddle, which had been presented to him some time previously; but Leopold would not consent, and told him to go away and not disturb the performers. This reproof, the child being always sensitive to the least cross word, brought tears into his eyes, and he stole away from the room. At Schactner's request, however, he was called back and allowed to play with him. "But remember," said the father, "so softly that nobody can hear you, or I must at once send you away." They began the trio, and Schactner soon perceived that his playing was superfluous, for Wolfgang was quite *au fait* at second violin. He gradually withdrew his instrument, and left Wolfgang to finish!

What new hopes were now held out to Leopold, blessed with two such wonderful children. Wolfgang was but seven years old, yet a wonderful clavier player, a violinist, and composer! Salzburg was not the place for any good to accrue to him from such prodigies, and Leopold left his wife at home and started on a journey which he hoped and believed would prove remunerative.

In the year 1762 they arrived in Vienna, and were everywhere received most enthusiastically. Their first visit to the Emperor's palace is thus described by the father: "We were graciously received by both their Majesties. . . . . . . Woferl seated himself in the Empress's lap, put his arms round her neck, and kissed her repeatedly. We were there from three o'clock to six, and the Emperor himself came and fetched me from the ante-room to hear Woferl play the violin."

Besides this interesting interview with the Emperor, they received many urgent invitations from princes, counts, and the highest ministers of the state; all of whom made much of the prodigies, and vied with each other in bestowing favours upon them.

From this successful expedition they returned in the spring of 1763; but only for a few months, for in the same year they set out on another tour, visiting Mayence, Munich, and other cities, all of which Master Wolfgang and his sister "set in commotion." Presents were showered on the young geniuses as large in number as they were varied in their selection. Swords and shoe-buckles, toilet bottles and lace, wigs and snuff-boxes, helped to swell their collection of treasures.

Paris and Versailles next opened their arms' to the juvenile wonders, and as the father wrote, "went crazy over his children, especially with Wolfgang's organ-playing." From Paris they came to London; and they had not been here many days, before they were summoned to St. James's Palace to play before George III. and Queen Charlotte. Writing to a friend concerning this visit, Leopold says: "On the 27th April we were with their Majesties from six to nine o'clock, and the present we received on leaving the palace was twenty-four guineas. Such was their friendly manner, we could not believe we were before the King and Queen of England. The king placed before Woferl some of Handel's and Bach's compositions, all of which he played faultlessly."

From England, Leopold Mozart and his children went to Holland. Here their fame had preceded them. Organs were thrown open for Master Wolfgang Mozart to perform upon, and all flocked to hear him and his sister play at their concerts. About this time (1765) Wolfgang composed six sonatas, which he dedicated to the Princess of Orange; the "Galimathias Musicum," for violins, viola, and cello, horns, oboes, bassoons, and harpsichord accompaniment; and also a small oratorio. From Holland they wended their way back to their loved Salzburg, visiting many towns on their way, and at length arriving at their home late in the year 1766.

With the new year they were again in Vienna, giving concerts, and introducing at them the musical effusions which were being constantly produced by this wonderful boy of eleven years old. The most notable of them are a Stabat Mater, the music to "Apollo and Hyacinth," and the operetta "Bastien and Bastienne," first performed in private at the summer residence of the Mesmers, at Landstrasse, a suburb of Vienna; also the opera "La Finta Semplice," about which Leopold Mozart had so much trouble with the cabals in Vienna, who had resolved to do all in their power to prevent the boy's inspirations from being heard. Writing of this proceeding, Leopold says: "The whole hell of music has risen to prevent the talent of a child from being heard." Still this did not damp the ardour of the young genius. He was commissioned by the emperor to compose a Mass for the consecration of the new Waisenhaus Church. This he soon accomplished, and at its first performance on the 7th December, 1768, before the whole of the imperial family, Wolfgang first appeared wielding the conductor's bâton.

The year 1769 was not remarkable. The family remained at Salzburg till December, when the plan which Leopold had previously formed of taking his son to Italy was carried out. They visited Milan, Bologna, Rome, and Naples, attending all the operas and concerts, and the marvellous sights these cities afford; in fact, it was more a holiday tour for Woferl than a professional circuit. His letters home during his absence are full of the sights and exploits of his travel. Writing from Rome, he says: "I had the honour of kissing St. Peter's foot at Pietro; but as I have the misfortune to be so short, your dear old Wolfang Mozart was lifted up."

It was while he was there that the marvellous boy performed the feat of appropriating Allegri's "Miserere," which was held in such high esteem that every one was forbidden, under pain of excommunication, to copy any portion of it. Attending the Sistine Chapel one day at matins, Master Wolfgang set all these injunctions at defiance, and made a rough sketch of this delightful composition while it was being sung by the choir! This was enough for one day. Shortly after he went on a finishing tour, and succeeded in completing his task! Beyond the opera "Mitridate, Rè di Pontes," Mozart composed but little during his journey. This work was performed with great success at Milan a few days before their departure for home.

We now pass on to the time when the youthful maestro produced "La Finta Giardinera." This work evinces a marked step in his progress as a composer, and though as nothing compared with his later operas, yet it possesses music of the most tender and satisfying nature. It was first performed at Munich on January 13th, 1775, with what success the following extracts from one of his letters will testify : " My opera was performed yesterday, and proved so successful that I cannot describe the commotion it caused. The whole theatre was crammed. After each air there was a deafening uproar of clapping of hands, and shouts of 'Viva Maestro,' in which the dowager and her highness the electress also joined."

The next few years of the life of the young genius were passed partly in Salzburg, and partly in travelling from one city to another, in the hope of obtaining some fixed appointment in the service of the first prince that would accept him; for, notwithstanding his powers as a composer as well as a performer on the piano-forte and organ, he was allowed to remain with barely sufficient to live upon. On this subject he writes : " I was requested to go to Count Savioli to receive my payment. It was just as I expected—another watch. Ten Carolins (£10) would have been more acceptable just now, although the watch and its appendages are valued at twenty. Money is wanted in journeying." Augsburg, Mannheim, Munich, and Paris, were visited, each in its turn, without either succeeding in the object he had in view when he and his mother left Salzburg in 1777, or deriving from it any especial benefit. At Munich on his way home, he fell in love with Constance Weber, whom he afterwards married; while, to counterbalance this piece of good fortune, he and his family sustained an irreparable loss; for on July 3rd, 1778, it was the will of God that he should pen the following sad words: "I write to inform you that my mother, my dearest mother, is no more. God has called her to Himself."

For the next few years little of importance occurred till the production of "Idomenio, König von Creta," which work may be said to be the commencement of Mozart's classical period. It was written at the request of the Elector of Bavaria, for the Carnival at Munich; was performed there for the first time on January 29th, 1781, and was most favourably received. Mozart himself regarded this opera as one of the best of his compositions; yet, notwithstanding this much in its favour—and profound musicians are not apt to judge their own effusions in any prejudiced light—"Idomeneo" has not kept the stage. Nor can this be attributed to anything but the libretto, which, without doubt, lacks variety. How sublime is the music in "Idomeneo's Prayer," or the "Lover's parting," and in the grand and sparkling choruses to this opera! But seldom is such music of any avail if the libretto be deficient in dramatic situation or interest.

Mozart's next work of any importance was the comic opera, "Die Entführung aus dem Serail." After some amount of opposition it was produced for the first time on July 12th, 1782, and met with a most hearty reception, notwithstanding the disadvantage which the composer laboured under of having his music interpreted by singers who were for the most part unable, from want of rehearsals, to do it full justice. In Mozart's time and later still, composers had by no means the power they now have. The singers ruled them, and often obliged them to alter airs to suit their own particular whims or fancies, and to refuse their request was but courting ill success for the work. Of the reception of "Die Entführung," Mozart says: "My opera was given yesterday with great success; and, despite the fearful heat, the theatre was crowded. It is to be performed again next Friday. . . . . The people are quite mad after it."

Here is another example of the genius and fertility of Mozart. How different is "Die Entführung" to anything he, or any before him, had yet written! In it he makes both surprising and successful innovations, and rids himself of the accepted trammels and formalities to which opera till then had been subjected, and creates what may be called a landmark in music by this work which, though the first of its style, is still looked upon as a model in this form of composition. It is replete with music of the most beautiful kind, resplendent and humorous, and for the most part totally different from what had hitherto flowed from his pen. Can it be that the thoughts of his fast-approaching and long-looked-for union with his beloved Constance were foremost in his breast when he penned the joyous music of "Die Entführung"—The Abduction? In all probability such thoughts were prominently before him and inspired this music, for in the next month "Die Entführung" is practically carried into effect—he marries on the 4th August, 1782.

Writing to his father a day or two after the happy event, he says: "My beloved Constance—now, thank God! my wife—knew my affairs long ago, also that I had nothing to expect from you; but her love and devotion for me were so great, that she joyfully trusted herself to my keeping. . . . . No one attended the wedding but her mother and youngest sister, Herr von Thorwath as guardian, Herr Zetto who gave her away, and Herr von Gilowsky. When the service was over we both shed tears. . . . . Our only festivity was a supper, given by Baroness von Waldstadten."

After his marriage Mozart remained with his wife in Vienna till the end of July, 1783, when they set out on a journey to Salzburg, to pay a visit to Leopold Mozart. This visit extended over three months, during which time he completed the "Davidde Penitente," which he had commenced in the beginning of the year, and had it performed at Salzburg, his wife rendering the solo passages. He also began the comic opera "L'Oca del Cairo," but on his return to Vienna he laid it aside, and neglected to give it the finishing touches. The reason assigned for this is, that he could not induce the Abbate Varesco, the author of the text, to adopt his suggestions for alterations; and, rather than write to a libretto distasteful and uninteresting to him, he preferred to sacrifice what he had already composed, notwithstanding that on December 6th, 1783, he wrote to his father in the following strain respecting this music. "There are only three arias required to complete the first act of 'L'Oca del Cairo.' I can truly say that I am quite pleased with the aria, the quartet, and finale of the first act, and I should much regret if I had written such music to no purpose—I mean, if we cannot agree as to what is absolutely requisite." As we have already seen, they could not agree.

We now come to that period in Mozart's life (1784) when he very wisely commences a record of his productions, and thus leaves us without a doubt of the order in which the compositions of the last eight years of his career were composed. The first of these we shall refer to is the sonata in B flat major for piano and violin, for the history and adventures of the score of this delightful composition are by no means uninteresting.

At the same time that Mozart was playing at the Imperial Palace at Vienna, there was also engaged there one Signora Regina Strinasacchi, an excellent lady violinist. He soon made the acquaintance of this gifted lady, and undertook to compose something in which they might appear together at her Court concert. The result of this promise was this sonata in B flat major; but by some means or other Mozart did not write a note of it till the night before that on which the concert was to take place. Madame Strinasacchi, of course, became anxious, and wishing to make a successful appearance, applied to Mozart, at any rate, for the violin part. This he set about, and on the morning of the concert it was in her hands to study. His own piano part, however, he could not find time to do, and the result was that they met at the concert without any rehearsal, and he, for his part, without anything on paper wherewith to guide him beyond a copy of the violin part, and an accidental here and there to mark the modulation he intended; however, he seated himself with his all-but blank paper before him. The sonata was commenced, and concluded amidst the applause of the delighted audience! But Mozart did not get clear off yet. The Emperor Joseph, who was seated near him, discovered with the aid of his opera glasses that Mozart was imposing upon the audience, for he could see no notes on the score but those for the violin. He instantly sent for both the composer and the mock score, but on questioning him the only reply he could get was, "May it please your majesty there was not a single note lost." Yet this is not all. This, one of the most beautiful of Mozart's writings, was afterwards filled in and guaranteed by his autograph, and very recently has again been prominently before the public, not only at the Monday Popular Concerts, where it is always a favourite, but at Messrs. Sotheby's salerooms. There, the very identical score which the emperor sent for was put up for auction in July, 1872, and went down with the hammer for the sum of ten guineas!

By the way, why should such a valuable treasure as this be allowed to be put up and knocked down as though it had no more claim on the universe than a ricketty old bedstead, or the fittings of an eel-pie shop would have? Is there no museum, no musical society who could spare ten guineas to rescue a treasure like this, and thus preserve it from the oblivion of private collections and the like? Into them, such scores, &c., too often fall and are then lost to the world—excepting the select family circle—until the death of the possessor causes them to be again brought to light, once more to be associated, perhaps in company with pots and kettles, with that irrevocable little hammer which again is employed to seal their doom, and consign them to that world of secrecy—private collections—from which but a transient escape has been made. Cannot something be done?

Passing over the year 1785, in which Mozart completed the six well-known quartets dedicated to Haydn, and in which year also he was busy for the Freemasons, composing for them the cantata, "The Joy of Freemasons," some masonic songs, and the music for a masonic funeral, we come to the production of "Le Nozze di Figaro," which, from a dramatic point of view, may justly be styled as Mozart's *chef-d'œuvre*.

"Figaro" was first performed on May 1st, 1786, and, notwithstanding the merits which a work must possess to stand the stage as this opera has done, it met with but an indifferent reception. This, however, was only what was expected, as the following extract from a letter shows: "It will say much for the opera if it succeeds, for I know there is a deal of opposition got up against it. Salieri and his followers will move heaven and earth to injure it." So they did, and produced rival operas, submitting them to the emperor. He, however, selected "Figaro," and gave it the benefit of his favour, if nothing else. All their opposition, too, proved of but little avail beyond its first performance. "Figaro" laid hold of the people. Its melodies were whistled and hummed through Vienna, placing Mozart still higher in the ascendant than he had previously been. Of its next representation he writes: "At its second performance there were five pieces encored! and at the third, seven—one little duet was repeated three times." Thus much for the first two or three representations of "Figaro" before the Viennese audience. Without pausing to name the many other works of Mozart's prolific pen during 1786, including three piano concertos, various trios and quartets, the symphony in D, many sonatas and variations, let us notice how the sprightly and playful "Figaro" was welcomed elsewhere.

Early in 1787, Mozart received a pressing invitation from Count Thun, to pay him a visit at his château at Prague. This he joyfully accepted, and was soon a guest at the old count's castle. In a letter to his friend, Herr von Jacquin, he says: "Directly we arrived, which was at twelve o'clock, it was as much as we could do to get ready for dinner at one o'clock; this over, we had some music by the duke's private band. . . . . At six o'clock I went to a ball with Count Canal, where we should meet all the Prague beauties. I fancy I can see you hopping after the pretty creatures. . . . . I neither danced nor flirted with them, because I was too tired for the first, and my natural reserve preserved me from the latter. I watched them, however, with great pleasure, tripping about to the music of my 'Figaro' transformed into various forms of dance music. Nothing is talked of here but 'Figaro,' nothing whistled and hummed but 'Figaro;' and no opera so well attended as 'Figaro;' very flattering, certainly." On the first night also of his stay at Count Thun's, Mozart attended the theatre where "Figaro" was playing, and where it had had a most successful run. No sooner was his presence discovered at the theatre, than the whole excited audience rose and greeted him with long deafening shouts of "Viva Maestro." Such a reception as this, to his work which through party intrigues had been so indifferently received at its first representation in Vienna, gave Mozart very much pleasure, and it was this that gave rise to his next opera, "Don Giovanni."

One day Mozart happened to be talking to the manager of the theatre of "Figaro's" success, when he said, "As the Bohemians understand me so well, I must compose something expressly for them." The result was, they agreed there and then for "Il Dissoluto punito ossia il Don Giovanni." Mozart then returned to Vienna, and although he did not put a note of "Don Giovanni" on paper till September, only a month before it was performed, there is no doubt that he at once set his mind to work on the subject, and that when he did begin to write, his plan was well matured. But his pen was not idle all this time. Quintets for stringed instruments, sonatas, much piano-forte music, and many songs, flowed continually from his prolific pen during the "Don Giovanni" year.

In May of this year, too, a sad calamity fell on him. He had the misfortune to lose his valued father, and he informed his friend, Herr von Jacquin, of this event in the following words:—"On my return home to-day, I received the sorrowful news of the death of my excellent father. You can conceive the condition I am now in."

On the 16th September, Mozart made another journey to Prague, there to write out "Don Giovanni" and to put it on the stage. In the course of a few weeks he completed it. The first performance took place on October 29th, 1787, and enjoyed a most brilliant reception from the enthusiastic audience. Herr von Jacquin had the first news from Mozart of his new effort. He says, "My opera was played here on the 29th October, with brilliant success. Yesterday it was performed for my benefit. . . . . When I come back you shall have the aria to sing. . . . . Every effort has been made to induce me to stay here for two months longer, and to compose another opera, but I cannot accept the proposal." Such was the reception accorded to Mozart's best opera—the opera of which he said, "It was not for the Viennese, more than the Praguers, but chiefly for myself and friends."

Spohr regarded it as the best and most energetic of all Mozart's operas, and so it is. It ingeniously combines both sides of life—the light and the dark—in perfect reality, whilst the wonderful style in which this comedy and tragedy are alternately delineated, the great variety of situation, and, above all, the sublime and irresistible music which Mozart has added to Da Ponte's adaptation, combine to place "Don Giovanni" foremost on the list of all musical dramas.

Holmes, in his excellent life of Mozart, gives some interesting anecdotes connected with this opera. "Dussek's house," he states, "was a scene of great resort and revelry while Mozart was his guest, and it is to be remembered that there was often considerable playing of bowls in his grounds. In the midst of all the talk and laughter with which this amusement was attended, the composer pursued his work, but rose from time to time when it came to his turn to take part in the game." Another he relates is that "in rehearsing that part of the finale of the first act, where Zerlina is seized by Don Giovanni, there was some difficulty in getting Signora Bondini to scream in the right manner and place. It was tried repeatedly and failed. At length Mozart, desiring the orchestra to repeat the piece, went quietly on the stage, and awaiting the time that she was to make the exclamation, grasped her so suddenly and so forcibly, that, really alarmed, she shrieked in good earnest. He was now content. 'That's the way,' said he, praising her. 'You must cry out just in that manner.'"

We now come to the year 1788, interesting for the production of Mozart's grandest symphonies—the E flat major, G minor, and the C major, also known as the "Jupiter," composed in the order they are named, and all in the short space of six weeks! These three symphonies, each being quite complete and distinct in itself from the others, yet seem to be three stages of one gigantic musical structure, in which we see the reflection of Mozart's life-long struggle with a world that neither understood nor appreciated him, and of which he was far in advance. The one in E flat major—the first—seems to take us over the years of his boyhood, passed under the guidance and care of his esteemed father. It is quiet and calm throughout, subdued and submissive as he was known to be; repose distinguishes every movement, excepting perhaps the two joyous allegros, beautifully illustrative of the occasional breaks of success which marked his early years. The second, the G minor symphony, presents us with his period of struggle with the world, after he had left his father's protection, and started on the journey in 1777, to give his services to the first prince who would accept them. The music effectively describes this period of his life. Struggle, sorrow, and anguish is evident throughout the whole of it, and as Jahn says, "the gentle murmur of sorrow continues with ever-increasing intensity, till it becomes a raging passion, striving to drown its own devouring grief." In the last, the "Jupiter" in C major, all the struggle and anguish are over. His "Figaro" and "Don Giovanni" period, with its brilliant successes and enthusiastic receptions, is gloriously depicted. Success, joy, and triumphant victory, crown this splendid musical structure which Mozart has reared—the story of his life told in sound.

We must pass over the fruitful year of 1789, with the exception of one item—the instrumentation of Handel's "Messiah."

This was a delicate task for even Mozart to undertake; but yet what additional beauty has he not lent to this sublime oratorio by his superb and masterly scoring! We now have the combined efforts of two giant musicians on this significant subject, and some of Handel's best writing is wedded to instrumentation unknown in Handel's day, and above all by a master who revered Handel, and in a style which, when heard, leaves no doubt as to its being an eminently successful and truly welcome addition.

The next year, 1790, was productive of but six compositions, the most notable of which are the opera "Cosi fan tutte," first performed at Vienna, on January 26th,

1790; the instrumentation of Handel's "Alexander's feast," and the "Ode on St. Cecilia's Day." This paucity of work can, to some extent, be accounted for by his having in that year again made the journey to Frankfort, Mannheim, and Munich, going over the old ground which he had visited thirteen years or so before. This journey proved a most disastrous one. Mozart fell in with bad companions, and allowed himself to be carried away by their excesses; to which, and to the unsettled state of his affairs during that period, we must attribute the fewness of his compositions.

Mozart returned at the end of 1790, and with the new year 1791—alas, his last—resolutely set about to redeem the promise he had made to his "sweet, darling, beloved wife," as he calls her, while he was away on the journey, when he said, "I am quite determined to do all that I can here, and shall be delighted to return to you. What an enjoyable life we will lead! I will work, and work so hard that I may never again get into such a distressing position." That he did, indeed, strive to overcome the pecuniary difficulties which surrounded him, his list of works for this year shows. He persistently carried out his promise, and never laid aside his pen till death stepped in to arrest it. It is impossible within the limits of a short sketch like this to notice these compositions separately, for nearly fifty are recorded as produced during the first six months of this most fruitful of all Mozart's years. Minuets and dances, songs, variations, quintets for strings, the grand pianoforte concerto in B flat, the "Ave verum Corpus," a cantata, fill the long list till we come to his last great opera, "Die Zauberflöte"—the "Magic flute."

This opera was written at the earnest entreaties of one Schikaneder, who by reason of the non-success of his theatre, had got into very reduced circumstances. Mozart, ever ready to help others, was touched by his tale of woe, and promised to write something in the hope of reviving the fortunes of the theatre. The above-named opera was the result, and all Mozart asked in return, was that Schikaneder should sell no copy of it to any other theatre. In a very short time the composer had redeemed his promise. The "Zauberflöte" was produced, spreading his fame far and wide through Germany, and retrieving the fortunes of Schikaneder and his theatre. Yet how did the wretch show his gratitude? He was not satisfied yet in his greedy desire for gain, and would not even reserve for Mozart the very trifling condition on which he supplied the opera, but sold the work to as many theatres as he could possibly get to buy it, and from the noise it had caused, these were not a few.

After "Die Zauberflöte" came "La Clemenza di

Tito;" and another cantata for the Freemasons, entitled "The Praise of Friendship." Mozart then commenced his last work, "The Requiem," which, for depth of devotional feeling, the religious sentiment it expresses, and its whole character as a sacred composition, is undoubtedly the finest and most sublime of all his contributions to church music. Many were the circumstances, too, which tended to produce this solemnity of character. Death was staring him in the face ere he penned a note of it. Long before, Mozart had a presentiment of his approaching end; and besides this, there was the mystery attending the origin of such a work. One day Mozart was much surprised by the announcement that a stranger wished to see him. A tall messenger, dressed in gloomy gray, was shown in. He was the bearer of a letter without any signature, the purport of which was to inquire if Mozart would engage to compose a mass for the dead, and when it would be finished. Mozart consulted his wife; and, after informing her of the strange proceeding, and saying that he would like to undertake such a work, he agreed with the stranger, but would not name the exact time that it would be finished. He then inquired where the score should be sent to when ready; but the stranger said he would call for it, and that it would be in vain to attempt to discover who sent him. From that day thoughts of death haunted Mozart incessantly. On parting with friends, he would tell them they should never meet again. Oh, how true this was! He worked on "The Requiem" unceasingly, from the day of his interview with the mysterious messenger, but with such bad result on his health, that his wife called in Dr. Clossett to induce him to discontinue writing. He at once insisted on his giving up so exciting a subject. A marked improvement was soon apparent, and all hoped that he would be restored to health; but shortly after, he earnestly entreated to have the score back, that he might fulfil his commission. His kind Constance complied with this request, and he again set vigorously to work, and soon fell into a deep reverie over it. He now felt more strongly than ever that he was composing it for himself, and told his wife so.

On the 20th November, Mozart was carried to his bed, suffering dreadfully from a violent sickness, and with swollen hands and feet. From this bed he was destined never to rise again. During the fifteen days preceding his death he still retained consciousness, his wife and children continually occupying his thoughts during that time. Frequently he would exclaim, "Must I go, just as I am able to live in peace? Must I leave my wife and my poor children just when I should have been able to provide better for them?"

or, he would allow his fancy to run on the performance of his "Flauto Magico," which he loved so much. He would follow his watch, and exclaim, "Now the first act is over. Now is the time for the Queen of the Night." During this time, too, the heavenly "Requiem" was drawing near to completion. The score lay continually on his bed, and his pupil Süssmayr was constantly by his bedside receiving instructions as to the kind of effects he intended.

The night before his dissolution was a fearful one. At his bedside stood Constance and her sister, Sophie Weber, who had come to see how he was. Mozart on seeing her, exclaimed, "Oh, my dear Sophie! it is well you are here. I have the taste of death on my tongue. Who can comfort my Constance if you do not stay?" Thus he passed the night.]

The next day he was worse, and felt that his end was fast approaching. He said to Constance, "Oh, that I could only once more hear my 'Flauto Magico!'" About two o'clock he was visited by three intimate friends, to whom he showed the score of "The Requiem." After giving Süssmayr his final directions with regard to it, he once more glanced through it; and, with tears in his eyes, exclaimed, "Did I not always say that I was writing it for myself?" He then expressed a wish to have it sung. Poor Mozart took the alto part, and his friends the three remaining ones. They proceeded as far as the Lacrymosa, when suddenly Mozart burst into tears, and the score was put aside. He then fell into a delirium from which he never rallied. Cold applications were ordered to his burning head by Dr. Clossett; but it was all of no avail, and towards midnight he started up from his pillow, with his eyes fixed. His head then sank gently back, and the spirit of the great master had taken its flight.

Thus died Wolfgang Amadeus Mozart, on the 5th December, 1791. His body was clothed in the black dress of the Masonic Brotherhood, and after a benediction had been pronounced over it, it was carried on a snowy, stormy day along the Schuller Strasse to the churchyard of St. Mark, near Vienna, and deposited in a common grave. When his sorrowing Constance and friends, some time after, came to erect a cross over it, no one was to be found who could point out where his remains were lying! But what of that? His spirit is in heaven, and the monument he himself has raised, for worlds yet unborn, will perpetuate and immortalize his memory when the highest and fairest of marble columns shall have crumbled into dust.

PRINCIPAL INCIDENTS IN THE LIFE OF MOZART.

Born at Salzburg, 27th January	1756
First Visit to Vienna	1762
Played before George III.	1763

Mozart.

First compositions	1765
First public appearance as a Conductor	1768
Journey to Italy	1770
"La Finta Giardinera" produced	1775
"I Domeneo" performed	1781
"Le Nozze di Figaro" performed	1786
"Don Giovanni" first performed	1787
Instrumentation of the "Messiah"	1789
"Cosi fan Tutte" performed at Vienna	1790
"Die Zauberflöte" first performed	1791
"The Requiem" composed	1791
Mozart died	1791

Beethoven.

AMONG the many noble tombs and monuments in the secluded cemetery at Wahring, near Vienna, may be seen one of striking and stern simplicity—a stone with but one word upon it. No date of birth or death, no word of praise or regret, only a name—Beethoven. Beneath this stone lie the remains of the great tone-poet whose name it bears, and who stands out "a miracle of man," among all other musical composers.

Ludwig Van Beethoven was born on the 17th December, 1770, at the lovely town of Bonn, on the Rhine, where his father, Johann Van Beethoven, was tenor singer in the Elector of Cologne's private chapel. Very little is known authentically of Beethoven's infant years, except that they were passed in the midst of poverty and misery, the result of the wretchedly small income which his father received, and of the drunken and dissolute habits to which he was a victim. However, this sad deficiency was to some extent counterbalanced by the kindness and liberality of Ludwig's grandfather, who was spared to behold the first three years of Ludwig's existence.

On his father's death, Johann had to confront matters, and consider how he could best make up the deficit it caused in his income. This, no doubt, led him to form a plan respecting Ludwig, who had already evinced a liking for the clavier. Urged by the poverty staring him in the face, now more deplorably than ever, and also by the glowing accounts of the successes of Mozart as an infant prodigy, Johann resolved to make a similar wonder of the infant Ludwig, and at once commenced his musical education. At first the lessons were given in play, but were soon made sad and wearisome, for the poor child was kept at the piano day and night. Often, when his father and Pfeiffer returned from the tavern, the child was called from bed to sit at the instrument till daybreak. Of course, with this kind of tuition, he made but little progress, and it soon became evident that if he was to become as wonderful as Mozart and others had been, a change must be made in the mode of instruction. Fortunately for the world, it took place in time to save the first sparks of genius in the baby boy from being extinguished by the inhuman Johann, and Ludwig was placed under the care of Pfeiffer, an excellent pianist, to whom we have already referred. Under his kind instruction, the child made wonderful and astonishing progress, and acquired a most passionate love for music. But when Ludwig was nine years old, Pfeiffer obtained an appointment as bandmaster in one of the Bavarian regiments, and was compelled to leave Bonn. Before doing so, however, he generously saw the young genius provided for, and handed over to the Court organist, Van den Eeden.

This change was of very short duration, for Eeden, dying shortly after, the boy once more changed hands, and this time fell into those of Eeden's successor, Christian Gottlob Neefe, a masterly musician, and at one time cantor at the Thomas-Schule at Leipzig. From what Beethoven afterwards said, he does not appear to have been on very harmonious terms with Neefe; and he also relates that he did not profit by his instruction. Whether this be so or not, the master seems to have been proud enough of his pupil, for, writing in *Cramer's Magazine* of that time, he says of him:—"Louis Van Beethoven, son of the Court tenor singer of that name, a boy of eleven years old, possesses talent of great promise. He plays the piano with wonderful execution, and reads very well at sight—in short, he plays almost the whole of Sebastian Bach's 'Wohltempirte Clavier,' which Herr Neefe has put into his hands. All who know this collection throughout all the keys (which might almost he called the *ne plus ultra*) will understand what this implies. Herr Neefe has also given him, so far as his other engagements will permit, some instruction in thorough bass. He also exercises him in musical composition; and, to encourage him, has had his nine variations on a march published at Mannheim. This young genius deserves help, that he may travel. He will certainly be a second Wolfgang Amadeus Mozart, if he continues as he has begun."

Under Neefe, Ludwig remained till 1787. During that time, though he was chiefly engaged in teaching, he filled the post of assistant organist at the church of St. Remigius—to which he was appointed by the Elector Max Franz, at a salary of a hundred thalers a-year—and conducted the rehearsals of the Grossman Operatic Troupe, in the room of Neefe.

In the spring of 1787, young Beethoven started on a visit to the great art capital, Vienna, where Mozart and other great artists were living, the chief object of this visit being to obtain an interview with Mozart. This was soon accomplished, and Ludwig was requested to play before the then great idol of the musical world. A theme was laid before him, on which he was requested to improvise: with what result we all know. Mozart was struck by it, and stood watching with speechless wonder every movement of the lad; till at last, while the genius was winding up amid a labyrinth of melodies, Mozart crept stealthily to another room, where both critics and friends had previously assembled, and, with his face full of wonder and excitement, exclaimed: "Take care of this youth; some day he will make a stir in the world." Such was the verdict of the great Mozart!

Ludwig did not remain long in Vienna, for, receiving information that his mother's health was in a very precarious state, he at once returned home, and arrived there only in time to see his loving parent breathe her last. She died 17th July, 1787. This was a heavy blow to him. How his sensitive spirit received it, is best told in his own words. Writing to a friend, Dr. Schaden, he says:—"She was, indeed, a kind mother to me, and my best friend. Ah! who was happier than I when I could still utter the sweet name of mother, and it was heard? To whom can I now say it? Only to the silent form whom my imagination pictures to me."

Once more was our young genius surrounded with disheartenings which would have daunted the courage of many. Yet not so with him. He fearlessly and nobly looked matters in the face, and more earnestly than ever set about a task to which he never could, to the end of his days, inure himself—that of teaching.

Still, teach he must to provide for his younger brothers and sisters, who were now dependent on him for support, for the father was getting more extravagant than ever in his habits. For years was Beethoven compelled to succumb to this, to him, distasteful alternative. But he had his reward : for it was in the pursuance of that which he disliked so much, that he made such acquaintances as Count Waldstein, the Archduke Rudolphe, and the Breuning family. His associations with them were of the pleasantest kind, and especially with the Breunings, with whom he was as one of the family, and they were proud of him. It was at their house that he first became acquainted with that literature of his country, which afterwards he so much delighted to read, and to which he wedded some of his most splendid music.

In this cheerful society our artist lived till 1792, with but little to break the every-day round of teaching.

In the year 1792 Beethoven again started for Vienna, which he had so suddenly quitted some five years previously, and with a somewhat similar object as before. It was not, however, to see Mozart, but Haydn, and to receive the benefit of his instruction. Arrived in Vienna, our artist soon procured lodgings, and enrolled himself among the list of Haydn's pupils. Haydn instantly perceived his marvellous talent. Before long, however,

Beethoven did not feel satisfied with Haydn's instructions, and there is reason to fear that his discontent was only too well founded.

One day, returning from Haydn's house with his music under his arm, he came across his friend Schenk, who was not only a scholarly, but a conscientious musician. To him he confided his trouble; but Schenk, being unwilling to credit such an account of Haydn, went very carefully through the compositions in Beethoven's portfolio, and discovered serious errors passed over uncorrected. So enraged was Beethoven at this treatment, that he took the first opportunity that presented itself of severing his connection with Haydn.

He then placed himself under the tuition of Albrechtberger, for the purpose of thoroughly grounding himself in the mysteries of counterpoint and fugue. It was during this time that the young maestro made the acquaintance of another among the great *dilettanti* who flocked to hear and to see him. This was Prince Karl Lichnowski, who, together with his wife, took such an interest in Ludwig that they wished him to reside with them at the Lichnowski palace. This kind offer Beethoven accepted, on condition that he should not be compelled to observe court etiquette, and, for about ten years, this sort of friendly intercourse continued. So great a favourite did he become, that he used afterwards to say that "the Princess Christianne would have put a glass case over me, so that no evil might come nigh me." Many were the happy days passed in the Lichnowski palace, and many were the works penned within its walls. It was there that the three wonderful and unsurpassed trios for violin, violoncello, and pianoforte were first performed; also many of his quartets, the appealing Pathétique Sonata, his first Concerto in C major, for piano and orchestra, and other works more or less important. He remained a resident at the palace till the year 1795, when we find him appearing in public, as a *virtuoso*, for the first time. Hitherto he had confined his performances to palaces and private mansions. His fame, however, had spread so far and wide that the public *would* see him, and the curiosity of the Viennese was at length gratified on the occasion of his appearing at the "annual concert for the widows and orphans of musicians." From that time to the year 1827, when he died, he never quitted for more than a day or so the town in which he made his *début*.

Behold our colossal genius, but twenty-five years old —the greatest *virtuoso* of the day, and already overstepping the summit which others had reached as composers. How must the ardent young fellow have felt now? He must, indeed, have felt thankful and proud as he looked back on the cloudy past through which he had struggled. He was now sought after by the highest and noblest in Vienna. All strove to make his acquaintance. What a contrast to the time when he first arrived in the same city in 1787, to see Mozart!

But, what is this cloud before him? Beethoven has forebodings of a fearful nature. His hearing occasionally fails him. Gradually the cloud creeps nearer and nearer, till, in 1800, his fears culminate—Beethoven is deaf! Oh! how heavy a burden was now laid upon him! Other misfortunes he had got over. How was he to shake off this heaviest of them all? Such thoughts as these must have passed through the mind of the great *virtuoso*. What was his reply? "Resignation! what a miserable refuge, and yet the only one left for me." How keenly Beethoven felt his affliction will be best perceived by a few extracts from his letters. Writing to a friend, he says:—

"If I had not read that man must not of his own free will end this life, I should long ago have done so by my own hands. . . . I may say that I pass my life wretchedly. For nearly two years I have avoided society, because I cannot shout 'I am deaf!' . . . I have often already cursed my existence."

In his will, also, he refers to his fearful calamity in the following words:—

"Thus, with a passionate, lively temperament, keenly

susceptible to the charm of society, I was forced early to separate myself from men, and lead a solitary life. If at times I sought to break from my solitude, how harshly was I repulsed by the renewed consciousness of my affliction; and yet it was impossible for me to say to people, 'Speak louder—shout—I am deaf!' Nor could I proclaim an imperfection in that organ which in me should have been more perfect than in others. . . . What humiliation, when some one near me hears the note of a far-off flute, and I do not; or the distant shepherd's song, and I not."

Gradually was Beethoven compelled to give up his piano-playing and conducting, for he could not hear sufficiently what he or others played, and in the year 1802 he settled down to composition for the remainder of his life.

The first great work to which he directed his attention after his affliction, was the Third symphony, in E flat major, better known as the "Sinfonia Eroica." In this wonderful composition, Beethoven takes up the divine art where Mozart and Haydn left it, and carries it to a world in which neither they, nor any before or after them, have lived. This symphony establishes more distinctly than any of his former compositions his marvellous and unique originality, which shows itself still more prominently in his later works, than in this. At one time it was Beethoven's intention to publish it with the inscription "Buonaparte," in whose honour it was composed: but it wants no title to tell its meaning, for throughout the symphony the hero is visibly portrayed. The characteristic writing in the wonderful scherzo movement has never ceased to be the subject of argument since it was first heard. Critics ask, what does it mean? Some reply, "the pleasures of camp life;" others say it is intended to represent the "revels of unburied slain." But, however this may be, certain it is, that as a whole, the "Eroica" stands among the finest of Beethoven's nine symphonies.

After the massive "Eroica," Beethoven published a few piano sonatas, trios, and songs; then we come to that grand form of writing in which he has left us but one solitary specimen—"Fidelio."

On November 20th, 1805, this opera was given to the world, under the title of "Leonore, or Conjugal Affection," and met with quite an indifferent reception! After three representations, Beethoven withdrew it from the stage, but only to be brought out again in the following year, with one act completely taken out, and a new overture added to it. Still his enemies at the theatre would not have it, and succeeded in preventing its performance. Thus it was put aside for some years. In 1814, with several alterations, and another overture in E—the most beautiful and vigorous of the four Leonore overtures—it again made its *debut*, under the title of "Fidelio." Since then it has found a place on every stage in Europe, and Leonore, the heroine, has supplied the part in which some of the greatest singers have earned their laurels—Schroeder, Devrient, Milder-Hauptmann, Pasta, Malibran, and to come nearer the present day, Mdme. Titiens.

Although "Fidelio" is the only opera which Beethoven wrote, it is a sufficient example to prove his aptness for this branch of composition. The music to "Fidelio" stands above that of any other opera—shall we except "Don Giovanni?"—and it is to this alone that its success can be attributed; for, from a dramatic point of view, the opera possesses but little interest beyond the heroine Leonore. Why Beethoven wrote but one opera is hard to conceive, considering his immense fertility in writing, unless for the reason that he would not submit to the many whims and fancies of those who had the singing of his music; for in his "Fidelio" he had the greatest trouble to get the singers to sing his melodies as they were written; and he was not a man who would stoop and yield to singers, however great they might be.

This brings us to what is styled by some writers as the "matured period" of Beethoven's life, 1804—1814; that is, the period when his writings bear unmistakably the stamp of his individuality and genius, and to this period belongs a list of colossal works which cannot in this brief sketch be treated of singly. Among the most important are the music to Göthe's "Egmont"—alone sufficient to place its composer in the first rank, had he written nothing more—the Fourth symphony in B flat major, and the Fifth, in C minor, the most splendid symphony ever written. Opening in anguish, as of one in trouble, it wanders through many shadowlands, with gleams of hope and sunshine occasionally flitting across the gloomy path, and carrying the listener on to the *finale*, with its bright and joyous themes, like one who having long journeyed through anguish and sorrow, rejoices to reach at last a haven of rest and joy, where sorrow and sighing are unknown.

The Sixth symphony followed immediately after the one last referred to. It is in F major, and may be better known by the title given to it by the composer himself — "The Pastorale." It is noteworthy as being one of the very rare examples of the great genius attaching a descriptive programme to his music. But it is quite unnecessary; for the rustic merry-making, the storm, the shepherds' songs, and joy after the storm, are all wonderfully and faithfully depicted by the music. This symphony was followed by the mass in C, in which the composer made such a deviation from the path that Haydn and Mozart had trodden before him. Throughout the whole of it there breathes a grave and pathetic yearning. There is no ornate writing, such as is found in the works of the pious Mozart, to pave the path to piety, but a severity of treatment and conception, which, at the time, was neither understood nor tolerated.

The mass was first performed in 1810, at the palace of Prince Esterhazy, at Eisenstadt, where the prince, his kapellmeister Hummel, and a host of artists and *dilettanti* were assembled to hear this new mass, so different to those of the Mozart school to which they were accustomed.

They however reserved their opinions till the guests sat down to the *déjeuner* provided for them, The prince then made a remark which greatly irritated and hurt the susceptible Beethoven, who, glancing round the table, discovered that Hummel was laughing, as if enjoying very much the unflattering expression which had been made upon the mass. So enraged was Beethoven that a brother musician should thus treat him and his work, that he at once rose from the table and quitted the palace, and never, till he lay on his death-bed, was he reconciled to Hummel.

Five years elapsed between the "Pastorale" symphony and the Seventh, during which a long list of somewhat smaller works flowed without intermission from his prolific pen. These included sonatas, trios, and songs, the music to Kotzebue's "Ruins of Athens" and King Stephen;" till, in the year 1813, the Seventh symphony in A major, which he dedicated to Count Fries, was given to the world.

Of all the nine colossal symphonies written by Beethoven, this one in A major is the most majestic and powerful, and affords a splendid example of his wonderful originality and power of comprehension. What could be more striking and original than the powerful and pompous introduction, moving heavily on as it does to the point where the whole mass of instruments strike with the utmost power the *staccato* chord, leaving but one small voice—the oboe—to carry on the interest. Notable, too, in this symphony is Beethoven's unique and unparalleled use of the *crescendo*, as well as his total disregard of the trammels of the rules of writing. He makes a bold step, clear out of the then accepted path.

Many have been the hot words caused by this piece of orchestral writing and the innovations introduced into it; and no less warm has been the warfare on the question of what this splendid symphony is intended to represent. Some say "Moorish chivalry," others a "masquerade" or "wedding feast;" while, again, some maintain that, in this majestic composition Beethoven intended to represent himself, his life and circumstances, viewed in connection with the world; at that time the theatre of mighty events. It was first performed—together with the "Battle of Vittoria," composed by Beethoven in honour of Wellington's victory—at a concert given for the benefit of Austrian and Bavarian soldiers wounded in the battle of Hanau. At this concert Beethoven himself wielded the *bâton*, Schuppanzigh led the first violins, Spohr the seconds; Salieri marked the time for the cannonades and drums, while Hummel and Sivori occupied subordinate places. In a circular Beethoven afterwards wrote concerning it, he says:—

"It was a rare assemblage of distinguished artists; every one of whom was anxious to employ his talents for the benefit of the fatherland; and without any thought of precedence or merit, they all took their places in the orchestra. The direction of the whole was entrusted to me, but only because the music was of my composition. If any one else had written it, I would as cheerfully have taken my place at the big drum; for we had no other motive but the serving of our fatherland and those who had sacrificed so much for us."

The next year (1814) brought with it "Der Glorreiche Augenblick," a cantata for voices and orchestra, composed at the request of the authorities of Vienna, upon the occasion of the great Congress of kings and princes in that year. In recognition of his composition, Beethoven was presented with the freedom of the city of Vienna, and received also other marks of esteem from the gay throng of visitors who crowded the city.

But this joyous time came to an end, and Beethoven was doomed to have further burdens to bear. His brother Carl died, and left him his only child to support. Beethoven cheerfully undertook this charge, and the first thing he did was to place the boy out of the reach of his mother—the Queen of the Night, as he called her—who was considered by Beethoven an unfit person to train up the child. But this "the queen" would not submit to, and the result was, that, for four years, a lawsuit was pending between her and the great *maestro*, as to who should possess the boy.

Eventually, Beethoven gained the day, and at once sent his young relative to the university. But Carl was soon expelled; for the mother's character was firmly rooted in him, and he had chosen the path in which his father had walked. Yet after this, Beethoven got his ungrateful nephew admitted to a school where his co-guardian was supervisor. It was, however, of little use. Carl went from bad to worse; till, after attempting self-destruction, he was placed in an asylum, where, for the present, we must leave him.

During the years of the lawsuit, the composer published and wrote but little. The Eighth symphony, however, made its appearance in 1817; but it is most probable that it was composed some time before it was published. This symphony does not enjoy so high a degree of popularity as the others, which must, as we conclude, be partly owing to the high perfection to which the intellectual powers must attain before its beauty and merits can be conceived and appreciated. Although conceived in less vast proportions than its predecessors, it is far superior to either his first or second symphonies, and equal, both in form and instrumentation. to any he afterwards composed.

In the latter part of 1819, Beethoven sat himself down to the mass in D major, intended for the occasion of the installation of his friend the Archduke Rudolphe, as Archbishop of Olmutz, in the year 1821; but so engrossed did the composer become in this colossal work for solo voices and chorus, full orchestra and organ, that he did not complete it till two years had passed beyond the event it was intended to celebrate. By Beethoven it was regarded as his most successful effort; and certainly it is one of the grandest and profoundest works of art ever created—so grand, in fact, that there is but little scope left for devotional feeling and worship. It was first performed on April 1st, 1824.

The next and last great work with which Beethoven's name is associated is the Ninth symphony, better known, perhaps, as the "Choral symphony," or the "Jupiter," which the composer dedicated to Frederick William III. of Prussia. Like the eighth, it bears remarkable traces of the "mysticism" that pervades the latest of Beethoven's works. In this symphony he soars to a yet higher world than before. The resources of instrumentation seem insufficient to give vent to his marvellous imagination. In fact, of this last symphony the learned Marx says: "It exhausts the resources of instrumental music." What does the mighty genius that he may the better describe his creations? With instruments he combines voices, and thus raises a monument worthy the last efforts of so gigantic a genius.

Of its merits in relation to his other works there is much dispute. Spohr says of it: "The Ninth symphony, as regards the first three movements, is, in spite of occasional traits of genius, inferior to any of his former ones: and the conception of Schiller's Ode, in the fourth movement, is so utterly monstrous and absurd, that it is beyond my comprehension how Beethoven could write such a thing," Hans von Bulow says: "Not one in ten can understand it." Many call it a "monstrous madness;" while others see in it the most magnificent representation of Beethoven's genius. It was first performed at Berlin, under the composer's own direction, and met with unprecedented success. Such was the delight of the vast concourse assembled to hear it, that at times their shouts of joy completely overwhelmed the orchestra and singers. But Beethoven could not hear this!

About this time, he received an intimation that his nephew was in a fit state to be restored to him; and accordingly, Beethoven made a journey to the asylum, and brought Carl away with him. From the asylum they went to the house of Johann van Beethoven, where they were to reside during the arrangements that were pending for Carl to join Baron Stutterheim's regiment. A few days of his brother's company proved sufficient for Beethoven. He could not put up with his taunts, and on a wet and miserably raw day in December, 1826, Beethoven, with his nephew, started for Vienna in an open conveyance, for his brother would not lend him his close one. This exposure to the cold and rain brought about an attack of inflammation of the lungs, from which he never recovered.

On reaching his home at Vienna, he laid himself on

the bed which he was fated never again to leave. His friend, Dr. Wawruch, was in constant attendance, and performed several operations, which gave Beethoven partial relief; but dropsy set in, and made his case more than ever precarious. Still, his naturally strong constitution enabled him to linger on till March in the next year, 1827. It then became evident that he could not long battle against his disease, which was fast gaining the mastery over him; and on the morning of the 24th his friend Schindler visited him, and found him with a distorted face, sinking, and unable to speak more than a few words. His bedside gathering, which included Hummel, Schindler, Herr Ferdinand Hiller, Stephan Bruening, and, lastly, A. Hüttenbrenner, saw that he could bear up but little longer; and on the doctor arriving, they begged Beethoven that he would allow the holy sacrament to be administered to him, to which he calmly replied, "I will."

The pastor came, and the holy office was performed with the greatest solemnity. Beethoven then requested his friend Schindler not to forget to thank Herr Schott and the Philharmonic Society for the assistance they had rendered him during his illness; and in a few minutes afterwards he lost all consciousness. He continued gradually to sink, till, on the evening of the 26th, Nature sang her requiem over him. Amid a fearful storm of thunder and lightning, his spirit took its flight, soaring to another and more peaceful home.

His mortal remains were followed to their resting-place by over twenty-five thousand persons — kings, princes, poets, painters, artists, composers, and the public of Vienna—all anxious to pay their last tribute of respect. A simple stone was all that was deemed necessary to mark the spot where his ashes lie; but when time shall have swept that and all his associations away, his noble and sublime music will yet remain to preserve his name in every home, and in every heart.

PRINCIPAL INCIDENTS IN THE LIFE OF BEETHOVEN.

Born at Bonn on 17th December 1770
Assistant Organist at St. Remigius 1785
Played before Mozart in Vienna 1787
Under Haydn's Tuition 1792
His First Works—Three trios, and the "Pathétique"
    sonata—composed 1795
Afflicted with Deafness 1800
The "Eroica" Symphony composed 1804
"Fidelio" produced 1805
The C minor Symphony written 1807
The "Seventh" Symphony produced . . . 1813
Presented with the Freedom of Vienna . . . 1814
The "Eighth" Symphony produced 1817
The D major Mass first performed 1824
The "Choral" Symphony produced 1824
His Last Journey 1826
Died 1827

Spohr.

"THE first singer on the violin that ever appeared." Such was the judgment which the Italian critics delivered, when one of the truest of tone-poets first drew his bow to speak to, and kindle the emotions of, an audience in Italy. This was Ludwig Spohr. Great as a composer, great as a violinist, and beloved as a man, he has won the laurels of a master, and gained a place among the most illustrious musicians. Few have been more devoted to their art, or more ready to help a poor but promising student, than Spohr; few have appreciated the works of others as did the composer of the "Last Judgment" and the "Power of Sound."

He was born at Brunswick on the 5th April, 1784. Fortunately both his parents were musical; his father being an excellent flautist, while his mother possessed remarkable talent as a pianiste and singer. As might be supposed, they often passed their evenings in practising music, and the development of young Ludwig's high musical gifts was naturally due to these family concerts. Nature had endowed him with a very sensitive ear' and a fine clear voice, so that when he was but four or five years old, he joined with his mother in duets at the evening gatherings.

From a very early age the little boy evinced a disposition for the instrument on which he afterwards became so distinguished a performer. He had so long been teasing his father for a violin, that when he was six years old, he presented him with his first instrument. Great was the little fellow's joy on receiving this treasure. It was never out of his hands, and he would wander about the house with it, endeavouring to play some of his favourite melodies. In his autobiography Spohr says: "I still recollect that after my first lesson, in which I had learnt to play the G-sharp chord upon all the four strings, in my rapture at the harmony, I hurried to my mother, who was in the kitchen, and played the chord to her so incessantly that she was obliged to drive me out."

Young Ludwig received his first lesson on the violin from Dufour, an excellent amateur musician, who had settled at Seesen, in which town the Spohr family at that time resided. The progress the boy made fairly astonished Dufour, and induced him to ask the parents to allow the boy to devote himself entirely to music. This was agreed to, and little Ludwig was delighted. His progress was wonderful; indeed, so well did he play, that, although a boy, he obtained an appointment in the Court orchestra at Brunswick. Already, too, he had shown his inclination for composing, although as yet he had received no instruction either in harmony or counterpoint.

Spohr remained under the care of Dufour until he was about twelve years old, when, at his master's suggestion, he was sent to Brunswick, that he might there enjoy the advantage of better instruction. For this purpose he was placed under Kunisch, an excellent teacher of the violin, and under Hartung for harmony and counterpoint. The latter was one of those dry, surly old people, who are too often the ruin of young and ardent talent. Spohr refers to him in his autobiography, saying: " Not long after the commencement of the lessons I showed him a composition of my own. 'There's time enough for that,' said he. 'You must learn something first.'" However, the old man died, and Spohr received no more theory lessons from him or from any one else. What he learnt after this was from his own diligent and careful study of the scores of the great masters—a pursuit of the utmost advantage to both young and old musicians, and one which cannot be too forcibly instilled into the minds of young scholars.

Ludwig Spohr, now fourteen years old, was already an excellent solo player, and his father was of opinion that he should now be maintaining himself; so accordingly the talented youth set out for Hamburg to try his fortunes there. His bright hopes were soon dissipated, and, with the little money remaining from that which his father had given him at starting, Ludwig sent his violin and other things on before him, while he, weary and footsore, trudged back to Brunswick.

When he arrived, he began to consider what was best to be done to obtain a livelihood, for he felt half ashamed to apply to his father after so soon retreating from Hamburg. Ultimately he hit upon the idea of petitioning the Duke of Brunswick, who as he knew was a good amateur violinist. Accordingly, one morning, as the duke was walking in the palace grounds, Spohr took the opportunity of presenting his petition, which was favourably received, and the duke very kindly arranged a concert at the palace, at which Spohr was to play. Upon hearing him, the duke was much pleased, and immediately secured for him a post in the orchéstra, saying, " Be industrious and well-behaved, and if, after some time, you have made good progress, I will place you under a great master." The duke was faithful to his promise, for early in the year 1802 he placed Spohr under the care of Francis Eck, one of the finest violinists then living.

Shortly after this both master and pupil set out on an artistic tour, visiting, among other cities, Hamburg, Strelitz, Riga, and St. Petersburg; in all of which Spohr's fine playing won the admiration both of musicians and the public. It was not until July, 1803, that he returned to his native town, and his first meeting with his relations was a curious one. "I arrived," he says, "at two o'clock in the morning. I landed at the Petri Gate, crossed the Ocker in a boat, and hastened to my grandmother's garden, but on arriving there I found both the house and garden-doors locked. As my knocking did not arouse any one, I clambered over the garden-wall, and laid myself down in a summer-house at the end of the garden. Wearied by the long journey, I soon fell asleep, and, notwithstanding my hard couch, would probably have slept on for a long while, had not my aunts, in their morning walk, discovered me. Much alarmed, they ran and told my grandmother that a stranger was lying in the summer-house. Returning together the three approached nearer, and, recognizing me, I was awakened amid joyous expressions, embraces, and kisses. At first I did not recollect where I was, but soon recognized my dear relations, and rejoiced at being once again in the home and scenes of my childhood."

During his travels, Spohr had not only wonderfully improved in his playing, but he had also made good progress as a composer, having published a concerto for the violin, and some duets, which had attracted much attention. Upon his return to Brunswick, therefore, he took the first opportunity of arranging a concert, so that his friends might see the progress he had made. The concert took place, and the duke was so pleased with the violin concerto and the way in which Spohr now played, that at the conclusion he sent for him, and warmly congratulated him. Moreover, he appointed him first violinist in the Court orchestra, with an additional salary of two hundred thalers, a small, yet welcome amount.

Shortly after this Spohr made a tour to Leipzig, Dresden, and Berlin, where he charmed all who heard him, and gained fresh laurels as a composer, by producing his splendid D minor and E minor concertos.

In the spring of 1805 he had returned from this journey; but hardly had he settled down again before he received a letter, inviting him to compete for the directorship of the ducal orchestra at Gotha, which had become vacant. Spohr was successful, and was duly introduced to his new duties, which consisted in the arrangement of a Court concert once a week throughout the year, and in practising and rehearsing the orchestra. For these duties he received a salary of five hundred thalers per annum.

Now occurred an interesting event in the great artist's career. At the house of Madame Scheidler, one of the Court singers at Gotha, Spohr made the acquaintance of this lady's daughter, Dorette, an expressive and beautiful player upon the harp. The attachment grew stronger. He and Dorette often played together at concerts, and, returning from one of these given by the minister Von Thummell, where the young musicians had been overwhelmed by the praises of the delighted company, Spohr, during the drive home, asked, "Shall we thus play together for life?" "Bursting into tears," he says, "she sank into my arms; the contract for life was sealed." On the 2nd February, 1806, they were married in the palace chapel, in the presence of the duchess and a large assemblage of friends.

In the following year Spohr and his young wife set out on their first artistic tour, "by which," he says, "we not only earned a rich harvest of applause, but saved a considerable sum of money." His friends in Gotha had heard of his success, and what was Spohr's surprise when, yet some miles from the town, he was met by a band of his pupils, who had come out to escort their beloved master home in triumph. For some time he remained at home, applying himself assiduously to composition. An opera, entitled "Alruna," was among the most important of his writings at this time, which, although its composer allowed it to disappear, possessed, nevertheless, much that was good. At its first performance it gave "general satisfaction," says Spohr, and its composer was overwhelmed with congratulations.

The month of October, 1809, found Spohr and his talented wife again leaving their home—this time for a journey to Russia. However, they had only proceeded as far as Breslau, when Spohr received a letter from the Court chamberlain, inviting them to return, as the duchess could no longer spare them from the Court concerts, and would willingly indemnify them, if they would give up their proposed journey and return at once. This request was acceded to, and soon the gifted musicians were once again in the Court orchestra at Gotha. Here they remained for some time, during which Spohr was chiefly engaged in composition. Among the works of this time may be mentioned "Der Zweikampf mit der Geliebten," "Das Jüngste Gericht," first performed at the festival held at Erfurt in 1812, in honour of Napoleon's birthday; a symphony, and some sonatas for the harp and violin.

In the autumn of 1812, however, Spohr again applied for leave to take another journey. This was granted, and in December of this year he and his wife were charming the Viennese by their exquisite playing. It was a most satisfactory journey for Spohr, and it enabled him to resign his Gotha appointment. While at Vienna he was offered the directorship of the Theatre An der Wien, at a salary three times the amount of that which he was receiving at Gotha. This, and Count Palffy's assurance that he intended making it the finest orchestra in Germany, induced Spohr to accept the offer.

Now came the necessary search for a domicile in Vienna. This was at length found, and with it there came another piece of good fortune. One fine morning Spohr was waited upon by a gentleman, who, it turned out, was a wealthy cloth manufacturer, and a passionate lover of music, who never failed being present at every public concert. What he wanted was this—that Spohr should hand over to him all that he might compose, or had already written, in Vienna, for three years; the original scores to be his sole property during that time: Spohr not even to retain a copy of them. "But," said Spohr, "are they not to be performed during those three years?" "Oh, yes: as often as possible, but each time on my lending them for that purpose, and when I can be present," was the reply. The two struck a bargain. Thirty ducats was the price the enthusiastic connoisseur was to pay for a string quartet, five-and-thirty for a quintet, forty ducats for a sextet, and so on, according to the kind of composition.

Soon Spohr had two compositions ready for his customer, and, in handing them over to him, remarked that he should apply the money to the furnishing his lodgings. Hereupon Von Tost willingly undertook to provide the furniture complete in every respect; and, on an early day, a tour was made among the shops of Vienna, Tost ordering costly mahogany furniture, curtains, pots and kettles, provisions, tables and crockery-ware, as Spohr has it, "more suitable for a merchant than an humble artist." All Spohr's expressions that such and such a thing would not be required were met by, "Make yourself easy, I shall ask no cash payment;" or, "You will soon square all accounts with your manuscripts." So Spohr's new home got well furnished, and, let us hope, the enthusiast's interests served. He had two objects in view. "First," he told Spohr, "I wish to be invited to the musical circles in which you will play your compositions, and to do this I must have the scores in my possession; secondly, in possessing such treasures of art, I hope upon my business journeys to make a large acquaintance among lovers of music, which I may turn to account in my manufacturing interests!"

In the midst of his new duties Spohr now gave to the world two important works—his opera of "Faust," and the cantata "The Liberation of Germany." "Faust" was composed for the An der Wien Theatre, but circumstances arose which resulted in its finding its way to the shelves, and not getting performed till Weber brought it out at Prague in 1816. However, the score created a stir in musical circles long before it was publicly performed, and such musicians as Meyerbeer and Hummel predicted for it much success. Curiously enough the cantata, which was written to celebrate the return of the army that had liberated Germany, shared something like a similar fate. When the work was completed, not a building could be obtained wherein to perform it, and thus it did not get a hearing till it was performed at the musical festival at Frankenhausen in 1815, on the anniversary of the battle of Leipzig.

The year 1815 brought with it a change in Spohr's arrangements. There had been a rupture between him and Count Palffy, the proprietor of the An der Wien Theatre, which ended in their cancelling their agreement. Now free, he decided on making a long journey, visiting Germany, Switzerland, and Italy. Preparations for the tour were begun. Von Tost's little matter was satisfactorily arranged, and his furniture and household properties were put up for auction. "Immediately," says Spohr, "that the sale was announced, a host of purchasers presented themselves, and as our furniture was very elegant, and also nearly new, they bid warmly against each other, and the sum we realized was far beyond our expectations." On the 18th March, 1815, Spohr, with his beloved Dorette and young family, bade adieu to Vienna.

It was late in the year 1817 before they returned from this long artistic tour, and on their way home Spohr received a letter, inviting him to accept the post of director of the opera and music of the Frankfort Theatre. He did so, and for nearly two years laboured zealously to improve his new orchestra. "Zemire and Azor" was the most important work he produced during this period. This opera, founded on Grétry's "La Belle et le Bête" ("The Beauty and the Beast") was first performed at the Frankfort Theatre in April, 1819, under the composer's direction, and met with a most favourable reception. "Indeed," writes Spohr, "a more successful one than did 'Faust.'" That lovely song which Zemira sings, "Roses softly blooming," is an excellent sample of how much there is to charm in this opera.

On the 5th April, 1831, it was produced at Covent Garden Theatre, under the title of "Azor and Zemira," or "The Magic Rose." The caste on this occasion included Miss Inverarity, the two Miss Cawses, Mr. Wilson, and Mr. Morley—by no means so strong or effective a one as the opera demanded. The work created a great stir in musical circles, and was the subject of much discussion. All were agreed that "melody in the richest profusion" was to be found in the opera, but the prevailing opinion was that it was too "scientific." The public and critics could not feel happy with the harmonies, and declared they were "obscure and overstrained."

While at Frankfort, Spohr received an invitation from the Philharmonic Society to come to London for the season of 1820, and appear at one of their concerts. He accepted this, and early in that year he and Dorette were in London, where he appeared at one of the society's concerts, playing a cantabile scena of his own composition, and also one of his quartets, both of which were much admired. The great violinist, Viotti, was present, and highly complimented Spohr on his brilliant playing.

While here he composed his D flat symphony (Op. 49), which was interpreted for the first time by the orchestra of the Philharmonic Society at their concert of April 10, 1820, its composer wielding the *bâton* on this occasion. Spohr says: "On this night the symphony was played with a better effect than I have ever since heard it." The following day most of the papers had something to say of the splendid new symphony, and brilliant performance overnight.

Moreover, while in London, Spohr gave a benefit

concert, which proved most advantageous to him, the receipts being very considerable. The following is a copy of the programme which our great artist provided for his audience on this occasion, and to some readers it may not be uninteresting :—

NEW ARGYLL ROOMS.
MR. SPOHR'S CONCERT.
Thursday, June 18th, 1820.

PART I.

Grand Sinfonia (MS.) ... ... Spohr.
Air—Mr. T. Welch—" Revenge ! Revenge ! Timotheus cries" ... ... Handel.
Grand Duetto (MS.)—Harp and Violin—Mad. Spohr and Mr. Spohr ... ... Spohr.
Aria—Miss Goodall—" Una voce al cor mi parla"— Clarinet Obligato, Mr. Williams ... ... Pœr.
Ses Stetto for Pianoforte, two Violins, Viola, Violoncello, and Contrabasso—Messrs. Ries, Watts, Wagstaff, R. Ashley, Lindley, and Dragonetti ... Ries.
Irish Melodies (MS.), with variations for the Violin— Mr. Spohr (composed expressly for this occasion) Spohr.

PART II.

Nonotto for Violin, Viola, Violoncello-Contrabasso, Flute, Oboe, Clarinet, Horn, and Bassoon— Messrs. Spohr, Lindley, Dragonetti, Ireland, Griesbach, Willman, Arnull, and Holmes ... Spohr.
Scena—Mrs. Salmon—" Fellon, la pena avrai"... ... Rossini.
Rondo for the Violin—Mr. Spohr ... ... Spohr.
Aria—Mr. Vaughan—" Rend i'l sereno "· ... ... Hande
Overture ... ... Spohr

    Leader of the Band ... ... Mr. Spohr.
    At the Pianoforte ... ... Sir George Smart.

With the London season over, Spohr turned his face towards his home, to make preparations for a winter tour to Paris. After conducting a musical festival at Quedlinburg, to the satisfaction of every one, he again parted with his children, and set out for Frankfort. Here he gave a concert, and produced his D minor Violin concerto (Op. 55), causing a great sensation. Other cities were visited before Paris was seen, in most of which he gave concerts, meeting with the same enthusiasm as always attended his performances. Early in December he was in Paris, and for two months did little else than attend the opera and theatres, pay visits to the virtuosi there, and accept the many pressing invitations which he received from most of the musical circles in this lively city.

On the 20th January, 1821, Spohr made his *début* before a Parisian audience, and with much success. The concert was given in the Grand Opera House, "and," says Spohr, "the satisfaction of the audience was unmistakably expressed by loud applause and shouts of 'bravo!'" This was the only concert he gave during this stay in Paris, as he found that the risk and expenses were too great in this a so full of attractions. He turned to his "dear fatherland," and busied himself with the composition of a ten-part vocal mass, and a clarinet concerto in F minor, composed for his friend, the celebrated clarinettist, Hermstedt. The mass was finished, and despatched to the director of the Choral Society at Leipzig, for performance there; but at the rehearsals it was found to be so extremely difficult, that the idea was given up, and the work laid aside. However, some years after, on St. Cecilia's Day, 1827, it was performed with great success by the Cassel Choral Society, under Spohr's own direction.

On New Year's Day of 1822, Spohr was in Cassel. He had been recommended by Weber for the directorship of the orchestra of the Court Theatre there, and had gone to see the elector with reference to the post. It was given to Spohr in the hope that by his exertions it would soon be one of the most celebrated in Germany, and with it the elector gave him the authority to do whatever would be requisite to accomplish this end. At a grand dinner, amid songs, speeches, and toasts, Spohr was introduced to his new orchestra, to which he remained so brilliant and useful an ornament for over thirty years.

It was not long before he laid before them a new composition written by himself. This was the opera of "Jessonda," first performed on the 28th July, 1823, at one of the Court concerts, "when," says Spohr, "the effect was great! The chorus and orchestra, scenery, storm, decorations, costumes—everything was most excellent. The work has made me very happy, and I believe it will be successful." Spohr's belief was realized. "Jessonda" was successful, and soon found a home on all the stages of Germany by reason of its peculiar gracefulness, and the masterly treatment of the text. Two of its duets alone would be sufficient to keep its composer's name ever before us.

Another opera, "Der Berg Geist" ("The Mountain Spirit"), followed upon "Jessonda." This work was composed to celebrate the marriage of the Elector of Hesse's daughter, the Princess Marie, with the Duke of Saxe-Meiningen. On that occasion the new opera was produced, and met with a most cordial reception from the brilliant assembly which filled the theatre.

The oratorio "Die Letzten Dinge" ("The Last Judgment"), more familiar perhaps to English people than any other of Spohr's compositions, came with the year 1826. On Good Friday of that year the Lutheran church of Cassel presented a most impressive appearance. It was evening. The sacred edifice was lighted up, and overhead hung an enormous cross covered with silver foil, from which were suspended hundreds of lighted lamps, shedding a brilliant ray of light upon the many hundreds of persons who filled the church. Here was heard, for the first time, Spohr's sublime oratorio— the "Last Judgment." What must have been the thoughts of the congregation, as in the "solemn stillness" which Spohr says prevailed, and in the light of that emblem of Calvary overhead, they awaited the solemn narrative of the "Last Judgment."

The performance was faultless; the singers and orchestra, numbering nearly two hundred performers, rendered their parts most effectively. "Never before," says Spohr, "did I experience such complete satisfaction from the performance of one of my works." The fame of the "Last Judgment" soon spread through Europe, causing a deal of excitement among the *dilettanti*, who were anxious to hear the new oratorio. To those in England an opportunity was afforded at the Norwich Festival of 1830, for here, under Mr. E. Taylor's direction, this work was first given in England. This performance fully endorsed all that had been said of the work. The critics were loud in their praise, and referring to it, a high authority of the day wrote, "It would be presumption in us, having heard it but once, were we to attempt a minute detail of all the beauties of this elaborate work, in which is embodied every passion, sentiment, and feeling that the power of music is capable of expressing; and however elevated the name of Spohr may justly be as a composer of the highest class of instrumental music, this sublime oratorio will add immensely to his reputation, and henceforward his name will be inserted in the list of those authors whose studies, efforts, and genius have been most successful in this, the noblest branch of art."

Such was the opinion of the merits of this oratorio then, and forty years have not lessened it; while, had it not been for the flashing of that brilliant meteor, Felix Mendelssohn, across Spohr's path, leaving behind it such gorgeous traces of its passage, there can be no doubt whatever that the merits of the "Last Judgment" would have won for the work many more admirers than it even now commands.

It is by no means a large work, containing in all but twenty-three numbers. All who have heard it, must ever remember such inspirations as the opening chorus, "Praise the Lord our God," or "Destruction is fallen on Babylon," and "Great and wonderful," with its joyous "Hallelujah," two more of its finest choruses. Nor is the duet for soprano and tenor, "Lord, remember my affliction," or the air and chorus, "Holy, holy, holy," less charming. The work is replete with such gems as these, and this, with the charming originality of the music, and the complete and masterly grasp of the subject, combine to render the oratorio worthy of a place among the masterpieces of Handel or Mendelssohn.

Spohr was now assiduous at composition. After "Die Letzten Dinge" came the B flat minor quintet, some quartets for strings, his third symphony—the C minor—the opera "Pietro von Abano," till we come to the opera of "The Alchymist," first performed in Cassel on the 28th July, 1830, where it was received with the greatest enthusiasm. With the year 1832 came another great work, better known in England, perhaps, than any other of Spohr's orchestral works. This was the symphony "Die Weihe der Töne" ("The Power of Sound"). Spohr had been reading through a volume of poems which his deceased friend Pfeiffer had left behind him, when he alighted on "Die Weihe der Töne," which pleased him so much that he thought of taking the words for a cantata. However, he did not do this, but decided to delineate the subject of the poem in an orchestral composition. Thus originated that masterly and colossal conception, "The Power of Sound," a composition which, had Spohr written nothing else, would have secured a lasting fame for its gifted composer.

In the year 1834 a sad calamity overtook the great master—the death of his beloved wife. For some time she had been suffering from nervous fever, and to this she succumbed on the 20th November.

Dorette's illness and death had interrupted Spohr's work upon his new oratorio, "Calvary," and it was some time before he felt fit to resume his labours. Yet Dorette, during her illness, had taken such an interest in the work, that for this reason he felt anxious to complete it as soon as possible. He fell to work upon it, and on Good Friday, 1835, the oratorio was first publicly performed. "The thought," says Spohr, "that my wife did not live to listen to its first performance, sensibly lessened the satisfaction I felt at this, my most successful work." It was first heard in England at the Norwich Festival of 1839, and the success it then achieved was enormous, in spite of much opposition hurled at it from the Norwich pulpits.

Before Spohr's very face was one of these needless discourses delivered by a zealous clergyman from the cathedral pulpit; but, fortunately, Spohr was foreign to the English language, and he was spared the pain of sitting still under this ill-timed personal attack. Referring to this occasion, the *Monthly Chronicle* says :—"We now see the fanatical zealot in the pulpit, and sitting right opposite to him the great composer, with ears happily deaf to the English tongue, but with a demeanour so becoming, with a look so full of pure good-will, and with so much humility and mildness in the features, that his countenance alone spoke to the heart like a good sermon. Without intending it, we make a comparison, and cannot for a moment doubt in which of the two dwelt the spirit of religion, which denoted the true Christian!"

Notwithstanding the sermon, the performance took

place, and hours before the appointed time the doors of St. Andrew's Hall were besieged by crowds of people anxious to gain admittance. "From far and wide," says a journal of the time, "the auditory flocked in thousands, evincing a powerful feeling of excitement, and an enthusiasm which increased continually during the performance; and, beyond all expectation, a complete triumph was achieved."

Two lonesome years had barely passed, when Spohr began to long for another partner. This he found in the sister of his deceased friend, Pfeiffer; and on the 3rd January, 1836, their wedding took place. Soon after this, accompanied by his wife, more than twenty years younger than himself, he made a long journey, visiting Leipzig, Brunswick, Vienna, and many other cities, in all of which he and his young wife, a brilliant pianiste, were received with great rejoicings. Musical parties and feasts were arranged, and almost nightly were the talented artists to be seen in gayly-festooned rooms, charming the listeners by their wonderful playing.

In 1839 he gave to the world a work he had planned during this journey. This was another splendid orchestral composition—the celebrated "Historical" symphony, illustrating, in its first movement, the music and characteristics of the Bach-Handel period, 1720; in its adagio, the Haydn-Mozart period, 1780; and in its scherzo movement, the Beethoven period, 1810; while the concluding movement is devoted to illustrating the style and taste of playing at the time when the symphony was composed, 1838-9. No sooner was it heard in Cassel, than it was at once pronounced one of the finest productions from this great master's pen. The fame of it soon spread throughout Germany—indeed, throughout Europe. The Philharmonic Society introduced it in England, and here it created quite as favourable an impression as in Germany.

A pressing invitation from Professor Taylor brought Spohr again to England, to conduct the Norwich Festival of 1839; after which he returned to his home at Cassel, and set to work upon a new oratorio—"The Fall of Babylon." This was completed in time for the Norwich Festival of 1842, but unfortunately Spohr could not obtain permission from his employer—the Elector of Hesse—to visit England to conduct its performance. The work was produced, nevertheless, under Professor Taylor's direction, when it met with a most satisfactory reception. The performance took place in the St. Andrew's Hall, "and," says the *Morning Herald*, "the whole interior of the building was immediately filled; where a resting-place could be found for one foot only, fool-hardy individuals were to be seen located in the most dangerous situations; and every one seemed determined to endure the greatest inconvenience rather than forego the pleasure of hearing Spohr's oratorio. many persons clambered up to the roof, and from thence in at the window; but numbers were compelled to remain outside, and content themselves with looking down from their dizzy height upon the crowds below. This is no exaggeration, but strictly true; and that such a degree of interest should have been evinced for a new musical work, is certainly an event that stands alone in the history of music."

The following year gave the Londoners an opportunity of hearing "Babylon"—first at the Hanover Square Rooms, and shortly after at Exeter Hall, by the Sacred Harmonic Society. This latter performance was an eminently successful one. The large hall was crammed to overflowing, and no sooner did Spohr appear than there commenced a shouting of "bravo" and "hurrah," accompanied with a waving of handkerchiefs such as had never before been witnessed within its walls. The performance over, the applause of the audience knew no bounds, "and," says an eye-witness, "at a loss to find a new and further way of expressing their rapture, they demonstrated it more prominently by mounting at once upon the benches. When at length Spohr had made his way through the mass of those who pressed forward to shake hands with and congratulate him, as he passed on to the door of the hall, it was observed with astonishment that the whole company remained behind, and were whispering to one another, which induced the idea, as was the fact, that something extraordinary, or at least important, was still to take place. After a time the noise broke out afresh, and Spohr was again vehemently called for. Upon this two gentlemen led him back once more, and having informed him that the public much wished him to address a few words to them, he at length determined to do so, and made a short speech to them in German, which though it was not generally understood, was very enthusiastically received by the assembly. Hereupon, the President stepped forward, and having delivered an address to Spohr in English, presented to him, in the name of the company, a large silver salver, with a beautifully-engraved inscription, commemorative of the evening festival, &c.

"This gratifying concluding scene crowned all that Sphor had yet experienced, and no incident of his life was afterwards referred to by him with greater pleasure than this performance of 'Babylon:' none of the many objects of esteem possessed by him were more prized, or referred to with more gratification, than was this trifling testimonial presented to him by the Sacred Harmonic Society."

After this Spohr left London, and not only did crowds

of people assemble to witness his departure, but some actually followed the steamer in boats, carrying with them albums, in which they entreated the great man to inscribe his autograph, and which he joyfully acceded to.

He arrived safely at his house at Cassel, with his thoughts busy about a new opera, "The Crusaders," which was first performed on New Year's Day, 1845, and "met with an unexampled brilliant reception."

After this he made a journey to Oldenburg, to conduct a musical festival. Here he met with a most hearty greeting, the whole platform from which Spohr led the orchestra, and the steps leading to it, were strewn with the finest roses, the front of the stage being decorated with wreaths, while beneath his bust, crowned with laurel, were the words "Louis Spohr," in large letters, formed of roses and laurel, beautifully and artistically interwoven.

Berlin saw him next, whither he had been invited to conduct his opera of "The Crusaders." In his autobiography he relates two pleasing incidents, which occurred during this visit, which are not uninteresting. He had been invited to a select dinner-party given at the palace, and between the king and Spohr, who was seated opposite to him, rose an ornamental centre-piece of considerable height, in the shape of a costly flower-vase, which, whenever the king was desirous of addressing his conversation to Spohr, greatly interfered and prevented him from seeing his face. Upon each occasion the king was obliged to stoop in order to look round the inconveniently intervening object, until, growing impatient, after having made several signs to the servants to remove it, which they appeared not to have understood, the king seized it with his own hands, and, removing the obtrusive ornament, procured for himself an unimpeded view across the table to Spohr.

The other incident was a surprise from his colleagues in art. One evening while a guest of the Wickmann family, Spohr and other friends were seated in the illuminated garden-saloon in friendly chat, when they were greatly surprised by the sudden entry, from the obscurity of the garden, of several dark figures, which were followed by a constantly-increasing number, until the whole of the members of the Royal Orchestra, with Meyerbeer and Taubert at their head, assembled. The senior member then presented Spohr with a beautifully-executed golden laurel wreath, while [Meyerbeer, in a speech of much feeling, thanked him for all the grand and beautiful things which, in his enthusiastic love of German art, he had hitherto created, and especially for this his excellent work, "The Crusaders."

For Spohr, the year 1847 opened brightly—it being the twenty-fifth anniversary of his connection with

Court Theatre of Cassel; and a festival had long been talked about to celebrate the event; but, alas! it was also the year when his beloved friend, Felix Mendelssohn, closed his eyes for ever. Spohr had returned from a happy visit to England when he received the sad tidings. The last time he had seen Mendelssohn was a year before, as he sat in the train returning from a visit to Leipzig. Then, after all the assembled friends had parted with Spohr, the amiable Felix, as the train at first proceeded slowly, ran for a considerable distance by the side of the carriage, until he could no longer keep pace with it, and his kindly beaming eyes were the last that left their expression on the mind of the traveller, little anticipating, indeed, that it was to be their last meeting on this side of the grave. In the midst of his grief, Spohr and his colleagues prepared a grand musical festival in memory of their departed friend, as the best tribute of affection they could pay to one whom they loved and admired so much.

The year 1850 is an important one, for it gave birth to another splendid symphony by Spohr, known as "The Seasons," in which masterly work the freshness of Spring; the warm and sultry Summer; Autumn, with its characteristic music, and the joyous chase and vintage songs; old Winter, so monotonous and cheerless, are all faithfully depicted in this grand musical structure. This symphony was followed by Spohr's seventh quintet, in G minor, another string quartet—the 32nd—and a series of pieces for the violin and piano; till, in 1852, he fell to work remodelling his opera of "Faust" for Mr. Gye's house.

On July 15th it was given, the great composer himself wielding the *bâton* in the room of Mr. Costa, who volunteered to play the organ behind the scenes. "On this occasion," writes a very reliable critic, "There was a certain amount of heaviness about the performance which told very much against the probability of that opera ever becoming a favourite with the Royal Italian Opera subscribers. Nothing could possibly exceed the poetical grace of Ronconi in the title *rôle*, or surpass the propriety and expression of his singing. Madame Castellan's Cunegonda was also exceedingly well sung; and Tamberlik outdid himself by his thorough comprehension of the music, the splendour of his voice, and the refinement of his vocalization in the character of Ugo. Mdlle. Zerr, as Rose, was much out of voice, and entirely deficient in pathos and simplicity, and evidently neither felt nor took the slightest interest in a small part, which she appeared to think quite beneath her notice. The Mephistopheles of Formes was a remarkable personation, being truly demoniacal in the play of his countenance, and as characteristic as any one of

Retsch's drawings of Göthe's fiend-tempter. His singing, being specially German, was in every way well suited to the occasion. Upon the repetition of this opera a few nights afterwards, when Mr. Costa resumed the *bâton*, the spirit and vivacity which superseded the heaviness of the composer's direction could not fail to be marked by a crowded and intelligent audience."

At the invitation of Dr. Wylde, Spohr came again to London for the 1853 season, to conduct some of the New Philharmonic Society's concerts. He was a guest of Dr. Farre during this stay, and the hearty reception and greetings he received on all sides, and the many fine renderings of some of his works during this season must have been intensely gratifying to him, and especially as this proved to be his last visit to England. He returned home and spent the next few years at Cassel, pursuing his Court duties, and composing some new works; yet, not omitting to take advantage of the leisure which the vacations at Court afforded him.

On these occasions he made journeys to Switzerland and many of the larger German towns, in all of which his presence was soon discovered, and then followed public and private entertainments, serenades, and such like, in honour of the grand old master.

The masterly septet for piano, string and wind instruments, another violin quartet, and three splendid duets for the violin, were among his compositions up to the year 1855; and, notwithstanding that Spohr was now over seventy years of age, they are as charmingly fresh and original in character as are his earlier compositions.

But he lived to see the day when he could not give expression to the fancies and beautiful forms which occupied his brain. In 1857 he put his pen to his 34th quartet, but, alas! upon completion, it did not satisfy him. Again he tried it, but sorrowfully desired it never to be made public. The same with his tenth symphony. After he had heard it performed by his Cassel orchestra, it was condemned. How bitter must this have been for Spohr! Yet he had to bear more, for there soon came the following unexpected communication :—

"In pursuance of our most gracious will and pleasure, we have granted to the Director-General of Music and Kapellmeister at our Court Theatre, Dr. Louis Spohr, in consequence of his advanced years, the permission to retire into private life; and have been further pleased to grant him a yearly pension of 1500 thalers from our Court treasury, dating from next month. The department of our lord high marshal of the palace will make the further dispositions to that effect.

"FRIEDRICH WILHELM.

"Cassel, November 12, 1857."

Nor was this all. He had reconciled himself to the change; "although," he says, "I felt still perfectly competent to conduct the few operas which latterly fell to my share;" when yet another joy—almost a condition of existence—his violin was thrust from him, for he had the misfortune to fall and break his left arm, and never again did it recover its strength and elasticity. All that was now left to him was the enjoyment of making short excursions to hear his compositions performed, and occasionally conducting, for his health began to trouble him. He was getting weary of life now that he could do so little, and the low-spirited mood into which he fell, clearly proved this.

Two years passed thus, with but one important incident—his last composition. In October, 1858, at the request of many friends, he set a song of Göthe's to music for an "Almanack of the Muses," and the long-silent piano in his room was once again unexpectedly heard throughout the house. This fragment was all it was needed for—the usual stillness returned, never to be again broken by Spohr.

With the Spring of 1859, Spohr journeyed to Meiningen, to direct a concert which was to be given on behalf of the "Widows' Relief Fund." Upon this occasion a colossal bust of Spohr was placed upon the stage, surrounded and overhung with branches of palm and laurel. The conductor's desk also had been tastefully decorated by fair hands with ingenious devices and garlands of flowers. The house, filled to overflowing, awaited in breathless suspense the appearance of the famed old master. "He comes!" was whispered through the spacious house, and a burst of welcome greeted the honoured man from the assembled thousands. This was the last time this mighty genius wielded the conductor's *bâton*.

He returned to Cassel, and passed his time in reading, or in visiting the theatres and concerts, for his love for hearing good music remained as strong as ever. About the middle of October a change was observed in him. The miserable and gloomy feelings which had troubled him for some time disappeared, and a calm and tranquil expression overspread his features. There were no more complaints of his sufferings and increasing weakness; but for a day or two he wandered slowly about, half lost, as it were, in a dream of a distant world.

On the evening of the 16th he went to bed, hoping that, being so tired, he would have a good night's rest. He awoke, with all his pains gone, and too weak either to get up or to eat anything; but he asked that his wife should sit on the bed beside him. She immediately complied with his request, when he took her hand and kissed it tenderly. Thus he remained for some days, with his life slowly ebbing away, surrounded by his family and those most dear to him, all anxious to look as long as they could into his loving face—till, on the evening of the 22nd October, 1859, the grand old musician passed away to the realms of never-ending harmony.

PRINCIPAL INCIDENTS IN THE LIFE OF SPOHR.

Born at Brunswick, 5th April	1784
First lessons from Dufour	1790
Director of Duke of Gotha's Orchestra	1805
Married Dorette Scheidler	1806
Director of the An der Wein Theatre	1812
"Faust" first produced	1816
"Zemire and Azor" first performed	1819
Visited London	1820
Director of Cassel Court Orchestra	1822
"The Last Judgment" first performed	1826
The "Alchymist" produced	1830
The "Power of Sound" symphony composed	1832
"Calvary" first performed	1835
Last Visit to London	1853
Died 22nd October	1859

Weber.

To some composers has fallen the lot of creating what is called a style or school; but of the subject of this present sketch this can hardly be said to be the case; notwithstanding that his music unmistakably possesses a character entirely its own, and which is not to be discerned in any previous master, while its influence is very perceptible in the work of some after composers. However, if Weber has not founded a school, he has left good traces of the profound musician he was, and has associated his name with the theatre as few other composers have. As a dramatic genius he has never been surpassed, and his operas are looked up to as models; while his treatment of his overtures, his love of, and success in the introduction of national melodies, and, indeed, his whole private and artistic life, stamp him as one of the greatest and most original musicians ever given to the world.

Carl Maria Friedrich Ernst Weber, the first child of a second marriage, came into the world on the 18th December, 1786, at Eutin, a town of Lower Saxony; and, at a time when his once rich and honourable father, was strolling about the Duchy of Holstein at the head of a *troupe* of wandering theatricals, well known as "Weber's Company of Comedians."

His father, Franz Anton von Weber, a musician of no small merit, had ever possessed the desire of giving a wonder-child to the world; and before his new-born boy could speak, his future course was decided,—the father had determined on developing in him an extraordinary musical genius. For this, his own line of life at the time afforded him every facility. The infant Carl —with his mother of but seventeen summers, obliged to follow in the train of comedians—was brought up amid the accessories of stage business. Scenery, canvas and paint-pots, carpentry and stage-lights, were the food upon which little Carl's imagination was fed. No wonder that he afterwards wrote for the stage with such facility and effect!

Nor, as a boy, did the scenes of his infancy change. Instead of the field and garden for a playground, he had the stage and its surroundings. "As child of a theatrical manager," says his biographer, "his playfellows were actors' children; his woods, his meadows, and gardens were daubed on canvas; a painted palace was his street; his boyhood's mimic fights were fought, not with sticks cut from the forest bush, but with silvered swords and cardboard shields, with which the actors, as heroes or robbers, fought out their mimic fights upon the stage at night. It was not on the hill-side, beneath the air of heaven, that little Carl Maria stormed the imaginary fortress with his playmates. The stage represented the castle, which was to be defended against the assailants from the orchestra; the side-scenes and traps were the vantage points or pitfalls of the battle. Orchestra and stage arrangements were familiar to him before the first lessons of his primer, half-understood theatrical intrigues his first glimpses of life."

Before the weak and sickly boy was six years old, a fiddle and a bow had been thrust into his hands by his impatient father. At first little Carl made too little progress to please, and received more raps on the knuckles than halfpence; for the father's wonder-child did not promise well. Teacher after teacher was tried; but, no sooner did master and pupil begin to understand each other, than the pupil was snatched away, to go whithersoever the comedy company thought they saw money. In time it was Michael Haydn that was the teacher; and, with him, the connection was not so transient. He was brother to the great symphonist, and himself a learned musician, who seldom gave lessons to any one; and Franz Anton knew the boy, and he, too, perhaps, would profit by the relation, so he would not sever it.

About this time, Carl Maria's astonishing genius began to unveil itself; and, before long, there came two compositions—of course for the stage—the comic operas "The Dumb Girl of the Forest" and "Peter Schmoll and his Neighbours." Neither of these made any very great hit, notwithstanding that of "Peter Schmoll" Michael Haydn wrote:—"I certify that this work has been composed in the truest rules of harmony, combined with much fire, delicacy, and appropriate feeling."

With the year 1803 came a change. The father had determined that Carl should go to Vienna, for there the flower of the musical and art world resided; and, amid its intoxicating life, the lad, now seventeen years of age, was left. He had grown gay and vivacious; and, with his amiable disposition and talent, soon became a great favourite in the highest musical circles. He could not long resist the allurements which his associates put before him, and soon made one of a band of gallant roysterers, to be met with wherever excitement ran the highest. "Wine, women, and song," was the strain with which the irresistible Carl and his gay companions plunged into the very vortex of the gay and licentious life and society which surrounded them. A year of this noisy life, and then Carl had to bid adieu to it, as well as to his reckless companions; but, the hardest parting of all was with a lady of title, whose acquaintance he had made, and who had grown desperately fond of our young musician.

During his brief stay in Vienna, Weber had studied under the Abbé Vogler, and it was at his recommendation that he was now leaving to undertake the conductorship of the Breslau Opera House. At his new post, the youth of eighteen summers met with but little success, for the older musicians did not care for the boy-conductor, whatever his qualities might be. A year's work amid opposition, jealousy, and the like, and then young Weber threw up the place in disgust. However, in spite of all this he found time while here to compose the greater part of his opera, "Rubezahl." It was in connection with this opera that the event occurred which was well-nigh debarring the world of the charming "Der Freischütz" and his other music.

In reaching from his piano to the table for a bottle of wine to refresh himself as he played the work over, poor young Weber unconsciously took up, and drank of, a bottle of powerful acid, which his father had carelessly left on the table. In fearful agony he fell from his stool. The first to enter the room was his friend Berner, when he stumbled over the apparent corpse of his beloved Weber. "Carl is poisoned!" he shouted through the house. Doctors were sent for, and, just as they were giving up all hopes, the poor fellow revived a little. It was some time before his burnt throat and mouth healed sufficiently to enable him to tell the tale, and to express his gratitude to his friend for his timely arrival.

The next few years of Carl's life saw many "ups and downs." From the Breslau Opera House he entered the service of Prince Eugène, of Würtemburg, and for nearly a year formed one of the brightest stars of his lustrous Court at Carlsruhe. Then came a cloud. War broke out, and the golden hours at the Silesian palace vanished.

His art at this time did not afford him so much as the means of subsistence, so altered had the social state of Germany become. In this plight, Carl appeared in quite a different character—that of private secretary to Prince Ludwig, of Würtemburg, whose palace was at Stuttgard. Here Carl learned little that was good, and much that was bad; nor was it long before he became more dissolute in his habits than he had been before. Still, all his spare time was not wasted, as it might easily have been. The darling art was not forgotten; for it was here in Stuttgard that he wrote his opera of "Sylvana," besides several smaller compositions. But all did not end well at Stuttgard. Carl Maria had been living high, and had run his finances into a serious state. So embarrassed, in fact, were his affairs, that before he left the place he found himself escorted by the police to the prison for debt, and there detained for some days. Mannheim, Darmstadt, and Baden, saw our talented artist after this. In these cities he gave concerts, producing many new effusions from his fruitful pen, and just pocketing enough to carry him on for a few weeks, when he could recruit his finances by the profits of another concert, or by the sale of a composition to Simrock, the music publisher.

1811 was an important year. The opera, "Abu Hassan," which he commenced while at Darmstadt, had been completed, and, by the advice of Vogler, his venerable master, young Weber was about dedicating it to the Grand Duke. Writing of this to a friend, Weber said: "I have dressed up the fellow in smart red binding, and sent him with the dedication to the Grand Duke. Who knows what he will say to it? Perhaps, if he is in good humour, '*Musje je tiens bocup de cè.*'" Had the Grand Duke heard this slur upon his imperfect French, he would hardly have accepted the dedication with such pleasure as he did, or have sent Carl the substantial evidence of this pleasure—a purse of forty golden carolins (£40).

On the 6th February the opera was performed, and the reception accorded to it, on this its first hearing, was most gratifying to Weber. The Grand Duke took a hundred and twenty tickets, and, altogether, Carl Maria netted something like two hundred florins clear profit by the performance.

After this, Weber set out on a long artistic tour. München, Prague, Berlin, Dresden, and other cities were visited, in all of which he gave concerts, which proved most advantageous from an artistic, as well as pecuniary, point of view. On all sides he was in request, for his wonderful talent, straightforward and charming manner, won all hearts. By the time his tour had extended to Prague, where his popularity had preceded him, he found princes and the highest families in the place ready to give him a hearty welcome.

One of the first visits Weber paid was to the invalid Liebich, director of the Prague Theatre, whom he found in his bedroom. Stretching out his hand and smiling, he said, "So you are *the* Weber! a capital fellow, I hear, and a very devil on the piano. Of course you want me to buy your operas. Very well; I hear they are good. One fills up an evening, the other doesn't.

I'll give you 1500 florins Viennese for the two. Is it a bargain?" "Yes," said young Weber, and the two musicians parted with the promise that Weber should return in the following spring to conduct his operas.

From Prague he moved on through Leipzig to Berlin, where he found his opera of "Sylvana" in anything but good favour. "Crazy stuff" was the music pronounced by the Berliners, whom, in turn, Weber described as being a "cold people, full of talk, but with no hearts; regular reviewer souls, carping at everything." The next we hear of "Sylvana" is in another strain. Weber soon proved to them that his music was not such "crazy stuff." On the 14th July, 1812, in a letter to his friend Gansbacher, Weber says: "It was given on the 10th, and is to be repeated to-day. I directed myself, and, besides the applause given to the music, after each act there were loud cries of 'Bravo, Weber!' It did indeed go off admirably, and the singers and the orchestra vied with each other. . . . . . . It secured for me the utmost possible triumph over all cabals," &c., &c.

True to his promise, the spring of 1813 found Weber again in Prague, where he met Liebich as friendly as ever, and a host of other admirers awaiting him. They had a pleasant surprise in store for him. The appointment of music director at the Prague Theatre had become vacant, and all were desirous that young Weber should have it. A salary of 2000 florins, a benefit concert guaranteed at 1000 florins more, and leave of absence for three months in each year, were the allurements held out to Weber, and which enticed him to accept the post, "Though," he wrote in his diary, "I find it very difficult to renounce my darling plans of travel; but in order to have the delight of paying all my debts, as an honourable fellow, what would I not do!"

Forthwith Weber threw all his energy into the reorganization of his orchestra, which he soon brought to a rare pitch of excellence, and for three years continued to work assiduously for the promotion of his beloved art. New operas were put upon the stage with the most astonishing rapidity, and with such success that the envy of his enemies—for he had these here—became more bitter than ever against him, and it was no doubt, in some measure, due to this, that, in spite of the earnest entreaties of his dearest friends, Weber, in 1816, sent in his resignation.

During this three years' engagement his pen had not been idle. He snatched away sufficient time to give to the world several new and charming compositions, among which were some of the heart-stirring "National songs," the great A flat and D minor sonatas, and the cantata "Kampf und Sieg" ("Struggle and Victory ")—a work which spread like wild-fire through Germany, and raised its gifted composer to the highest degree of popularity.

There is one event that happened during this period which must not be forgotten—Weber's engagement to Caroline Brandt. His eyes first lighted on her in 1810, as she stood singing in the orchestra of the Frankfort Theatre. Then he saw her again, as, on its first performance, she filled the title *rôle* of his opera of "Sylvana," and with such success that the composer himself was loudly called for; on which occasion she had to drag the half-frightened youth before the curtain to receive the applause. How little did Weber dream, that the hand which then clasped his, was that of his future wife!

Weber was not long without a new post. He had many kind and influential friends, who had watched his untiring zeal at the Prague Theatre; and one of these, Count Vitzthum, was doing everything he could to secure Weber for Dresden. At last, on Christmas morning, 1816, the good news came. Weber was " Kapellmeister to his Majesty the King of Saxony." "Long," he wrote to his intended, "did I look on Count Vitzthum's letter, without daring to open it. Was it joy, was it sorrow? At length I took courage. It was joy! So round I went to all my friends, who laughed, and made the new Royal Kapellmeister the most reverential bows. I must fig myself out now in true Court style. Perhaps I ought to wear a pigtail to please the Dresdeners! What do you think? I ought to have an extra kiss from you for this good news."

This was the sunny side of things. A visit to Dresden soon after, and a look round at what was going on, put another and somewhat more clouded picture before Weber. He found a rival faction in strong opposition against him and his new German opera scheme, and, moreover, they were well represented, and stood in high favour at the Court. Nothing but Italian opera had ever been thought of at Dresden, and the brilliant and talented Italian artists stood aghast at the new-comer and his sweeping innovations. Still, Weber was buoyed up by the newly awakened spirit of national feeling in favour of German opera, and with this was determined to overcome every difficulty. And so he did. "The Italians," he wrote to a friend, have "naturally worked heaven, earth, and hell to swallow up the whole German opera. But they have found a precious hard morsel to digest in me. I am not so easy to be swallowed."

Mehul's "Joseph and his Brethren" was the first work taken in hand by the new establishment; and, although during the rehearsals some of the orchestra and chorus had often gone home sulky and growling at the sharp and precise manner in which the new conductor went through the business, yet, by the time for its performance, these were all on his side, feeling a love and pleasure in their playing, and performing their parts in the most artistic manner, in place of the careless fashion to which they had been so long accustomed.

On the 30th January, 1817, "Joseph" was publicly performed, and on this occasion the king honoured the performance with his presence. It went off remarkably well, far exceeding the most sanguine expectations. Moreover, the king was pleased too. He had a knack of coughing when anything was not to his liking, yet never once during the evening had this ominous sign been heard by any one. But there was one little scrimmage. Genast, the tenor, had taken upon himself to introduce a bravura passage in the Italian style, which Weber did not fail to take account of. The tenor saw this, and, after the performance, attempted a hasty retreat home. But Weber was too quick for him. "What's that you were doing?" he thundered out. "Don't you think that, if Mehul had wanted any such crinkum-crankum, he would have put it in better than you? No more such tomfoolery for the future! Good-night. Go home, and sleep off your fit of Italian intoxication."

So things went on. Amid all the opposition from the

rival opera company, Weber's venture continued to establish itself, and to gain favour, till, ultimately, it became a State establishment, and Weber was appointed musical director for life. This enabled him to fulfil his long-cherished desire of marrying Caroline Brandt, and on the 4th November the wedding took place. An entry in his diary shows what an earnest man the great musician had become:—"May God bless our union, and grant me strength and power to make my beloved Lina as happy and contented as my inmost heart would desire! May His mercy lead me in all my doings!"

Further on is another, made at midnight on the last day of this, to him, important year. "The great important year has closed. May God still grant me the blessing, which He has hitherto so graciously accorded to me, that I may have the power to make the dear one happy, and, as a brave artist, bring honour and advantage to my fatherland! Amen!"

We now arrive at the most brilliant period of Weber's life, for it is that when his marvellous creative powers were at their highest: that period when he penned the sublime music which travelled almost with lightning speed over Europe, and made the name of Weber a "household word." His happy marriage had put new life into him; and, after a short trip, he returned home to the "comfortable sweet nest" which he had provided for his "little birdie." Now, with his fondest hopes realized, the great man poured forth some of those choice fancies with which his fruitful brain was teeming. First, there was the great E flat mass, a work of striking beauty and originality, full of religious feeling. This masterly composition was followed by the incidental music for one or two small dramas, when the master jotted down some of the best known of his exciting national songs. The notes of these latter had barely time to dry, before the fertile pen was again at work, this time upon a festal cantata, "Nature and Love," to celebrate the Queen of Saxony's name-day.

Still the rich melodies continued to flow, and the "Jubilee" cantata was given to the world. It was written to celebrate the fiftieth year of the reign of Augustus III., of Saxony; but the Italian faction prevented its performance, and only the overture was given. However, subsequently the whole work obtained a hearing, and made a "great sensation." The overture to this cantata is universally known and admired. It opens with an *adagio* of the most striking character, which, having developed, leads by an effective scale passage for the basses, to the *presto assai*, its chief movement. Some exquisite themes for the violin, carefully worked out with a master hand, carry the listener on to the brilliant *coda*. All has been happiness and joy, and in this movement this feeling reaches its highest pitch. An ever-exciting ascent of the violins through another scale of three octaves, and then bursts out in *fortissimo* the inspiring strains of the national anthem—"God save the King."

In the opinion of some this overture is an entirely distinct work from the "Jubilee" cantata, being written in the key of E, while the cantata begins in the key of E flat, and, moreover, from its bearing a later opus-number. Whether this opinion be right or wrong, will probably ever remain a mystery, but it must not be forgotten, that, while in support of the above notion there is the further evidence that it was not Weber's usual custom to write his overtures *after* the completion of whatever works they were intended for, yet, on the other hand, it is difficult to conceive that his son and biographer would not have been acquainted with the fact, had they been distinct works.

The pen was not laid down yet. A Jubilee mass, the noted E flat rondo, some pieces for four hands for the piano-forte, and his charming, world-famed "Invitation to the Waltz," followed in quick succession.

Many must be struck with Weber's great activity at this period, but what will be their surprise at learning that very shortly after these works, another, and that the great "Der Freischütz," was completed. Slowly, but surely, had this work drawn towards completion during the last two or three years of this great creative period; and little did the world at large know that the same hand that was penning so many beautiful compositions was also at work upon one, compared with which they seem to be but mere diversionary studies.

On the 8th of May, 1820, the score of "Der Freischütz" was despatched to the director of the Berlin Theatre, of which more presently, for before "Der Freischütz" had received many rehearsals, Weber, the great and indefatigable worker, had set to, and finished the important opera of "Preciosa;" and on the 20th July of the same year the score of this work followed in the same track as did that of "Der Freischütz." Unfortunately the new opera-house in which these works were first to be performed, was still uncompleted, and Weber saw this year out before either of his operas was upon the stage.

"Preciosa" appeared before "Der Freischütz," and well it might; for the Berlin public needed to be prepared for the "Freischütz" music. "Preciosa" just did this, as it contained many of the innovations and daring effects which Weber had introduced into the larger work.

In spite of all that was new, the opera was very successful, and found great favour with the Berliners, notwithstanding the slight notice the newspaper critics took of the music. Perhaps it was too much for them.

"Preciosa" is founded upon Cervantes' pretty tale, "The Gypsy of Madrid," to which Weber has wedded some of the most charmingly characteristic music he ever penned. The true Spanish colouring which pervades the whole of it, is as faithful as it is masterly: with what fine effect, too, has not the gifted composer introduced the Spanish melodies and dances! This opera is now rarely, if ever, heard, but its overture is often played. The "Gypsy Chorus" also is universally known, and this is a sample of what the rest of the music is.

It may as well be related here, that the overture to "Preciosa," and all his subsequent ones, contain the leading melodies and ideas of the operas themselves— a by no means uninteresting fact to know—as being completed before the text had been graced with a single note, these overtures clearly prove with what marvellous skill Weber worked; and how the whole opera, acts, songs, and choruses, reached maturity in the composer's mind, before they ever came to the mechanical work of being written down.

No wonder that the glorious score of "Der Freischütz," which Weber's widow presented to the Royal Library at Berlin, is without a single alteration or erasure, when all had been corrected in his mighty mind! No wonder that when, in 1824, the management of Covent Garden Theatre offered him three months to write an opera for them, he exclaimed, "Three months! that will no more than allow me to read the piece, and decide the plan in my head!"

At last the long-looked-for day came—the day of the first performance of "Der Freischütz"—June 18, 1821. For hours before the time of opening, the doors of the new theatre were besieged by anxious crowds; and, when they were at length opened, there was a fearful rush to get in. In a few minutes pit, boxes, and galleries were filled to overflowing: the excitement was intense; and when Weber entered the orchestra there came from the thousands of people a burst of deafening applause which seemed to have no ending. Three times was he obliged to let fall his *bâton*, and to bow, before he could give the signal to begin. The overture was commenced, and the last notes had barely been played, before the whole theatre rose *en masse*, and broke out with such a tumultuous *encore*, that Weber was compelled to accede to the request.

So the opera proceeded: the excitement and applause increasing as each beauty of the work unveiled itself. The handsome Frau Seidler as "Agathe," made a marvellous impression in the great scena, "Wie nahte mir der Schlummer," while the wonderful scene of the Wolf's Glen completely carried away the audience; and this excitement continued till the curtain at length fell. What then ? Not a soul left the house! Thunders of applause burst from the delighted audience. Weber. was loudly called for; and when he came on, leading "Agathe" and "Aennchen" by the hand, flowers and verses were showered upon the stage from all directions. The success of " Der Freischütz " had been enormous!

"Der Freischütz" soon laid hold of the people, and there was not a melody but was soon heard in every street. Further representations were demanded, which filled the treasury of the theatre in the most satisfactory manner; and, not only at this, but at every other house—in Germany. So popular did it become, that there was not a stage upon which it was not played. Its fame soon spread over Europe, and before long it was on the French and English boards. In London the very atmosphere vibrated with its music. Street boys evinced a strong predilection for it. The melodies were whistled and hummed by every one; and, indeed, so familiar did it become, that, in advertising for a servant, a gentleman is said to have found it necessary to stipulate that he should *not* be able to whistle the airs from " Der Freischütz."

On the Parisian boards, however, it was hissed on its

first hearing at the Odéon; though, when it was put on again some time after, under the title of "Robin des Bois," it saw something like three hundred and fifty representations, before it was withdrawn.

Two years or so after the production of "Der Freischütz," "Euryanthe" made its appearance. When Weber undertook this work his intention was to produce the very best opera he possibly could—a work which should silence the critics who spoke so disparagingly of his "Der Freischütz," and declared that it owed its success to "devilry and fireworks." By some inexplicable means, Weber managed to obtain the libretto of this opera from a crazy old dame, Helmine von Chezy by name, who, on the first night of the performance of the work, did not hesitate to squeeze her great fat self into the benches of the pit, shrieking out in the most lusty manner, "Make room! make room! I'm the poetess! the poetess! I tell you I'm the poetess! make room!" Unfortunately for Weber, the text which this old lady supplied had about as much interest as a libretto, as she had as a woman, and to the very day of its performance caused Weber endless trouble. However, he did the best he could with it, and reared a work which he always regarded as his favourite one. "I rely on God and my 'Euryanthe,'" were the words he wrote to his beloved wife two hours before its first performance.

It was at the Kärnthnertor theatre in Vienna, on the 25th October, 1823, that this opera was first produced; and on this occasion, Weber, though suffering intensely from his chest disease, made the long journey to the great capital, that he might himself introduce the favoured "Euryanthe" to the public. What a reception it met with, is best conceived from a letter to his "dearest and best"—his wife. "Thank God, as I do, beloved wife, for the glorious success of 'Euryanthe.' Weary as I am, I must still say a sweet 'good-night' to my beloved Lina, and cry 'Victoria!' .... All the company seemed in a state of ecstasy: singers, chorus, orchestra—all were drunk, as it were, with joy."

On this occasion the title *rôle* was filled by Mdlle. Sontag, then a girl in her teens, but who had already manifested that promise of the great artist and *prima donna*, which, in a few years after, was so fully confirmed. Strangely enough, after the eighth representation or so of "Euryanthe," it failed to attract anything like a house—a fate which Weber could only account for by the utter disregard which he had paid to the spirit of the age in this opera; though the wretched libretto must have had something to do with this failure. Moreover, some strange criticisms on "Euryanthe" were going the round of Vienna, one of which was that the opera was "a collection of diminished sevenths," and this from no less an authority than the great Beethoven.

Weber took an early opportunity to lay the score of the work before the great lion of the musical world, if possible to dissuade him from this judgment; but he was not to be gainsaid. "You should have come to me," said Beethoven, "before the representation, not afterwards. .... Nevertheless, I advise you to treat 'Euryanthe' as I did 'Fidelio'—that is to say, cut out a third." Weber took Beethoven's advice, and really did apply his pruning-knife to the music, for he himself saw the necessity of it, and used to say, on account of the length of the work, "My 'Euryanthe' should be called *Ennuyante*,—a piece of facetiousness, by the by, which is often erroneously attributed to others.

The excitement and strain upon his already feeble health, consequent upon the production of "Euryanthe," left Weber in a very exhausted state, so that he returned to Dresden suffering dreadfully from his inward malady, and, alas! with cruel traces of the mastery it was fast gaining over him. Here there was no rest, for his official duties pressed unusually hard upon the weak and sickened man about this time; and there was no one to whom he could look for assistance. Gamely the brave artist struggled on, to the detriment of his health and powers, till, at last, the pen of this "ready writer" was laid down, apparently never again to be taken up to note fancies such as those which once filled his soul.

"I have not the slightest yearning for piano or music-paper," he wrote to his beloved wife. "I never could have believed that I should ever feel this disgust for work. But, oh! if it should always continue so, shall I ever again find a single thought within me? Now there is nothing—nothing." Nor was this state of apathy and ill-health all that the great musician suffered from. A presentiment that death was not far off had overtaken him, and he was haunted incessantly with fears for the future of his beloved wife and little ones, till at last his chief thought was that of providing for them against the time when he would not be there to look up to.

No doubt, then, it was this feeling which spurred Weber on, once again to take up his pen, and to shake off the antipathy for work which had taken possession of him. At this period he had no need to seek for patronage, for the "Freischütz" and "Euryanthe" had travelled round Europe, and tempting offers came in from all directions. The only one of these that can be dealt with, is that which came from Charles Kemble, the lessee of Covent Garden Theatre, in the summer of 1824—leading as it did to the last great work which emanated from

Weber's prolific pen; and, moreover, to his only visit to the English capital.

Kemble's proposition was accepted, and the two illustrious men were soon in communication with each other as to the libretto. At last this was settled. "Oberon," founded by Mr. Planché upon the old romance of "Huon de Bordeaux," was to be the subject of the new opera. Weber at once set to work, and, barring the overture, completed the work in time to bring the score with him to London in 1826.

It was at dawn, on the 7th of February, that Weber and his friend Furstenau—the celebrated flute-player—set out on this eventful journey, from which one of the twain was never to return alive. A sorrowful parting from Weber's dear home was this. "The time was come," says his son and biographer, "for the separation of the husband, who scarcely hoped to see his home again, from the loving wife, who felt that he was a dying man. Another tear upon the forehead of his sleeping children—another long, lingering kiss—the suffering man dragged his swollen feet into his carriage, huddled feverishly in his furs—the door was closed—and he rolled away from home, on that cold winter's morning, sobbing till the shattered chest might burst at once. Caroline rushed back to her room, and sank on her knees, with the cry, 'It is his coffin I heard closed upon him!'"

'After a pleasant journey, and a short stay in Paris, Weber arrived in London at the beginning of March; and, at the earnest request of Sir George Smart, took up his residence at his house, in Great Portland Street. A letter to his wife upon his arrival gives his own account of it. "Here, in Smart's house, I am excellently well taken care of. Every possible comfort is provided—a bath-room in the house. We dined at six, and by ten o'clock I was in my bed, where I slept charmingly till seven. . . . . One of the first piano-forte makers has provided me with an admirable instrument, which, in a charming note, he begs me to make him happy by using during my stay. . . . . I am allowed to be alone the whole day until five; then we dine and go to the theatre, or into society. . . . . People are all so good to me with their anxious care. No king can be served with greater love or affection in all things than I am. I am as much cosseted and caressed as a baby in arms. . . . . I cannot be sufficiently grateful to Heaven for the blessings which surround me."

Here it was then, that Weber composed the well-known overture attached to the opera of "Oberon," and which was only completed three or four days prior to the night of the first performance of the work. Like his other overtures, this one is a sort of epitome of the opera itself, and contains many of its leading themes.

The notes of the charmed horn open it, and these soon attract the fairies, who assemble with their lovely music —such as Weber alone knew how to write. A glimpse of a march is then heard, to which Sir Huon returns with his valued bride. The fairy music continues till a *fortissimo* chord breaks the charm, and the quartet "Over the dark blue waters" follows, furnishing the scene of the knight and squire urging their lovers to sail with them. Then comes another well-known air, "From boyhood trained," given out by the clarionet, and followed by a passage from Rezia's great scena, "Ocean, thou mighty monster;" after which is worked out an episode from the chorus of spirits who are commissioned by Puck to use their powers, and raise the storm which shall wreck the fugitive lovers' bark. With the joy and laughter of the spirits, this last inspiration from Weber's soul ends; and truly too may we call it the divine song of the dying swan, for it was the last music poor Weber ever wrote.

On April 12th Covent Garden Theatre was packed to the ceiling by an audience anxious to hear "Oberon." Weber's appearance in the orchestra was the signal for a burst of hurrahs, clapping of hands, and a hammering of feet and sticks, which lasted well-nigh a quarter of an hour. Then the great work was commenced, and was gone through amid the noisiest signs of approbation that could be conceived. At the end the whole house rose and demanded to see Weber before the curtain, when he met with a greeting such as few other composers have ever received.

Of course, he poured all this out before his beloved wife. "My dear Lina," he says, "thanks to God, and to His all-powerful will, I obtained this evening the greatest success in my life. The emotion produced in my breast by such a triumph is more than I can describe. To God alone belongs the glory. When I entered the orchestra, the house, crammed to the roof, burst into a frenzy of applause. Hats and handkerchiefs were waved in the air. .... All went excellently, and every one round me was happy." On this, its first performance, the chief characters were sustained by Miss Paton, Madame Vestris, and Braham.

Now comes the worst part of all. The morning after this successful *debût* of "Oberon," found the great musician, in an exhausted state, lying in his easy-chair. "The machinery is shattered," he murmured, as Furstenau entered the room; "but ah! would but God, in His mercy, grant that it might hold together till I could embrace my Lina and boys once more." Though ill-health was weighing him down, yet Weber would not break his promise with Kemble, but conducted each of the first twelve representations of "Oberon."

He was then busy about his concert, which he hoped and prayed would bring him in a good store to take back to his wife and little ones. Alas! the 26th May came—a pouring wet night—and the concert-room was almost empty. What a blow this was to him, in his then tottering state! After the concert he had to be led from the room, when, almost breathless and in despair, he fell upon a sofa. All the musicians gathered round; but they could hear nothing, save his faint voice murmuring out, "What do you say to that? That is Weber in London!"

He was driven home to Sir George Smart's house, and for a time was a little better, when his friends prevailed upon him to give up his benefit concert at Covent Garden, and return home. This Weber agreed to; and on 30th May he wrote to his wife, saying:—"You will not have many more letters from me. Answer this, not to London, but to Frankfort. I see your astonishment. I will not go to Paris. What could I do there? I can neither talk nor walk. What can I do better than go straight home?" Alas! the next day he was worse, and physicians were called in. They ordered a postponement of the journey home; but the dying musician sobbed incessantly, "I must go back to my own,—I must. Let me see them once more, and then God's will be done." The following day his trembling hand traced a few words to his wife,—the last letter he ever wrote. It concluded with "God bless you all, and keep you well! Oh! were I but amongst you all again! I kiss you with all my heart and soul, my dearest one! Preserve all your love; and think with pleasure on him who loves thee above all, thy KARL."

On the evening of the 4th, Weber was worse; and, as he sat panting in his easy-chair, with Sir George Smart, Moscheles, and two other friends around him, his cough became so bad that they urged him to retire to bed, when he left them with the tender words, "God reward you all for your kind love to me." Furstenau led him to his room, and helped him to undress. For this customary service Weber thanked him, and murmured. "Now let me sleep,"—the last words that mortal ear heard escape from the great artist's lips.

"The next morning," writes Weber's son, "at the early hour when Weber generally required his aid, Sir George Smart's servant knocked at his chamber-door. No answer came; he knocked again, and louder. It was strange; for Weber's sleep had always been light. The alarmed servant rushed to Sir George, who sprang out of bed, and hurried to the room. Still to his repeated knocking no answer was returned. . . . . It was now resolved to force the door. It was burst open. All was still within. The watch—which the last movement of the great hand which had written 'Freischütz,' 'Euryanthe,' and 'Oberon,' had wound up—alone ticked with painful distinctiveness. The bed-curtains were torn back. There lay the beloved friend and master,—dead. His head rested on his left hand, as if in tranquil sleep,—not the slightest trace of pain or suffering on his noble features. The soul, yearning for the dear objects of its love, had burst its earthly covering and fled. The immortal master was not dead : he had gone home."

The cause of death was an ulcer on the windpipe and tubercles on the lungs. Arrangements were at once made for his funeral; and on the morning of the 12th June the long procession made its way to Moorfields Chapel, where, to the solemn strains of the Dead March in " Saul," the body was lowered to its last resting-place. No, not its last! Weber's long-cherished desire had been to return to his wife and little ones. They could not have this, but they longed to have his precious ashes near them; and, after eighteen long years of waiting, the coffin was brought to Dresden. Weber was at last at home !

A funeral service was performed over the remains;

and when the vast concourse had left, when all was quiet, by the dim light of two tapers yet burning in the chapel, there were seen two forms still lingering about the bier,—the beloved wife and the eldest son.

On the following day the father was laid in his grave, side by side with his youngest son, who had died but a fortnight before, and whose face the great musician had last seen as he stood by his cot on the eventful morning that he left his home eighteen years before, and, with tears in his eyes, pressed a kiss on the forehead of his then helpless, sleeping baby-boy.

PRINCIPAL INCIDENTS IN THE LIFE OF WEBER.

Born at Eutin, 18th December	1786
First opera produced	1801
Went to Vienna	1803
Conductor of Breslau Opera	1804
"Abu Hassan" first performed	1811
Music Director to the Prague Theatre	1813
Kapellmeister to King of Saxony	1816
"Preciosa" first performed	1821
"Der Freischütz" first performed	1821
"Euryanthe" first performed	1823
"Oberon" first performed	1826
Died June 5th	1826

Rossini.

OF all sunny Italy's composers, not one can claim so prominent a place as the subject of this sketch is entitled to amongst the great tone-poets; and it may be safely asserted that no composer, either of Italy or any other country, ever enjoyed in his life-time such a degree of popularity as did Rossini. At one time his music solely occupied nearly all the operatic stages of Europe, and none other would be listened to. Less learned and elaborately constructed, with fewer pretensions to all that is grand, majestic, or severe, with nothing that is dry or difficult to understand, nothing suggestive of vast study, his music differs widely from either that of Beethoven, Mozart, Haydn, or Bach. Here then, must lie the secret of Rossini's popularity. His music appeals to the million, not alone to the educated class, and his great purpose seems to be to please, and not to try his listeners with learned modulations, or masterly illustrations of his learning.

Rossini.

It is perfectly natural, and in keeping with Rossini's character. Full of melody, sweet and beautiful, it never fails in its purpose of captivating. No one, probably, could listen to the "Stabat Mater" without becoming an admirer of Rossini, or without experiencing a feeling of enjoyment, as page after page of its music glides on, gratifying the listener with its suavity, and leaving the mind impressed with the sense of the pleasure which such agreeable music has aroused. Oulibicheff once declared, that when listening for the first time to one of Rossini's operas, he forgot, for the time being, all that he had ever known, admired, played, or sung—it seemed as though he had never heard music before.

It was on the 29th February, 1792, that Gioachino Rossini first saw the light, at the small town of Pezaro, in the Romagna, where his father, Giuseppe Rossini, filled the office of herald, or town-crier. But this was not all he did for a living. He could play the horn; and, in Signora Rossini, the old man had married a singer of some pretensions, so the two were to be frequently met with at fairs and other musical gatherings —she sustaining small parts on the stage, while her nobler half played the horn in the orchestra. No doubt their little son was also to be brought up as a musician, and for this end the zealous parents soon commenced to train him. At seven years of age he made his *début* at

Bologna. Paer's "Camilla" was produced there in 1799, and the subject of our sketch was chosen to fill the part of the child. "Nothing," said Madame Giorgi-Righetti, "could be imagined more tender, more touching, than the voice and action of this extraordinary child in the beautiful canon of the third act, 'Senti in si fiero istantè.'" Beyond this incident little more is known of Rossini's early life, save that while a boy he joined his parents in their musical excursions, when he generally played second horn in the orchestra.

About this time young Rossini came under the notice of Tesei, of Bologna, who gave him lessons in piano-forte playing, and singing, and, moreover, put him in the way of earning money by singing solos at churches. It was this latter which led to the Countess Perticari's patronage. She had heard young Rossini sing, and loved his voice, so she sent him to the Lyceum at Bologna, there to study counterpoint and fugue at the feet of the strict Padre Mattei. Rossini was no sluggish or dull student. A year's study, and he was chosen, at the early age of sixteen, to write the cantata which was annually expected from the best pupil at the Lyceum. The result was "Pianto d'Armonia per la Morte d'Orfeò," which, on its production at Bologna, met with the greatest success. Passing over various juvenile efforts which followed it—such as "La Cambiale di Matrimonio," written for the Sinigaglia Theatre for eight pounds; "L'Equivoco Stravagante," an opera buffa in two acts; "L'Inganno Felice;" "Ciro in Babilonia," for the Teatro Communale of Ferrara, in which was the air for the second *donna*, who, Rossini said, had but one good note in her voice, which he accordingly made her repeat, and none other, while the melody of her solo was played by the orchestra; "La Pietra del Paragone," which so pleased one of Napoleon's generals, that in consideration of it, he exempted Rossini from the conscription; "La Scala di Seta;" and, lastly, "L'Occasione fa il Ladro"—we come upon the first opera which made Rossini's name celebrated throughout Europe, that is "Tancredi."

"Tancredi" was written for the Fenice Theatre in 1813, and it at once laid hold of the Venetians. Its airs were sung everywhere, the gondoliers shaped them into serenades, and they even crept into the law courts, so that the judges had more than once to forbid their being hummed. It is to this opera that belongs the exquisite cavatina, "Di tanti palpiti," far better known than is the little anecdote which gave to it the title of "Aria del rizi." The day before the opera was to be given, Madame Malanotte took it into her head to dislike her opening air, the consequence of which little whim was, that Rossini had either to write another, or

17—2

put aside the work. Sorely perplexed, he returned home from the rehearsal, wondering how he could meet the caprices of his *prima donna;* and it is said that while the servant was preparing some rice which he had ordered, Rossini noted down this beautiful air within the few minutes required for the frying and serving of the rice; and thus appeased the dissatisfied Malanotte.

"L'Italiana in Algeria," written for the San Benedetto Theatre at Naples, also came to light this year, and is important as being the first essay in that style, which reached perfection in "Cenerentola" and "Il Barbiere." It never met with any very great success, but it has brought Rossini the reputation of being a delightfully lazy individual, for, as was his wont, he frequently wrote his music in bed, and it was when he was upon this opera that a part of the score fell from his bed, and rather than take the trouble to get out for it, he wrote the piece over again, and had just completed it as a friend was announced, to whom Rossini related the affair, and requested that he would fish out the previous piece from somewhere under the bed, and see which of the two he preferred. Both thought the original piece was the best, and accordingly that was adopted.

This opera was followed by " L'Aureliano in Palmira," which only saw one representation before it was withdrawn; but this was Rossini's own doing, to get rid of Velluti's company.

The fact is, in "Aureliano" there was a cavatina which the celebrated Velluti had to sing. "At the first rehearsal with full orchestra," says Stendhall, "Rossini heard Velluti sing it, and was struck with admiration. At the second rehearsal Velluti began to embroider. Rossini found some of his effects admirable, and still approved; but at the third rehearsal, the richness of the embroidery was such that it quite concealed the body of the air. At last the grand day of the first representation arrived. The cavatina and all Velluti's part were enthusiastically applauded, but Rossini could scarcely recognize what Velluti was singing; he did not know his own music." After this Rossini had no more to do with him, and told him to take his "embroidery" elsewhere, which he did, and could afford to do, if the following anecdote from Eber's "Seven Years of the King's Theatre" be true. At Milan, Velluti was the idol of the people; he was received *con furore*, and his fame spread on every side. A Milanese gentleman, who had a rich uncle, who was ill, met his friend in the street. "Where are you going?" "To the Scala to be sure." "How! your uncle is at the point of death." "Yes; but Velluti sings to-night!"

In the year of the production of "Aureliano" its composer was visited by the famous *impresario* Barbaja, which ended in Rossini's packing up his goods, and making a journey to Naples, where he shortly afterwards made his *début* at the San Carlo, having signed a contract with Barbaja for several years, to conduct at his theatres, to write two new operas annually, and to rearrange the music of any old works to be produced; in return for which he was to receive two hundred ducats a month, and a share in the profits of the bank in the San Carlo gambling saloon.

"Elizabetta Regina d'Inglitera" was the first opera composed here, and when it was produced, found very great favour with the warm Neapolitans; but, notwithstanding this and its beautiful music, it never travelled much farther than Naples. In connexion with this opera there is a very interesting story told, which may not be out of place here. Rossini was fond of saying that the form of his person was the best in the world; and there are not a few anecdotes current of his influence among the ladies of his time. Here is one. On the eve of the production of "Elizabetta," Rossini was sitting in his chamber at Naples, singing one of its airs, when a note was brought him by apparently the ugliest Mercury who ever carried one, and who instantly withdrew. The note contained an invitation of the most tender nature, and the place of assignation was a romantic spot a little way from the city. He went, gave the required signal, and immediately heard sung his aria. When it was concluded, a lady, beautiful as day, made her appearance from a grove surrounding a small villa, to which she introduced him. They were mutually pleased with each other's discourse, and, on parting. it was agreed that the next time of meeting should be signified by the Mercury as before. Rossini, full of surprise at having heard his aria sung, came, after much pondering, to the conclusion that the ugly messenger must be the lady herself in disguise; and when the envoy next came, his observations confirmed his suspicions. When the messenger retired, Rossini followed, and, unobserved as he thought, traced her to a dwelling at a little distance from the city, well known as the residence of a Sicilian and his beautiful wife. Satisfied with his discovery, Rossini returned. Soon afterwards, on a renewed appointment, he went again, but had hardly arrived on the spot, when the report of a carbine, and a ball whistling past his ear, gave him notice to retreat, a suggestion which he obeyed too rapidly to observe whether or not he was pursued.

Who also has not heard of Rossini's speech to the beauty standing between him and the Duke of Wellington—" Madame, how happy should you be to find yourself placed between the two greatest men in Europe."

Shortly after this Rossini went to Rome, where he was engaged to write two works for the Carnival of 1816, and thus were created "Torvaldo e Dorliska" and "Il Barbiere di Siviglia." Of "Torvaldo" nothing shall be said beyond that it was not successful; but the immortal "Barber of Seville," his happiest effort, deserves much more attention.

Years before Rossini thought of the "Barber of Seville" Beaumarchais' subject had been set to music by Paisiello; and, moreover, had become celebrated throughout Italy, so that there was no small stir when it became known that the young Rossini had applied to Paisiello for permission to re-set the subject. Of course he was accused of presumption and the like, but it must not be forgotten that Rossini had no choice in the matter, he having agreed to compose music to whatever text was supplied him. That this particular one was chosen might at the time have appeared inopportune; but what shall be said now? Where is Paisiello's "Barber of Seville;" and how many know it? Paisiello having granted the required permission, Sterbini set about writing a new libretto, and in justice to Rossini, let it be stated that it was as totally different from Paisiello's libretto as it was possible to make it. It took Rossini but thirteen days to compose this masterpiece, during which time he never left Luigi Zamboni's (the original

Figaro) house; but as Sterbini handed him over the wet pages of the libretto, so they were wedded to the joyous music which abounds in this opera, and then passed on to the copyists to work from. "Not even did I get shaved," he said to a friend. "It seems strange," was the reply, "that through the 'Barber' you should have gone without shaving." "If I had shaved," explained Rossini, "I should have gone out, and if I had gone out I should not have come back in time." If this be true the world must certainly feel indebted to the *maestro* for this instance of self-denial.

The night of the first representation at length arrived, and the Argentina theatre was crammed with friends and foes, the latter not hesitating to declare openly what they hoped and intended should be the fate of Rossini's "Barber." In his "History of the Opera" Sutherland Edwards gives an account of this first performance, and says the composer was weak enough to allow Garcia to sing beneath Rosina's balcony a Spanish melody of his own arrangement. Garcia maintained that as the scene was in Spain, the Spanish melody would give the drama an appropriate local colour; but unfortunately the artist who reasoned so well, and who was such an excellent singer, forgot to tune his guitar before appearing on the stage as "Almaviva." He began the operation in the presence of the public. A string broke. The vocalist proceeded to replace it, but before he could do so, laughter and hisses were heard from all parts of the house. The Spanish air, when Garcia was at last ready to sing it, did not please the Italian audience, and the pit listened to it just enough to be able to give an ironical imitation of it afterwards. The introduction of Figaro's air seemed to be liked; but when Zamboni entered also, with a guitar in his hand, a loud laugh was set up, and not a phrase of *Largo al factotum* was heard. When Rosina made her appearance in the balcony, the public were quite prepared to applaud Madame Giorgi-Righetti in an air which they thought they had a right to expect from her; but only hearing her utter a phrase which led to nothing, the expressions of disapprobation recommenced. The duet between "Almaviva" and "Figaro" was accompanied throughout with hissing and shouting. The fate of the work seemed now decided. At length Rosina came on, and sang the cavatina which had so long been looked for. Madame Giorgi-Righetti was young, had a fresh beautiful voice, and was a great favourite with the Roman public. Three long rounds of applause followed the conclusion of her air, and gave some hope that the opera might yet be saved. Rossini, who was at the orchestral piano, then turned towards the singer, and whispered "*oh natura!*" This happy moment did not last, and the hisses recommenced with the duet between Figaro and Rosina. The noise increased, and it was impossible to hear a note of the finale. When the curtain fell, Rossini turned towards the public, shrugged his shoulders, and clapped his hands. The audience were deeply offended by this openly-expressed contempt for their opinion, but they made no reply at the time : the vengeance was reserved for the second act, of which not a note passed the orchestra. The hubbub was so great that nothing like it was ever heard at any theatre. Rossini in the meanwhile remained perfectly calm, and afterwards went home as composed as if the work, received in so insulting a manner, had been the production of some other musician. After changing their clothes, Madame Giorgi-Righetti, Garcia, Zamboni, and Botticelli, went to his house to console him in his misfortune. They found him fast asleep. But there were other troubles. Don Basilio, on entering, stumbled over a trap, which had been left open, bruising his face terribly, and appearing on the stage with his handkerchief up to his nose. The letter duet miscarried in some way ; and, to crown all, a cat appeared on the stage while the grand finale was going on, and in the attempts to drive it off, got so bewildered as to excite the laughter of the *artistes* themselves.

Such was the reception accorded to Rossini's happiest

work on its first hearing. A week afterwards it was applauded up to the skies, and was speedily played on every operatic stage in Europe. All the remuneration Rossini received for composing the "Barber" was about eighty pounds, besides his thirteen days' board and lodging in Zamboni's house, less, probably, than some pettifogging arrangers of the present day would receive, for adding a few pages of musical gymnastics to one or two of its most popular airs.

This same year (1816) saw the production of another grand opera, "Otello," first brought out at the Teatro del Fonda, at Naples; and, apart from its capital music, celebrated for Rossini's reforms in opera seria which it marks. Its orchestration shows what strides the "innovations," as they were termed, and which first showed themselves in "Tancredi," were making. Sigismondi, of the Naples Conservatory, is said to have been horror-struck on first seeing the score of "Otello." The clarionets were too much for him; but, on seeing third and fourth horn parts, he exclaimed, "What does the man want? The greatest of our composers have always been content with two. Shades of Pergolesi, of Leo, of Jomelli! How they must shudder at the bare mention of such a thing! Four horns! Are we at a hunting party? Four horns! Enough to blow us to perdition!" Moreover, in "Otello" there were other reforms, among which was the banishment of the piano-forte as an orchestral instrument, the accompaniments being played instead by the orchestra, and the increased importance given to the chorus.

On its first hearing, Mdlle. Colbran, afterwards Madame Rossini, sang the principal female part, while the celebrated tenor, Davide, created the part of "Otello," and played it for many years afterwards. From all accounts, Davide must have been a great artist, notwithstanding his faults. He had the prodigious compass of three octaves, which he displayed to the utmost advantage.

M. Edouard Bertin describes him as "a singer full of warmth, *verve*, expression, energy, and musical sentiment; alone he can fill up and give life to a scene; it is impossible for another singer to carry away an audience as he does, and when he will only be simple, he is admirable; he is the Rossini of song. He is a great singer; the greatest I ever heard."

This opera much pleased the Italians, who considered it the *chef d'œuvre* of lyric tragedy. Barbaja, too, must have been pleased at it, for it benefitted his coffers greatly.

"La Cenerentola," another of Rossini's most successful operas, followed closely upon "Otello." It was written for the Theatre Valle, at Rome, where it was not very successful, though shortly afterwards it became a favourite in all the capitals of Europe, and at one time bid fair to surpass even the popularity of "Il Barbiere." Madame Giorgi-Righetti was the original Cenerentola —the last opportunity she had of creating a great *prima donna* part; for, after this opera, Rossini composed no more of these for the contralto voice.

It is not generally known that Rossini had one principle in which he was very persistent—this was, not to allow a good piece of his music to be lost through the fault and weakness of a libretto; so that throughout his works, it is not an uncommon thing to find the music of some very impassioned love song again doing duty to the words of a prayer, or some other scene with a totally different expression of sentiment to that which the music was originally written for. "La Cenerentola" is not without its examples of this principle. For instance, the air "Miei Rampolli" first appeared in "La Pietra del Paragone," afterwards in "La Gazzeta," and on the failure of that opera, Rossini married it to "La Cenerentola," where it must ever now remain. Other passages of its music have also gone through a similar process, such as the reproductions from "Il Turco in Italia."

No sooner did Rossini get "La Cenerentola" off his hands, than he fell to work upon "La Gazza Ladra," from a libretto which the composer, Paer, intended treating, but which, through the treachery of his librettist, came into Rossini's possession. "Gazza Ladra" was written for the frequenters of La Scala, who were somewhat displeased at "Il Turco in Italia," their last opera from the *maestro*. "La Gazza Ladra" removed all this. Directly the overture was played, the whole of the Scala audience rose and greeted Rossini in the most enthusiastic fashion, calling out "*Bravo, maestro!*" "*Viva Rossini!*" This was continued throughout the opera, and so frequently did the applause come, that Rossini afterwards said the acknowledging it caused him a great deal more fatigue than did the direction of the opera.

Four years afterwards (1821), "La Gazza Ladra" was first performed in England at the King's Theatre, in the Haymarket, during Mr. Eber's management. It was chosen as a novelty for the opening night, after one of those collapses so frequent in operatic history, and the choice proved to be a right one. "As I entered the stage door," says Eber, in his "Seven Years of the King's Theatre," "I met an intimate friend, with a long face and uplifted eyes. 'Good God, Eber! I pity you from my soul! This ungrateful public!' he continued. 'The wretches! Why, my dear sir, they have not left you a seat in your own house!' Relieved from the fears he had created, I joined him in his laughter, and proceeded, assuring him that I felt no ill towards the public for their conduct towards me." Madame Camporese sang the part of Ninetta, and after its first representation, Eber says, " the opera continued to be played for many nights successively, without any apparent loss of attraction." Thus its success here, in Paris, and, indeed, in all the other great cities in Europe, was as spontaneous as it had been at La Scala, and this, notwithstanding its further innovations.

Of these Lord Mount Edgcumbe speaks in his valuable book of reminiscences, after hearing it performed in England: "Of all the operas of Rossini that have been performed here," he says, "that of 'La Gazza Ladra' is most peculiarly liable to all the objections I have made to the new style of drama, of which it is the most striking example. Its finales, and many of its very numerous *pezzi concertati*, are uncommonly loud, and the lavish use made of the noisy instruments, appears, to my judgment, singularly inappropriate to the subject, which, though it might have been rendered touching, is far from calling for such warlike accompaniments."

Now came " Armida," written for the opening of the San Carlo after it was rebuilt, and notable as being the only one of Rossini's Italian operas containing ballet music; "Adelaida di Borgogna," for the 1817 carnival at Rome, and "Adina," for a Lisbon theatre, all of which are now forgotten, and need no further notice than just a record; moreover, we must pass on to two far more important works—"Mosè in Egitto," and "Donna del Lago."

"Mosè" appeared in 1818 at the San Carlo with a *caste* which included Mdlle. Colbran as *prima donna*, Nozzari as tenor, Porto as Faraone, and Benedetti as Mosè, and proved a success, except at the crossing of the Red Sea, which nightly moved the audience to laughter, instead of producing the totally different effect Rossini had anticipated. Undoubtedly, this scene spoilt the conclusion of the opera, and the *maestro* was at his wit's end to know how to remedy it; till, one morning the librettist presented himself in Rossini's bedroom and suggested a prayer for the Israelites before and after the passage of the sea. Rossini at once saw the use of it, and on looking over the words with which Tottola had provided him, exclaimed, "I will get up and write the music," and instantly jumping up, and sitting down in his shirt, he finished the piece in eight or ten minutes. The same evening it was played with the opera, "when," says Stendhal, "the audience were delighted as usual with the first act, and all went well until the third, when the passage of the Red Sea being at hand, the audience as usual prepared to be amused.

The laughter was just beginning in the pit, when it was observed that Moses was about to sing. He began his solo, 'Dal tuo stelato Soglio' (To Thee, great Lord). It was the first verse of a prayer which all the people repeat in chorus after Moses. Surprised at this novelty, the pit listened and the laughter entirely ceased. The chorus, exceedingly fine, was in the minor. Aaron continues, followed by the people. Finally, Eleia addresses to Heaven the same supplication and the people respond. Then all fall on their knees and repeat the prayer with enthusiasm: the miracle is performed, the sea has opened to leave a path to the people protected by the Lord. This last part is in the major. It is impossible to imagine the thunders of applause that resounded throughout the house: one would have thought it was coming down. The spectators in the boxes standing up and leaning over to applaud called out at the top of their voices, '*Bello, bello! O che bello!*' I never saw so much enthusiasm nor such a complete success, which was so much the greater, inasmuch as the people were quite prepared to laugh. . . . I am almost in tears when I think of this prayer. This state of things lasted a long while, and one of its effects was to make for its composer the reputation of an assassin, for Dr. Cottongna is said to have remarked—'I can cite to you more than forty attacks of nervous fever, or violent convulsions on the part of young women fond to excess of music, which have no other origin than the prayer of the Hebrews in the third act, with its superb change of key.'"

In 1822 Mr. Bochsa brought out "Mosè" as an oratorio at the Covent Garden house, but it failed. In the same year it was again produced, this time at the King's Theatre in the Haymarket; and, under another title, "Pietro l'Eremito," proving an immense success. Ebers says "Lord Sefton, one of the most competent judges of the day, pronounced 'Pietro l'Eremito' to be the most effective opera produced during his recollection; and the public confirmed the justice of the remark, for no opera brought out during my management had such unequivocal success. It was, indeed, the strong point of the season, to strengthen which every effort was made. The subordinate aids of scenery and decoration were unsparingly resorted to, to give effect to this opera; and the nature of the story rendered these important. A gentleman well known in high life, indeed, not satisfied with telling me that I deserved well of my country, positively testified his admiration of the opera, by avowing a determination to propose the manager at White's!"

"La Donna del Lago," Rossini's next opera, was brought out at the San Carlo, Naples, in October, 1819, and notwithstanding the fine *caste*—Colbran, Pisaroni, Davide, Nozzare, and Benedetti—proved a signal failure on the first night, owing to the further new effects and innovations which it contained, and with which the San Carlo frequenters were not at all "agreeably impressed." Rossini did not take this reception so coolly as that of the "Barber;" and instead of going home to bed, made a journey the same night to Milan, informing every one along the *route* that the new opera had quite delighted the Neapolitans, and which proved to be true by the time he reached Milan, for upon his arriving there he learnt that at its second performance the San Carlo frequenters were in ecstasies with it. This, however, did not remove from Rossini's mind the impressions of the first night, or this opera would probably not have been the last important one he wrote for Naples. Certainly, he did write something more in 1820—"Maomette Secondo;" but, as Sutherland Edwards points out in his "Life of Rossini," he was already under an engagement to furnish it to Barbaja for the carnival of 1820, when "La Donna del Lago" was brought out.

Following "La Donna del Lago" came two works, "Bianco e Faliero" and "Matilda di Sabran," neither of which met with any fresh degree of success at their first representations. Of their after receptions Rossini did

Rossini.

not stay to acquaint himself; but, with Mdlle. Colbran, took himself off to Bologna, where they were married by the archbishop in his palace. After a short stay at Bologna, Rossini and wife went to Vienna, where they met with a flattering reception from the nobility and others. In this city Barbaja had another opera house; and it was for the purpose of conducting one of his new operas, that Rossini visited the capital.

"Zelmira" was the title of the new work, and it is considered as the most satisfactory of his compositions, with regard to invention and the ingenious manner in which the ideas are developed. Carpain says, "It contains enough to furnish not one, but four operas. In this work Rossini, by the new riches which he draws from his prodigious imagination, is no longer the author of 'Otello,' 'Tancredi,' 'Zoraide,' and all his preceding works; he is another composer—new, agreeable, and fertile as much as the first, but with more command of himself, more pure, more masterly, and, above all, more faithful to the interpretation of the words. The forms of style employed in this opera according to circumstances are so varied, that now we seem to hear Glück, now Traetta, now Sacchini, now Mozart, now Handel; for the gravity, the learning, the naturalness, the suavity of their conceptions live and blossom again in 'Zelmira.' The transitions are learned and inspired more by considerations of poetry and sense than by caprice and a mania for innovation. The vocal parts, always natural, never trivial, give expression to the words, without ceasing to be melodious. The great point is to preserve both. The instrumentation of Rossini, is really incomparable, by the vivacity and freedom of manner, by the variety and justness of the colouring."

In Vienna it was not quite a success, nor yet when it was brought out in 1824 at the house in the Haymarket. Then, "Zelmira," says Ebers, "was much admired by musical amateurs, but failed to make an impression on the public at large. As a dramatic performance, it did not excite much interest, and those who did not relish or understand the science of the music, and the skill displayed in its combinations, found the piece languid and heavy."

After the Vienna season Rossini returned to Bologna and produced "Semiramide," the last of his Italian operas. This was first performed at the Fenice Theatre at Venice, on 3rd February, 1823, when the original *caste* included Madame Rossini as *Semiramide*, Madame Mariani as *Arsace*, Galli as *Assur*, Mariani as *Oroe*, and Sinclair as *Idreno;* but it was not much liked, although, unlike his other operas, it had the advantage of frequent rehearsals before it was publicly performed.

Nor was it hurriedly composed. "It is the only one of my operas," said Rossini, "that I was able to do a little at my ease; my contract gave me forty days, but I was not forty days writing it." The Venetians were wrong in the seal they set upon it. Half a century of time has declared it to be one of the finest of his works —in short a masterpiece, wherein is met in combination all his "innovations," or "crimes," both which they were called, that had gradually appeared in its predecessors. For the score the manager of the Fenice paid the *maestro* something like two hundred pounds.

We now reach a new phase in Rossini's life, that is, his English and French career. His first appearance in London was at the King's Theatre on the evening of the 24th January, 1824, when he stood in the orchestra to direct his "Zelmira." "When Rossini entered," says a writer of the time, "he was received with loud plaudits, all the persons in the pit standing on the seats to get a better view of him. He continued for a minute or two to bow respectfully to the audience, and then gave the signal for the overture to begin. He appeared stout, and somewhat below the middle height, with rather a heavy air, and a countenance which, though intelligent, betrayed none of the vivacity which distinguishes his music: and it was remarked that he had more the appearance of a sturdy beef-eating Englishman than a fiery and sensitive native of the South." No one could have received more attention upon his arrival than did Rossini. He was presented to his Majesty (George IV.) at the Pavilion at Brighton, where he found this monarch playing at *écarté* with a lady. Taking his arm the king walked with him to the concert-room to hear his band; which, in compliment to Rossini, had been ordered to play the "Il Barbiere" overture. The next piece his Majesty left to Rossini's selection, to which he replied with his natural good breeding, "If I might take the liberty of selecting the next piece it must be 'God save the King.'"

He was a guest at the most fashionable houses, where his talents as a singer and performer on the pianoforte were always called into action : and seldom without a handsome acknowledgment of the estimation in which they were held. He had a fine tenor voice and sang with much taste, besides which he was a remarkable pianist. Auber once saw him play and said, "I shall never forget the effect produced by his lightning-like execution. When he had finished I looked mechanically at the ivory keys; I fancied I could see them smoking." During this one season in London, Rossini and his wife were gainers to the extent of seven thousand pounds; after which they paid a visit to our neighbours across the Channel.

Arrived in Paris, Rossini soon perceived that the French were a more artistic people than the English; and one of the first proofs of this was the appointment which the Duke de Lauriston conferred upon him—that of director of the Italian Opera. With this and the Académie, Rossini was associated till the year 1830; when the Revolution broke forth, and put an end for a time to all musical arrangements. For Paris, Rossini wrote four operas—"Il Viaggio a Rheims," "Le Siége de Corinthe," "Le Compte Ory," and "Guglielmo Tell" —of which only the latter need be referred to.

"William Tell" was chiefly composed while Rossini was on a visit to M. Aguado at his *château;* a retired country seat some distance from Paris. This opera was first produced at the Académie Royale of Paris on August 3rd, 1829. It was partly successful, but after fifty-six representations, the opera ceased to draw; for it was perceived that the master had wedded his fine dramatic music to a somewhat imperfect libretto; and the work of cutting down was commenced. The music had saved it for a time, but what power music must have to give wings to an undramatic drama! In its new form the opera met with more favour and soon blazed into greater popularity, though of the beauty and power of the music there had never been two opinions. Fetis, the eminent French critic, writing immediately after its performance, said of it, "The work displays a new man in an old one, and proves that it is in vain to pretend to measure the action of genius. This production opens a new career to Rossini." "Guillaume Tell" is full of melody. Whether in its solos, or its massive choral and ballet music, we meet alike with that fine stream of melody which runs through the whole of this great opera. Its overture is a magnificent work of art—and must ever continue to charm and to be admired. The opening andante in triple time for the five violoncelli and double basses, at once carries the listener away to the regions of the snowy Alps, where all is calm and peaceful. We perceive that nature is awaking, and we seem to see the hazy atmosphere clearing off for the new-born day. In the next movement, this solitude is all dispelled. The raindrops fall thick and heavy, and a storm with thunder and lightning bursts upon us. But its fury is soon spent. The clouds clear away and all is bright again. The shepherds are astir—and from the mountain sides come the peculiar notes of the *Ranz des Vaches* from their pipes. Suddenly all is changed. Trumpets sound a call to arms. Troops are mustering, and the music cleverly marks their quick step as the soldiers and shepherd patriots march off to protect their country. A brilliant use of the violins and other instruments, depicts the joy and exultation of the victors upon their return, and their joyous shouts effectively close this grand tone-picture.

The original cast of "Guillaume Tell" included Nourrit, Levasseur, Dabadie, A. Dupont, Massol, and Madame Cinti-Damoreau, who were so delighted with the new work that the morning after its production they assembled on the terrace of Rossini's house, and performed a selection from it in his honour.

With this work Rossini's prolific career may almost be said to have ended—and this at the age of thirty-seven, when most great careers have but begun. Notwithstanding that he lived close upon forty years longer, a few songs, his "Stabat Mater," and the "Messe Solennelle," are all he wrote. Why he sank into this retirement it is hard to conceive. There have been many conjectures, but the thing remains as much a mystery as ever.

The "Stabat Mater" was originally written for a distinguished Spaniard, Don Varela by name, but upon his death Rossini secured it again, and sold it to his music publisher, and in 1842 it was publicly performed, bringing fame for Rossini as a church composer. That it is a masterpiece no one will doubt, nor would any one be insane enough to question the great beauty and tenderness of the melodious music in it; but, that there is a lack of devotional feeling and solemnity, which nothing can atone for, is also beyond doubt. Had Mozart taken the same words what would he not have left us! Rossini's fame will rest on his operas, not on his contributions to church music.

The "Messe Solennelle" first came to light in 1864, when it was played at Paris before Auber, Meyerbeer, and other private friends. As a sacred composition, it has not as much interest as the "Stabat," and can never become as popular.

The forty years of Rossini's retirement were spent partly at Bologna, and at Passy, near Paris. At this latter place he died. The great man had long been ailing, but it was only a fortnight or so before his death that his mortal illness began to show itself seriously; and then everything that science and devoted attention could do to save his life, was done, but in vain—"The Swan of Pesaro," as his compatriots delighted to style him, died after intense sufferings on the 13th November, 1868. After a grand funeral mass had been sung, his mortal remains were borne from the Church de la Trinité to their resting-place in the cemetery of Père la Chaise, followed by an immense concourse of mourners of all ranks.

Music, and especially operatic music, owes a very great deal to Rossini for the reforms which he made, both in opera buffa and opera seria. It was he who substituted singing for the endless recitatives, of which Italian opera before him chiefly consisted; it was he who brought the bass voice prominently to the front, and gave it a leading part; it was he who banished the piano-forte from the Italian orchestras, and laid down the principle that the singer should sing the notes the composer had given him, without any *fiorire* additions of his own. He it was who gave to the chorus a much more important place in opera than it hitherto had had. It was Rossini who made the orchestra what it is at the present day. Every new instrument that was invented Rossini found room for in his brilliant scores, and brought down the indignation and rage of all the Italian musicians. Hitherto their orchestras had consisted almost solely of strings: what must have been their surprise to see wind instruments added to the extent Rossini added them! This is best conceived, probably, by Sigismondi's behaviour on one occasion, when young Donizetti, then a student, pleaded to look at the Rossini scores at the Neapolitan Conservatory. That of "Otello" was selected, and the two sat down to examine it; but instantly old Sigismondi began raving about the "monstrous" score and its "buffooneries." Every instrument employed was severely commented upon; but when he came to the "wind" his indignation was terrible. Clarionets, bassoons, trombones, first, second, third, and fourth, had all been employed to swell a *crescendo* in one part; but when the *fortissimo* was reached, Sigismondi, it is said, uttered a cry of despair, struck the score violently with his fist, upset the table which young Donizetti had loaded with the productions of Rossini, raised his hands to heaven, and rushed from the room, exclaiming, "A hundred and twenty-three trombones! A hundred and twenty three trombones!" Donizetti followed the enraged musician, and endeavoured to explain the mistake. "Not a hundred and twenty-three trombones, but first, second, and third trombones," he gently observed. Sigismondi, however, would not hear another word, and disappeared from the library, exclaiming to the last, "A hundred and twenty-three trombones!"

PRINCIPAL INCIDENTS IN THE LIFE OF ROSSINI.

Born at Pesaro, the 29th February	1792
Performed in Paer's "Camilla"	1799
Under Padre Mattei	1804
"Tancredi" composed and produced	1813
"L' Italiana in Algeria" composed	1813
"Le Barbiere di Siviglia" produced	1816
"Otello" brought out at Naples	1816
"Mosè in Egitto" composed	1818
"Semiramide" produced at Venice	1823

Rossini.

Rossini visited London 1824
"Guglielmo Tell" produced in Paris 1829
The "Stabat Mater" first publicly performed . . 1842
The "Messe Solennelle" completed 1864
Died at Passy, 13th November 1868

Schubert.

SCHUBERT and song! These must ever be associated, and who, indeed, would wish to sever the tie. Song was the life-long object of this true tone-poet; for it he strove, and, above all, he accomplished. Many may know him by other music, but the world at large knows him only by those inspiring melodies which enkindle all the emotions appertaining to human nature—love and hatred, joy and sorrow, hope and despair, consolation, resignation, and the like. Those six hundred songs form a unique and precious bequest to music, and complete the last, and not least, of the stately and strong columns on which the vast edifice of modern musical art rests— the symphonies and sonatas of Beethoven, the operas of Mozart, the oratorios of Handel, the chamber music of Haydn, and the songs of Schubert.

Franz Peter Schubert was given to the world on the last day of January, 1797, at Lichenthal, near Vienna, where his father lived, and enjoyed not a little reputation and popularity as a schoolmaster.

Amidst the scenes and surroundings of the schoolhouse, baby Franz grew and thrived till he was four or five years old, when his father took him into his school. At first he was not made much more of by the grave schoolmaster, than were his other children. But Fortune had kissed the boy's brow—Franz soon became the favoured child. When he was seven years old, it was evident that nature had endowed him for a musician rather than a schoolmaster, the hereditary occupation of the Schuberts. At this early age, he had contracted a friendship with an apprentice, who often took him to a piano-forte warehouse, where he had frequently opportunities of practising on the instruments. Soon Franz became the delight of the family; the old harpsichord in the schoolmaster's house was often called into requisition, and gave forth wonderful music under the magic fingers of the performer. So much surprise did his performances excite, that the father determined to put him through a regular course of instruction, and thereupon placed him under a musician named Holzer, who resided in the neighbourhood. With him the boy's progress at theory-singing and organ-playing was astonishing, till at last Holzer could never speak of his pupil without evident emotion.

At the age of eleven years, Franz obtained an appointment in the emperor's chapel as a chorister, and exchanged his school-boy suit for a dazzling gold-bordered uniform. Here he remained for five years, during which time he made surprising strides in his art, and especially as a composer. A symphony in D major; a cantata in honour of his father's birthday; part of an opera; some string quartets; fantasias; an octet for wind instruments; many songs, including the well-known "Hagar's Lament," all belong to this early period of the life of our genius.

After leaving the imperial chapel, young Franz returned to his father's roof, and assisted him in the school. It was in vain, however, that the old man sought to make a schoolmaster of Franz, for the irresistible desire of composing oozed out even in school-hours, and whenever the old man's back was turned, he dashed down a movement, and suffered the scholars' lessons to pass unexamined. Music flowed from his brain far too quickly for the mechanical work of writing it down. The mass in F, composed for the Centenary Festival of Lichenthal Church; an opera, songs, pieces for stringed instruments, a piano sonata, came to light during this time, and carried the young composer's reputation a little farther than the school-house, notwithstanding he could get no music-seller to publish them.

Schubert.

The year 1815, when Schubert was but eighteen years of age, was the commencement of a prolific creative period, never equalled during the remainder of his life. To speak of all that was then written would be impossible. We can but glance at the most important productions.

In church music we have the masses in G and C, compositions most solid and thoughtful in character, and never surpassed even in his after-years. The songs of this period are legion. Those which breathe the spirit of Schubert most truly are the "Mignon Songs," the "Songs from Ossian," the "Erl-King," and the "Wanderer."

The "Erl-King" has a history. One afternoon Schubert was in his room, and, happening to take up a volume of Göthe's poems, read the "Erl-King." Again he read the poem, and with intense excitement. The howling wind and the terrors of the forest became stern realities to the youth, who instantly dashed down this wonderful tone-picture in the presence of a friend who had entered the room. Vogl, the singer, sang it, and produced a great sensation. This song has been the solace of the death-bed. Jean Paul requested that he might once more hear the "Erl-King" before he died; and, two years before Göthe's death, Madame Schröder Devrient called upon the aged poet and sang the "Erl-King." Taking her head between his hands, he kissed the songstress's forehead, adding, "A thousand thanks for this grand artistic performance! I heard the composition once before, and it did not please me, but when it is given like this the whole becomes a living picture."

This song was the first of Schubert's compositions that appeared in print, and this happened in the year of his death, thirteen years after the ballad was composed. The publishers for years refused to have it even at a gift, and probably would never have given the small trifle they did for it, had they not witnessed the demand for the copies Dr. Sonnleithner engraved at his own risk, and which were published on commission in 1821. They made thousands of pounds out of it, and published it in every conceivable form, even down to the "Erl-King Waltzes." What enterprise! How remarkable that the "Messiah Quadrilles" or the "Judas Galop" have not appeared long ere this.

The Abbé Liszt has arranged this song for the piano as he alone can; and no one who studies his superb instrumentation should forget this treasure of two great masters, as a piano-forte piece. Madame Schumann is the happy possessor of the original score of the "Erl-King."

"The Wanderer" belongs to the year 1816. Its score is still extant, and bears date October, 1816. The exact day has been erased, apparently by Schubert himself, and in some passages there are numerous marks of alteration in the piano accompaniment. The success of this song was even more spontaneous than that of the "Erl-King," and soon carried Schubert's name into distant lands.

The chief of the instrumental music of this time are two symphonies—one in B flat, known as the "Symphony without trumpets and drums;" the other in C minor, also called "the tragic."

Dramatic music was not forgotten. The operas, "Die Vicjährige Posten," with words by Korner; "Die bieden Freunde von Salamanka," in two acts, the words by the poet Mayrhofer, who one day threw himself from the top of a house and broke his neck; "Die Bürgschaft," in three acts; and many others, as well as a cantata in honour of Salieri, and another entitled "Prometheus," all flowed from Schubert's fertile pen during this wonderful period of production.

Nor are these mere precocious efforts, lacking the touch of a matured musician; they are the works of a genius of immense creative powers, with a rare sense of the beautiful and true, and a familiarity with the art of composition, which the study of a hundred years could never have made him more intimate with. The "Erl-King" and "Wanderer," as we have seen, are works of this period. No one will question the hand of a master in these songs; yet they were written when Schubert was but a youth, a youth, however, who had com῀ menced his matured period long before he entered his teens. Composing was no more a struggle to him than was breathing his native air; and the facility with which he wrote was so great that Schumann once said of him, "In time he would probably have set the whole of German literature to music."

Let us now look at Schubert's inner life at this time. There are no collected letters—those dearest and best relics of the beloved dead, that seem to speak to us with a living voice, and that recall familiar names, bright bygone scenes, and the once firm hand that penned them. We lose all this with Schubert; but he speaks to us in his music, and in this he comes to the terrified child, to the lover, the penitent girl, to the wearied and lost wanderer, and the girl at her spinning-wheel. Happily, too, fragments of a diary that Schubert kept about this time have been found, and from this a few lines may be quoted; for from letters or a diary so deep an insight may be obtained into the thoughts and feelings of a man. Here is an entry on June 13th, 1816:—
"This day will haunt me for the rest of my life as a bright, clear, and lovely one. Gently, and as from a distance, the magic tones of Mozart's music sound in my ears. With what alternate force and tenderness—with what masterly power—did Schlesinger's playing of that

music impress it deep, deep in my heart! Thus do these sweet impressions, passing into our souls, work beneficently on our inmost being; and no time, no change of circumstances, can obliterate them. In the darkness of this life they show a light, a clear beautiful distance, from which we gather confidence and hope. O Mozart! immortal Mozart! how many and what countless images of a brighter, better world hast thou stamped on our souls!"

Here is another, dated the following day:—"After the lapse of a few months, I took once more an evening walk. There can hardly be anything more delightful than, after a hot summer's day, to stroll about in the evening on the green grass. The meadows between Währing and Döbling seem to have been created for this very purpose. I felt so peaceful and happy as my brother Carl and I walked together in the struggling twilight. 'How lovely!' I thought and exclaimed, and then stood still enchanted. The neighbourhood of the churchyard reminded us of our excellent mother. Whiling the time away with melancholy talk, we arrived at the point where the Döbling road branches off, I heard a well-known voice, issuing as though from heaven —which is our home. The voice came from a carriage which was being pulled up. I looked round, and there was Herr Weinmüller, who got out and greeted us with his hearty, manly, cheerful-toned voice. How vainly does many a man strive to show the candour and honesty of his mind by conversation equally sincere and candid! How would many a man be the laughing-stock of his fellow-creatures were he to make the effort! Such gifts must come naturally; no efforts can acquire them."

Further on, Schubert writes, "Happy is he who finds a true friend. Happier still is he who finds in his own wife a true friend. To the free man, at this time, marriage is a fearful thought; he confounds it either with melancholy or low sensuality."

Another entry is:—"Light mind, light heart. A mind that is too light generally harbours a heart that is too heavy."

In 1817 Schubert was twenty years old; and not very prepossessing in his appearance. He was short, and stooped a little, and had short curly hair and a puffy face, bushy eyebrows and a stumpy nose; was pale, but not delicate. At this time he bade adieu to his father's roof, and took up his abode in the house of his friend Schober, in the Landskrongasse. His daily work was usually begun in the forenoon, and continued without intermission till dinner-time.

When writing, his whole being is said to have been absorbed in music; his compositions had such an effect on him, that eye-witnesses affirm they could frequently observe, in his flashing eye and altered speech, that he was labouring under intense excitement. The rest of the day was almost invariably devoted to social pleasures, and in summer to country excursions with his friends.

When visiting at the houses of the great, Schubert was reserved and shy. No sooner had he finished his exquisite playing of the accompaniment to his songs than he put on a serious face, and withdrew to an adjoining room. Indifferent to applause, he avoided all compliments, and sought only the approbation of his intimate friends. Though he never danced, he was sometimes present at private parties given at friends' houses, when he would obligingly seat himself at the piano, and, for hours together, extemporize the most beautiful dance music. When not invited out he would spend the evening at the inn with his friends. He was fond of wine, and at these meetings at the inn, which were often prolonged into the small hours, he frequently indulged in more than was good for him, when he became noisy and rather unpleasant society. Another place Schubert was fond of frequenting after dinner, was the Bognersche coffee-house, not alone to sip and enjoy his coffee, but to watch the odd movements and manner of the quaint waiter there, who used to send

Schubert into fits of laughter by the original style in which he called out to the kitchen, the customer's orders.

Schubert had only lived with Schober a twelvemonth or so, when he met with Count Esterhazy, a Hungarian nobleman, who offered him the post of music-master in his family. Schubert did not care for teaching, in fact had an aversion to it; but the two gulden a lesson, the wintering in town, and the stay at the estate at the foot of the Styrian hills during the summer, induced him to waive his objections to accept the count's offer, and to accompany him to Zelésy. The family were all musical, and, under Schubert's direction, sedulously set to practising the works of Haydn, Mozart, and some pieces of his own.

Soon after entering into the family he felt a growing passion for Caroline Esterhazy, the count's youngest daughter. The pretty features, the sweet voice, and careful piano accompaniments of the girl of eleven charmed the young genius. The flame increased, and he loved her ardently. She did not return his love, and could do no more than appreciate his genius. Yet she would coquet with him, and once reproached Schubert for never having dedicated any piece of music to her. "What's the use," replied the poor fellow, "when you have already got all?" To the last day of his life he entertained the same feelings towards his little love, but they were always hopeless and unrequited.

We turn again to Schubert and his works. Under Schober's roof he composed five masterly piano-forte sonatas—those in E flat, A flat, A, F, and B minor— works only inferior to those of Beethoven, which precious treasures had already been given to the world. These, and two overtures in the Italian style—on the success of which hung the fate of his having a good glass of wine from his companions—were composed immediately preceding the period of his entering the service of the Esterhazy family. While there, his pen did not lie idle, for at Zelésy was produced, among many minor works, his sixth symphony in C, interesting as marking a state of transition from Mozart and Beethoven to his own true style, so perfected in the next and last symphony he composed, and which probably would have been even more perceptible had he lived longer and completed another: a pianoforte quintet, with the song "Die Forelle," and variations to it; a cantata, in honour of his friend Vogl's birthday; and many splendid settings of Göthe's songs, which he sent to the aged poet, who, however, would have nothing to do with them, and laid them aside.

By this time (1820) Schubert was living with his friend, Mayrhofer, in the Wipplingerstrasse. At No.

420 in this street, the two geniuses rented in common a third-floor room, from one, dame Sanssouci, a tobacco seller. Mayrhofer once described it as being in a dark gloomy street, with house and furniture the worse for wear, the ceiling beginning to bulge, the light obstructed by a huge building opposite, and containing an old worn-out piano, and a shabby book-stand as chief part of the furniture. Most probably it was in these quarters that Schubert composed the dramas "Die Zwillingsbruder," and "Die Zauberharfe," for the An der Wien Theatre; the cantata "Lazarus," a work of striking beauty and originality, most impressive, and full of thoughtful and religious music; "Sakontala;" an unfinished opera; and a setting for female voices of the 23rd Psalm, which deserves to be better known.

The year 1821, if it was not productive of much that was great in the way of composition, was none the less an important year of the few allotted to Schubert, for it was that in which he first became known, out of his own circle of intimate friends, as a great composer and song writer, by his "Erl-King," and other pieces being privately engraved and given to the world. For new works we must look to the following year.

"Alfonso and Estrella," one of Schubert's two greatest operas, was conceived and chiefly composed while he and his friend, Schober, were enjoying a short stay amid the beautiful country which surrounds the town of Ochsenburg. Its gifted composer's eyes never saw it upon the stage, nor indeed did any others, till, in 1854, Dr. Liszt secured a performance, which was not remarkable as a success, either for the opera, or for the treasury of the theatre. The original score of this opera is in the library of the Musik-verein, at Vienna.

The other important effusions of this year were a mass in A flat, of great beauty, and parts of an unfinished symphony in B minor, which, judging by what there is in existence, had it been completed, would have been a most wonderful and interesting work. These fragments were first performed in London at one of the Crystal Palace concerts, on the 6th April, 1867, and the beauties then unravelled have warranted their frequent performance since, both there and elsewhere.

An event now occurred which must not be passed over. For well-nigh thirty years Schubert and Beethoven had lived in the same town, had breathed the same atmosphere, but had never met. All the world knew of Beethoven, and those who understood him and his music, worshipped him—though at a distance, for the great genius was difficult of access. Among these was Schubert, who from his earliest years possessed the deepest reverence for the master. What were his words when, but a mere boy, an admiring friend was praising him for his cleverness? "Who can do anything after Beethoven?" he replied. Beethoven, however, seems never to have heard of Schubert, or his wonderful "Lieder," and other works. This year changed all this. The two men met. Here is the account, which Schindler, Beethoven's biographer, gives of their meeting:—

"In the year 1822, Franz Schubert set out to present in person the master he honoured so highly, with his variations on a French song (Op. 10). These variations he had previously dedicated to Beethoven. In spite of Diabelli accompanying him, and acting as spokesman and interpreter of Schubert's feelings, Schubert played a part in the interview which was anything but pleasant to him. His courage, which he managed to husband up to the very threshold of the house, forsook him entirely at the first glimpse he caught of the majestic artist; and when Beethoven expressed a wish that Schubert should write the answers to his questions, he felt as if his hands were tied and fettered. Beethoven ran through the presentation copy, and stumbled on some inaccuracy in harmony. He then, in the kindest manner, drew the young man's attention to the fault, adding that the fault was no deadly sin. Meantime the result of this remark, intended to be kind, was to utterly disconcert the nervous visitor. It was not until he got outside the house that Schubert recovered his equanimity, and rebuked him unsparingly." Never, till Beethoven lay dying, did Schubert go to see him again, for he had not the courage to do so.

This interview most favourably impressed Beethoven with Schubert's worth, and in the last days of his life the dying musician commenced to study Schubert's works. On his death-bed lay numbers of his songs, some only in manuscript. "For several days," says Schindler, "he could not tear himself away from perusing them, and he pored for hours daily over the 'Iphigénie,' 'Grenzen der Meuschheit,' 'Allmacht,' 'Junge Nonne,' 'Viola,' the 'Mullerlieder,' and several others. He exclaimed repeatedly, in a voice of rapturous delight, 'Certainly a god-like spark dwells in Schubert! Had I had this poem, I, too, would have set it to music!' He could not say enough in praise of most of the other poems, and Schubert's original way of handling the subject." A few days after this Beethoven lay dying. Around his bed-side were many kind friends, among them Schubert, to whom the dying man addressed a few unintelligible words. Schubert turned his face, and burst into a flood of tears. A little later he and others bore the remains of the kingly musician to the grave. On their return home, after the German fashion, they drank to the memory of the recently departed one: it was then proposed to drink to him who should first follow Beethoven. Hastily filling up his cup, Schubert drank to himself! This was in 1827. In the following year Schubert was laid by the side of Beethoven!

But we must turn back and follow out the last few years of Schubert's existence. The year 1823 is one of the most conspicuous in his life. Dramatic compositions appear to be the order of the day with him, for these form the staple part of the works which this year has the merit of producing.

The first to be referred to is "Rosamunde," the words of which were supplied by that same restless old lady, Helmina Chezy, who supplied the words to Weber's "Euryanthe."

"Rosamunde" was composed for the An der Wien, where it was announced to be played on Saturday, December 20th, 1823, for the benefit of an actress of the theatre. The music was announced as by the popular and talented composer, Herr Franz Schubert. It was produced, and met with a success which one more performance decided not sufficiently marked to suggest repetition. One critic wrote of it: "Herr Schubert shows originality in his compositions, but unfortunately 'bizarrerie' also. The young man is in a period of development. We hope that he will come out of it successfully. At present he is too much applauded; for

Schubert.

the future, may he never complain of being too little recognized."

The music after these performances disappeared, and was not heard again for more than forty years, when, thanks to the energy of Mr. George Grove, of the Crystal Palace—an ardent admirer of Schubert's music —the original scores were discovered, and the "Rosamunde" music was performed at the Saturday concert of March 28th, 1868. To that gentleman and distinguished amateur, are our best thanks due for the service he has rendered art, and for the pleasure which his introduction of more of Schubert's works, has been the means of providing for us. He was in Vienna when he made the discovery of this "Rosamunde," and other of Schubert's supposed lost music. His narrative says: "It was on Thursday afternoon, and we proposed to leave on Saturday for Prague. We made a final call on Dr. Schneider, to take leave and repeat our thanks, and also, as I now firmly believe, guided by a special instinct. The doctor was civility itself; he again had recourse to the cupboard, and showed us some treasures which had escaped us before. I again turned the conversation to the 'Rosamunde' music; he believed that he had at one time possessed a copy or sketch of it all. Might I go into the cupboard and look for myself? Certainly, if I had no objection to being covered with dust. In I went, and after some search, during which my companion kept the doctor in conversation, I found, at the bottom of the cupboard, and in its farthest corner, a bundle of music-books, two feet high, carefully tied round, and black with the undisturbed dust of nearly half a century. It was like the famous scene at the monastery of Souriani, on the Natron lakes, so well described by Mr. Curzon: 'Here is a box,' exclaimed the two monks, who were nearly choked with the dust; 'we have found a box, and a heavy one, too!' 'A box!' shouted the blind abbot, who was standing in the outer darkness of the oil-cellar; 'a box! where is it?' 'Bring it out! Bring out the box! Heaven be praised! we have found a treasure! Lift up the box! Pull out the box!' shouted the monks in various tones of voice. We were hardly less vociferous than the monks, when we had dragged out the bundle into the light, and found that it was actually neither more nor less than what we were in search of. Not Dr. Cureton, when he made his truly romantic discovery of the missing leaves of the Syriac Eusebius, could have been more glad or grateful than I was at the moment, for these were the part books of the whole music in 'Rosamunde,' tied up after the second performance in December, 1823, and probably never disturbed since. Dr. Schneider must have been amused at our excitement; but let us hope that he recollected his own days of rapture; at any rate he kindly overlooked it, and gave us permission to take away with us and copy what we wanted, and I now felt that my mission to Vienna had not been fruitless."

"Fierrabras," another opera of this year, was written to the order of Barbaja, who at this time was *impresario* of the Imperial Opera-House at Vienna. It was never performed, however, but extracts from it have since then been played at various concerts in Vienna. The score, which contains something like a thousand pages of closely-written music, is in Dr. Schneider's collection. From dates on it, it appears that its first three hundred pages were composed in the short space of seven days.

"Der Häusliche Krieg," an operetta in one act, first performed in 1861 at a concert by the Musikverein at Vienna, and afterwards with much success at Frankfort; the charming "Müller-lieder" series; and that exquisite piano sonata in A minor, which was dedicated to Felix Mendelssohn, are the remainder of the productions of this year, which, with more space, might easily be dwelt upon longer.

Mention must now be made of a sad change that came over our artist about this time. Suddenly poor Schubert was seized with a dreadful feeling of depression, which at times drove him almost to despair. No doubt the failure of so many hopes, his long-continued struggle with the music publishers, the broken promises to perform his operas at the theatre, his want of money and the common necessaries of life, in spite of his constant activity and working, these, and perhaps the sad memories of his unrequited love, which a visit to the Esterhazys at Zelésy at this time again brought before him, all tended to bring on this unhappy and desponding state of mind. "Picture to yourself," he wrote to a friend, "a man whose health can never be re-established, who from sheer despair makes matters worse instead of better; picture to yourself, I say, a man whose most brilliant hopes have come to nothing, to whom the happiness of proffered love and friendship is but anguish, whose enthusiasm for the beautiful (an inspired feeling at least) threatens to vanish altogether, and then ask yourself if such a condition does not represent a miserable and unhappy man?"

The entries in his diary at this time are just as gloomy. Here is one:—"Grief sharpens the understanding and strengthens the soul, whereas joy seldom troubles itself about the former, and makes the latter rather effeminate or frivolous." Another says:—"My productions in music are the product of the understanding, and spring from my sorrow; those only which are the product of pain seem to please the great world most."

How did Schubert get consolation? He turned to his music, and despite his melancholy state, poured forth more works—an octet for stringed and wind instruments, for Count Troyer at Vienna; three stringed quartets, in A minor, E flat, and E major; a duet for piano and flute; and many other pieces and songs. Early in 1825, too, Schubert and his old friend Vogl set out on a ramble amid the mountains and blue lakes of Upper Austria, which had a most beneficial effect upon him.

On his return he applied for the place of vice-kapellmeister at the Imperial Chapel, but here was another failure. They had never heard a mass of Schubert's, consequently he was not chosen, and one Weigl secured the post. Soon afterwards came another opportunity of obtaining a settled appointment, but this he allowed to slip by. The conductorship at the Kärnthnertor Theatre was vacant, and Schubert's election to it depended upon his setting to music an operatic *scena* or two. He accomplished his task, which by-the-way contained an air which the chief soprano found it impossible to render. She and all concerned entreated Schubert to simplify it, which he refused to do. The general rehearsal came, and all went well up to this air, which the *prima donna* could not sing. Here Duport, the manager, stepped up to Schubert, and politely asked him to make the necessary alterations for Fräulein Schechner. This was enough for Schubert. After calling out at the top of his voice, "I alter nothing," he shut up his score with a bang, put it under his arm, and walked out of the place as fast as he could!

The string quartets in D minor and G major are both works of this year (1826), and are remarkable as showing the perfection the prince of lyrists had reached as a composer of chamber music. They are of the most delicate and tender character, a rich stream of melody runs through them, which, with the invention and learning they contain, stamp them as two of the most important effusions from this genius's pen.

The year preceding that of his death was productive of but little beyond the E flat trio, a work which met at once with the heartiest reception, and was frequently performed in private circles; the second part of the "Winterreise," and a quantity of dance music. Far more important are the compositions of the next and last year of Schubert's short life. 1828 was the beginning of a time which Schubert had longed for, for nearly thirty years—a time when the music publishers would take notice of him and his works. At last they were doing this; but, alas! it was too late. Had they come earlier they might have saved the wrecked constitution, shattered for the want of bread, and life's commonest necessaries; they might have assisted him

Schubert. 311

in his cherished desire of once again enjoying the beautiful scenery and air of the Styrian hills. But no! he could not go for the want of funds, so he stayed in town, and put up with his second-floor lodging, in a damp and newly-built house in the Neuen Wieden.

Most likely he frequently sat for hours in the chilly atmosphere of this room, absorbed in his beloved work of composing, and unknowingly sowing the seeds of that disease which so soon terminated fatally.

The works of this year are numerous, and unmistakably bear marks of progress, which leave one in doubt as to whether Schubert really did reach his climax as a composer. The "Seventh symphony" is a striking illustration of this advance. According to the original score now in the Vienna Musikverein, it was composed in March, 1828. Soon after this, Schubert presented it to the committee of the Musikverein, who were going to perform it, and actually had the parts copied out, and the rehearsals begun; but soon it was laid aside, as being "too long and too difficult," and was never played till after his death. Of all his symphonies this one in C is the grandest and most masterly work, besides being that most characteristic of him. For some listeners it must appear too long, and probably it is, but this will never materially affect its popularity. Mendelssohn and

Schumann both pronounced it to be the finest orchestral composition after Beethoven's.

The mass in E flat, generally considered the finest of Schubert's masses; the splendid quartet for strings in C; the cantata "Miriam's Battle Song," and many other lesser works and songs, belong to this year.

About the beginning of September poor Schubert began to sicken, and doctors were called in. For a while he was better, and able to go out, but in October he became a dreadful sufferer from giddiness and pains in his head. Late in this month he was dining at an hotel, but had hardly swallowed the first morsel of fish than he suddenly dropped his knife and fork, and would eat no more, declaring it was poisoned. From that time he took little more than his medicine, and continued to get so bad that about the 11th November he was compelled to keep his bed. A nervous fever came on, and after lying for some days in a raving and wandering state of mind, he succumbed to the fever at three o'clock in the afternoon of the 19th, surrounded by several of his friends.

A day or two after, his mortal remains, covered with wreaths of flowers, were borne to the Währing cemetery, and placed near Beethoven, as he wished. A bust marks his grave; and on the pediment beneath it is the following epitaph :—

Schubert. 313

> Music buried here a rich treasure,
> But still more glorious hopes.

Here lies
FRANZ SCHUBERT,
Born on the 31st January, 1797,
Died on the 19th November, 1828,
Aged 31 years.

Schubert has left behind him works in every style—symphonies, operas, church-music, piano-music, and songs. In song he is prodigious, and stands apart from every other composer, but in the other branches he has his superiors. The "Seventh" is the only one of the symphonies that at all approaches the finest known examples in this form, and before these, Schubert's last and best pales. In opera Schubert is nowhere; he lacked the vital faculty of knowing when to stop, and this would ever have shut out from him the opportunity of obtaining such salient points in opera as a "crisis" and "situation." The piano music Schubert has left certainly entitles him to an exalted place, for it is a most valuable contribution to the *repertoire* for this instrument; but despite such masterly works as the fantasias in C and G, the two sonatas in A minor, the bold and vigorous one in D major, no one could ever think of comparing Schubert's piano-music with that which the monarch Beethoven has left behind him. It is too thin. Where Schubert stands out in bold relief is in his songs, and to these we love to turn, and in fancy soar with him whithersoever his passionate and soul-stirring melodies lead us.

Oh, Schubert! thy life was spent for us, and the works of thy distress give us pleasure. Thou shalt not be forgotten. This and future generations shall sing thy lofty strains, and full of unspeakable happiness join in the loving words of one who was as dear to thee as a brother :—

"All bliss be thine, thou pure angelic soul!"

Principal Incidents in the Life of Schubert.

Born at Lichenthal, 31st January	1797
Placed under Holzer, his First Master	1805
The "Erl-King" composed	1815
The "Wanderer" composed	1816
Music-Master to Prince Esterhazy	1818
The "Sixth" Symphony written	1819
"Alfonso und Estrella" composed	1822
"Rosamunde" Music written	1823
The "Seventh" Symphony composed	1828
The E flat Mass composed	1828
Died 19th November	1828

Mendelssohn.

But very briefly indeed, within the limits of a few pages, can we sketch the career of one upon whose short life volume upon volume might be written; whether in dwelling upon the artistic side of it, with its long series of brilliant achievements as a composer, conductor, pianist, and organist, or in viewing it from a social aspect, and recording all that was great in him as a man—tracing the development of those sterling qualities which he possessed in so rare and high a degree. Mendelssohn's was a noble nature; spurning all that was base, mean, and insincere; full of fiery energy, yet as simple and lovable as a child's. Let those who wish to become acquainted with it, read his collected letters; and there is for those who desire to know him as a musician, his sublime music.

Felix Mendelssohn Bartholdy's birthday was the 3rd

February, 1809. Unlike most of our great musicians, he had none of the evils of poverty to contend with. Everything was in his favour; for his father, Abraham Mendelssohn, was a wealthy banker, his mother a highly-gifted and distinguished woman. Under her tender influence little Felix was educated, and it was she who gave him his first lessons in music. His loving teacher proved an excellent one. The first lessons were short ones, for she was careful not to check the inclination which her little son exhibited for music. However, they gradually became longer, as it was Felix's highest delight to be perched up before the keys of the piano-forte, wandering over the long range of notes before him. He was soon so far advanced, that his mother put him through a complete course of instruction, and so astonishing was the progress he made, that before he was ten years old he was well acquainted with some of the best works, and showed evident signs of great musical promise.

About the year 1817 his father moved from Hamburg to Berlin, and in a year or so after he placed little Felix under the care of Berger, for the piano-forte, and under the learned Zelter, Sebastian Bach's great disciple, for the theory of music. He entered upon his studies in high spirits, and was not long in unravelling the mysteries of harmony and counterpoint. With the piano-forte also, he made similar wonderful strides, for ere long he accompanied regularly at the Friday practices of the Singakademie at Berlin, where Zelter conducted. His playing soon attracted the attention of the musical circles in Berlin, and there were few who did not notice the handsome boy as he walked through the streets of that city.

Sir Jules Benedict, in his charming sketch of his friend's life, relates his first meeting with Felix, and says:—"It was in the beginning of May, 1821, when walking in the streets of Berlin with my master and friend, Carl Maria Von Weber, he directed my attention to a boy, apparently about eleven or twelve years old, who, on perceiving the author of 'Freischütz,' ran towards him, giving him a most hearty and friendly greeting. ''Tis Felix Mendelssohn,' said Weber, introducing me at once to the prodigious child, of whose marvellous talent and execution I had heard so much at Dresden. I shall never forget the impression of that day on beholding that beautiful youth, with his auburn hair clustering in ringlets round his shoulders, the ingenuous expression of his clear eyes, and the smile of innocence and candour on his lips. He would have it that we should go with him at once to his father's house; but as Weber had to attend a rehearsal, he took me by the hand, and made me run a race till we reached his home. Up he went briskly to the drawing-room, where, finding his mother, he exclaimed, 'Here is a pupil of Weber's, who knows a great deal of his music of the new opera. Pray, mamma, ask him to play it for us;' and so, with an irresistible impetuosity, he pushed me to the piano-forte, and made me remain there until I had exhausted all the store of my recollections. When I then begged of him to let me hear some of his own compositions, he refused, but played from memory such of Bach's fugues or Cramer's exercises as I could name. At last we parted, but not without a promise to meet again."

By this time Felix had improved amazingly in his studies, and already the music meetings held at his home had been graced more than once with a sketch from his pen. His first symphony, that in C minor, was composed for one of these. After returning from his visit to Weimar in 1821, where the talented youth was introduced to the great poet Göthe, the meetings were resumed with more than their usual briskness, and for them he composed two or three one-act operas.

These were enjoyable occasions for the energetic and clever little musician. The *réunions* were held in the drawing-room, the grown-up singers sitting round the large table, doing good justice to the inspirations of the boy who was seated at the grand piano, sometimes accompanying, at other times leading and directing with all the ardour and power imaginable. The "Two Schoolmasters" and the "Wandering Minstrels" were the titles of these two one-act operas; and though the composer was so young, his friend Devrient says of them, that "the music was individual, the declamation of the words unsought and natural; there were no striking melodies, but the comic incidents were treated with skill and humour."

Nor as an extempore player was Felix at this time less known. On one occasion, while staying at Frankfort in 1822, he attended the meeting of the Cecilia Society, and, at the request of the director, sat down and extemporized, and in such a manner as to electrify the body of old musicians who gathered round him. Choosing his subjects from Bach's motets, which he had heard sung but a few minutes before, he worked them up with incredible ingenuity into the most elaborate fugues, astonishing all by his complete command of counterpoint and his brilliant execution.

The year 1825 was an eventful one for Felix; for he then accompanied his father to Paris, to see Cherubini, whose counsel was sought to ascertain if the boy had a decided genius for music. This severe judge spoke in very flattering terms of the boy's promise, and so his future career was decided upon. Felix's new opera, "The Wedding of Camacho," had for some time been finished, and produced at the home performances, and soon after his return from Paris it was brought out at the Berlin Theatre Royal. The public were favourably disposed towards it, but the gentlemen of the Press cut it up most unmercifully.

Mendelssohn could not understand this and used to say, "The opera was not bad enough to deserve such very scurvy treatment." Its composer, however, was but sixteen; and yet there is much of this music which bears traces of the accomplished and matured musician. The fitting Spanish colouring which pervades the whole of it, proves that already the composer knew the capabilities of an orchestra, and by his judicious employment of the instruments, that he knew well what would prove effective.

The overture to the "Midsummer Night's Dream" was the next creation of the young composer, and it marks a most important period of his life, inasmuch as in this characteristic masterpiece his genius frees itself from the fetters of the school he had studied in, and we first get the irresistible and charming Mendelssohn in its buoyant and incomparable music. It was an immense flight which his genius had now taken.

For the next two years Felix was a student at the

University of Berlin, attending many of the lectures of the various learned professors, and working indefatigably at his studies. But, with all this, he found time to compose many new pieces, among which was his second descriptive overture, "The Calm Sea and Prosperous Voyage," wherein is plainly discernible the marked progress the future master was now making.

Early in 1829, Moscheles advised the father to allow Felix to visit England, and accordingly preparations were made for this journey; but, before leaving there was one favour his friends begged of him. For some time, Bach's "Matthew-Passion" had been brought out at the Saturday vocal practices at Mendelssohn's home, and all shared the conviction that it was the grandest and most important of German musical works. The singers wished to revive it in public, and for this object sought the assistance of the youth of twenty as conductor. Even Mendelssohn was loth to attempt so important an undertaking as the revival of such a work. But his friend Devrient soon coaxed him over, and on an early morning the two set out for the Singakademie on a visit to Zelter, whose aid was needed in order to obtain the use of the large concert-room and the services of the singers of the Academy.

"Now mind," said Felix, on arriving at the door; "if

he grows abusive I shall go—I cannot squabble with him."

On being shown in, they found the gruff old giant hid in a thick cloud of smoke from his long pipe, through which, however, his deep bass voice easily penetrated. There he was in his drab-coloured knee-breeches, and thick woollen stockings, sitting before his favourite old instrument, a two-manual harpsichord. The old German theorist *did* grow abusive in right earnest. He got excited and paraded the room, pouring volley after volley upon the half-frightened enthusiasts. Felix more than once pulled Devrient by the sleeve, but he still went on, and eventually brought the old musician round. Zelter promised the required assistance, and on the 11th March, 1829, Bach's immortal masterpiece was resuscitated under the direction of Mendelssohn with ever-memorable success, after having lain dormant for one hundred years. To him, then, the world must ever be indebted for having thus brought to light this *chef-d'œuvre* of amaster, alas! even now too little known.

A day or two after this event, Felix sailed for the white cliffs of England. He arrived in London on the 20th April, and was received with open arms at the house of his life-long friend Moscheles. On May 25th, at one of the Philharmonic concerts, he made his first bow to an English audience, and on this occasion the *bâton* was entrusted to his care, while the programme included two of the youthful *maestro's* works—his admirable C minor symphony, and the overture to the "Midsummer Night's Dream." He created a marvellous sensation. Loud acclamations followed each movement of the symphony; especially was this the case with the sublime adagio, and Mendelssohn was compelled to repeat the scherzo and trio. The bewitching music of the "Midsummer overture" simply electrified the vast audience, and nothing was heard of for days but the successful *debût* of the young composer.

Before returning to Berlin, Mendelssohn accompanied his friend Klingemann on a tour amidst the romantic scenery of Scotland. How his richly-cultivated mind was fed by the impressions it received during this tour, is best told by the masterly overture to "Fingal's Cave," and the splendid Scottish symphony, both so full of what he saw, and of the charming atmosphere he breathed. He arrived home in time to celebrate the silver wedding of his parents, and for this occasion he composed the trifle, entitled "Return from Abroad."

Mendelssohn then undertook another journey—the eventful one to Italy. Full of life and spirits, he set out in May, 1830, on what proved a delightful tour to this "cradle of art." "Italy at last," he writes on

October 10th, "and what I have all my life considered as the greatest possible felicity, is now begun, and I am basking in it." Arrived in Rome, he found himself surrounded and courted by a brilliant *réunion* of talent and rank.

In this sunny climate he painted Göthe's "Walpurgis Night," with brilliant and harmonious colouring that can never fade. Besides this inspired music, there was the "Reformation" symphony, the bright "Italian" symphony in A, and the three exquisite motets for treble voices, written especially for the nuns of the convent, Trinità del Monto, at Rome.

Writing home to his sister, Fanny, he relates all that he had been doing. "Listen and wonder," he says. "Since I left Vienna, I have partly composed music to Göthe's 'Walpurgis Night,' but have not yet had courage to write it down. At the opening there are songs of Spring, &c., and plenty of others of the same kind. Afterwards, when the Watchmen with their 'Gabeln und Zacken, und Eulen,' make a great noise, the fairy frolics begin, and you know that I have a particular foible for them." Then he goes on, "I have once more begun to compose with fresh vigour, and the Italian symphony makes rapid progress. It will be the most sportive piece I have yet composed, especially the last movement. I have not yet decided on the adagio, and

I think I shall reserve it for Naples." However, this work was laid aside for something else, and did not come to light till it was interpreted by the Philharmonic band, on May 13th, 1833, under the composer's direction.

What a bright and happy effort it is: so teemful of the balmy southern atmosphere, and all the gay images which had settled on the composer's mind—an undying record of his Italian impressions. After its three delicious movements, we come upon one even yet more so—the last, marked "*Saltarello Presto*," fully verifying all that its genial composer wrote of it, and of so vivacious and charmingly distinctive a character as to captivate all hearers.

Returning by way of Florence and Milan, Mendelssohn passed into the fresh and bracing air of Switzerland. How he enjoyed its glorious scenery—its gigantic mountains of pure snow, towering amid the dark blue atmosphere! "Nowhere," he writes to his parents, "has Nature in all her glory met my eyes in such brightness as here, both when I saw it with you for the first time and now. . . . Yesterday, at sunset, I was pacing up and down in front of the house, and each time that I turned my back upon the mountains I endeavoured vividly to represent to myself these gigantic masses, and each time, when I again faced them, they far exceeded my previous conceptions."

Early in December, 1831, Felix was again in Paris, where he passed three delightful months amidst its pleasures. "I have," he says, "cast myself headlong into the vortex, and do nothing the whole day but see new objects—the Chambers of Peers and Deputies, pictures and theatres, dio-neocosmo and panoramas, constant parties, &c." During this exotic life he composed very little, but his overture to the "Midsummer Night's Dream" was performed at one of the concerts of the Conservatoire, and also his A minor quartet, "which," as Mendelssohn wrote, "they played with such fire and precision that it was delightful to listen to them. It appeared to make a great impression on the audience, and at the scherzo they were quite uproarious."

Towards the end of April he arrived in London. He had only been there a week when he strolled in unawares at one of the Philharmonic rehearsals, and had been in but a few minutes when one of the orchestra espied him, and cried out, "There is Mendelssohn!" on which they all began shouting and clapping their hands to such a degree that for a time he was at a loss to know what to do. When this was over, another called out "Welcome to him!" and the uproar recommenced, and he was obliged to cross the room and clamber into the orchestra to return thanks to the delighted musicians.

The great composer soon received an invitation to

perform at one of the Society's concerts, where he produced and played his brilliant "G minor concerto." It created an extraordinary impression; so much so, that he was obliged to repeat it at their following concert—an occurrence without precedent. Nor was his production of "The Hebrides" overture one whit less eventful. This masterly work, replete with exquisite touches of feeling, and so thoroughly characteristic of the glorious Highland scenery which suggested it, was given during the same season; and the applause which followed immediately after its performance was such as but few compositions before it had excited, but which its transcendent merits must fully have entitled it to.

In July, 1832, Mendelssohn bade adieu to London, and returned to his home in Berlin. His cheerful and intellectual circle were delighted to see him back again—the same warm-hearted merry Felix. Devrient relates that the children were as familiar as ever with him; he made the old, unforgotten jokes, insisted on their calling him "Mr. Councillor;" they likewise *would* call him "Mr. Horrid."

Not long after his return came the day for the long-talked-of election for the post of conductor at the Singakademie, rendered vacant by the death of Mendelssohn's old master, Zelter; and at the request of many of his friends, Felix became one of the candidates for the office. The contest lay between one Runenhagen and Mendelssohn, and after some noisy meetings Runenhagen was elected to the post in recognition of his long connection with the Academy, his partizans declaring that it was a private society, and they wanted some one who was popular with them in preference to his qualities as a musician. Perhaps it was as well that the great artist did not find himself conducting a choir the majority of whom possessed such sentiments as these.

In April, 1833, Felix again visited London, this time accompanied by his father, but it was not for long, for in the following month he conducted at the Düsseldorf Festival. This was attended with unprecedented success, and so much so, that the directorship of the concerts and theatre of that city was offered to him. This post he accepted for three years, and threw his life and soul into his new work: bringing the musical performances there to such a degree of perfection as to draw all Europe to hear them. To church music especially did he zealously apply himself, and it was in furtherance of this that he set about his great and beautiful work, "St. Paul." Moreover, his pen at this time was very fruitful. Apart from the oratorio which he was engaged upon, he composed many beautiful songs, and also much music for the piano-forte, including many of the charming "Lieder ohne Worte."

(Sir) Jules Benedict says: "At this period of mechanical dexterity, musical claptraps, skips from one part of the piano to another, endless shakes, and arpeggios were the order of the day. Everything was sacrificed to display. Passages were written for the sole purpose of puzzling and perplexing the musical dilettanti, causing amazement by the immense quantity of notes compressed into one page. Mendelssohn, who never would sacrifice to the prevailing taste, took, in this new species of composition, quite an independent flight; his aim was to restore the ill-treated, panting piano-forte to its dignity and rank; and in this view he gave to the world those exquisite little musical gems, the "Songs without Words."

As it was in Mendelssohn's day, so it is now, or even worse; and they who put upon paper these flimsy fantasias, arrangements, and such like, with their page after page of musical gymnastics, the more insurmountable, to them, the more musicianly, would do well to cease their claptrap, and allow Art to go merrily on her way rejoiced at the barrier which had so long impeded her being removed.

With the spring of 1835, Mendelssohn was in Cologne, arranging for the approaching festival there.

Among the works he produced were Handel's oratorio, "Solomon," the "Morgeneseng" of Reichardt, and Beethoven's 8th symphony. (Sir) Jules Benedict was present at one of the rehearsals of this latter work when Mendelssohn conducted, and in his sketch of his friend's life he relates: "The admirable allegretto in B flat of this symphony not going at first to his liking, he remarked, smilingly, that he knew every one of the gentlemen engaged was capable of performing and even of composing a scherzo of his own; but that *just now* he wanted to hear Beethoven's, which he thought had some merits." It was cheerfully repeated. "Beautiful! charming!" cried Mendelssohn; "but still too loud in two or three instances. Let us take it again from the middle." "No, no," was the general reply of the band; "the whole piece over again for our own satisfaction;" and then they played it with the utmost delicacy and finish, Mendelssohn laying aside his *bâton* and listening with evident delight to the now perfect execution. "What would I have given," he exclaimed, "if Beethoven could have heard his own composition so well understood and so magnificently performed!"

The festival went off with great *éclat*, and as a memento of his visit, he was presented with a collection of Handel's works. Writing home, he says: "They really are so beautiful, that I am charmed with them; thirty-two great folios, bound in thick green leather in the regular nice English fashion, and on the back, in big gold letters, the title and contents of each volume; and in the first volume besides there are the following words —'To Director F. M. B., from the Committee of the Cologne Musical Festival, 1835.'"

On arriving home there awaited him an invitation to take the conductorship of the celebrated Gewandhaus Concerts, at Leipzig. This important post which Sebastian Bach, whom he revered so much, had filled a hundred years before, Mendelssohn accepted; yet not before a satisfactory arrangement had been concluded with his predecessor, Polenz, who, as a brother-artist, he desired to see treated with the utmost delicacy and consideration. On the 4th October, 1835, he was rehearsing his new orchestra for their first concert under his direction; and in writing home he does not omit to speak of his "good and thoroughly musical orchestra," and of the friendly disposition the people in Leipzig show for him and his music.

Now occurred one of those sad calamities which break upon us when we least expect them. In the midst of all this sunny life at Leipzig, came the sad tidings of the death of Mendelssohn's beloved father, on November 19th. His grief was intense at this mournful bereavement, and so depressed and downcast did he become, that all grew anxious for the once light-hearted, merry Felix. Writing to his friend, Pastor Schubring, Mendelssohn says: "It is the greatest misfortune that could have befallen me, and a trial that I must either strive to bear up against or utterly sink under. A new life must begin for me, or all must be at an end—the old life is now severed."

Yet, amidst all this trouble, he found a solace in his music. "I shall," he writes, "work with double zeal at 'St. Paul,' for my father urged me to it in the very last letter he wrote to me, and he looked forward very impatiently to the completion of my work. I feel as if I must exert all my energies to finish it, and make it as good as possible, and then think that he takes an interest in it." Soon it was finished, and its first performance took place at Düsseldorf on the 22nd May, 1836.

"How shall I give you an idea of the beauty of the work?" writes a distinguished friend of Mendelssohn's. "I shall keep to that word—Beauty; it best conveys the character of the music, which never makes an effort, never is strained to produce uncommon sensations or novel effects, but only develops quietly, honestly, devoutly, the grand subject it treats." He says: "The room, the garden surrounding, the people flowing in to hear, inside or outside, as they might—all this in a bright May day was festive and cheering. Fancy to yourself a long room, of good proportions (only too low), an orchestra containing three hundred and sixteen singers, and two hundred and twenty performers, and an audience of one thousand persons—the director's place a sort of pulpit decorated with a golden lyre. All orderly, well-regulated, and harmonious, it began at seven o'clock, and lasted two hours and a half. You can have no idea of the splendour of the performance. . . . When it was over the young ladies showered flowers and garlands on him; they crowned the score, and, if they had no more to say, and no further applause to bestow, it was only because they had sung it and talked of it constantly since the preparations for the festival began."

It is, indeed, a beautiful work—truly a masterpiece. Whether in its choruses, airs, or recitatives, there is still that sweetness so characteristic of this master. "Stone him to death!" "Oh! great is the depth," and its final one, are three of its finest choruses; while the oratorio abounds in treasures for tenor and bass voices. Its recitatives—these predominate somewhat—have never been excelled, and some of its airs are most exquisite. "But the Lord is mindful of His own;" the fine bass song, "I praise Thee, O Lord my God;" and that heavenly tenor aria, "Be thou faithful unto death," are among these. In "St. Paul" its composer has soared to the highest realms of his art, and has left a work worthy to be classed with the greatest oratorios—one which, not forgetting "Elijah," is the finest oratorio this mighty genius has given to the world.

Mendelssohn spent the summer of 1836 at Frankfort, and here it was that he first met his future bride, Cecilia Jean Renaud, the daughter of a Protestant clergyman. His friend Devrient says: "Cecilia was one of those sweet womanly natures, whose gentle simplicity, whose mere presence soothed and pleased. She was slight, with features of striking beauty and delicacy; her hair was between brown and gold, but the transcendent lustre of her great blue eyes, and the brilliant roses of her cheeks, were sad harbingers of early death. She spoke little, and never with animation, in a low, soft voice."

In the spring of the following year he was married to his lovely Cecilia at Frankfort, and after a delightful wedding trip along the Rhine, he, with his young wife, set out for Birmingham, whither he had been invited to conduct his oratorio, "St. Paul." Passing through London on his way thither, he just dropped in at Exeter Hall, where the Sacred Harmonic Society were performing it. He sat in the gallery by the side of (Sir) Jules Benedict. Before the performance was over his presence was discovered, and it was with some difficulty that he made his way out at its conclusion, so great was the crowd that showered their congratulations upon him.

His reception next day at Birmingham was one of the most enthusiastic he had ever received. "St. Paul" was produced, and, writes Mendelssohn, "the applause and shouts at the least glimpse of me were incessant, and sometimes really made me laugh."

After a long and uncomfortable journey, Mendelssohn and his wife arrived at their home in Leipzig, and amidst its repose and pleasant surroundings he poured out many fine compositions, the most notable of which are the majestic inspiration, "When Israel out of Egypt came," the "Ruy Blas" overture in C minor, with its vigorous and gorgeously rich instrumentation; and the trio in D minor for piano-forte, violin, and violoncello.

With the new year (1840) came "Lobgesang" (Hymn of Praise), written for the celebration of the fourth centenary of the Invention of Printing, held at Leipzig on the 25th June, 1840. Soon after its performance on this occasion, this splendid work was repeated at the Birmingham Festival. Truly is this an outpouring of thanks and praise for the blessing yielded to the world in the form of the great discovery it was written to celebrate. What more shall be said of its exquisite duet and chorus, "I waited for the Lord," than that for beauty, expression, and sublimity of conception, it would be impossible to excel it. The composer must truly have soared to the seventh heaven of musical art when he penned this divine melody. "Lobgesang" is a superb creation, teeming with its characteristic feeling of subdued thankfulness, which was the composer's intent. By some it is regarded as tame, by reason of its want of something more exulting or triumphant, but surely its composer knew the colouring and treatment such a work needed.

In the spring of 1841 Mendelssohn visited Berlin, whither he had been summoned by the King of Prussia, to undertake the directorship of the music class of the Academy of Arts, and to conduct the great instrumental concerts held at Berlin. After a long correspondence Mendelssohn accepted the offer, yet not without a feeling of distrust. His inaugural address to the Court of Berlin came in the shape of the incidental music to "Antigone," first performed on the 6th November, 1841, at the new palace at Potsdam, and the successful and learned manner in which Mendelssohn treated this tragedy of Sophocles was such as to gain the commendations of that great scholar, Bökh, who said "he found the music perfectly in harmony with his conceptions of Greek life and character, and with the muse of Sophocles."

The celebrated symphony in A minor, known as the "Scottish," is a work we must just glance at now. This masterly record of the impressions Mendelssohn received, when, with his friend Klingemann, he made the delightful tour amid the wild scenery of Scotland in 1829, did not appear till the beginning of 1842, when it was produced at one of the Berlin concerts. It next appeared at one of the Philharmonic concerts—that of June 13th, 1842; and the applause it elicited was such as to completely drown the music. This was especially the case after the conclusion of its charming scherzo movement—a form of composition in which Mendelssohn was always peculiarly happy—when, in accordance with the composer's intent, the next—the adagio—movement was to be immediately taken; but the audience had been worked up to the highest pitch of excitement, and their acclamations were so deafening that, notwithstanding the orchestra was far advanced in the adagio, Mendelssohn was compelled to repeat the merry scherzo, and allow his delighted audience to once more hear the beautiful movement, with its familiar tones of the bagpipes. The melancholy adagio movement is a grand inspiration, teeming with sorrowful expression, and with its martial accent so suggestive of a last tribute of respect to a departed loved one. The concluding movement is remarkable for its brilliant and fiery orchestration, and the effects produced in some parts by the vigorous tone and strong accent of the violins are such as must strictly be styled Mendelssohnian.

Another composition, which this same year claims the merit of producing, is the vigorous sonata in D major for piano-forte and violoncello, a work in which this mighty genius shines out in all his resplendence, whether this be in the exalted joy of its allegro movements, or in the sublime adagio, with its earnest solemnity, which is to be found in this peculiarly beautiful sonata.

Yet one more event to make this year a memorable one, was the death of Mendelssohn's dear mother, in the month of December. His grief was inconsolable at this sudden and unexpected calamity. "Now," he wrote to his brother, "the point of union is gone, where even as children we could always meet, and though we were no longer so in years, we felt that we were still so in feeling;" and so it was—with her gone, the parental home was no more.

Early in the new year Mendelssohn was busy arranging for the opening of the Leipzig Conservatorium, and on the 3rd April, 1843, this now world-famed institution was inaugurated. The prospectus displayed a brilliant staff of teachers, including Mendelssohn and Schumann for piano-forte and composition, Hauptmann for harmonium and counterpoint, David for the violin, Becker for the organ, and Polenz for singing, besides other well-known musicians who assisted these. Thus, with his duties here and at Berlin, Mendelssohn was well occupied. Yet he found time to produce many fine compositions this year, although the unsatisfactory state of things connected with his post at Berlin—"that tedious, everlasting affair," as he calls it—was such as to almost make him ill. Notwithstanding all this, his impetuous nature led him to London in the following season, where there was yet more exhausting excitement awaiting him. During this visit, Mendelssohn conducted six of the Philharmonic concerts, and a performance of "St. Paul," at Exeter Hall, besides appearing at Moscheles' farewell concert, at which an extempore cadenza was given by Mendelssohn, which, for grandeur of conception as well as for the power with which its prodigious difficulties were overcome, exceeded any parallel effort in the recollection of living musicians.

This long-continued stream of excitement was not without its effect upon Mendelssohn, and he felt that he must take repose. Accordingly he repaired to Soden, near Frankfort, where his family had been staying during his visit to London. "I found them all well," he wrote to a friend. "Cécile looks so well again. . . . The children are as brown as Moors, and play all day long in the garden." Here he had the whole day free, lying under apple-trees and huge oaks. "Oh!" he says, "if this could go on for ever!"

His compositions for this year are by no means few. Besides many beautiful songs, there are the two fine psalms, the forty-second and forty-third, for eight-part choirs, four of his grand organ sonatas, the overture to "Athalie," and also that splendid violin concerto in E minor, composed for his friend, Ferdinand David.

Passing over the year 1845, spent chiefly at Leipzig, we come to the production of the splendid cantata, "Lauda Sion," composed for a festival held in the church of St. Martin, Lüttich, which was followed by his great masterpiece, the "Elijah," first performed at the Birmingham Festival of 1846.

On the morning of August 26th, the noble Town Hall of Birmingham was crammed by some thousands of anxious listeners eager to hear this latest work from the great master's pen. Exactly at the appointed time, Mendelssohn was seen approaching his seat, and instantly there burst forth from the assembled thousands a deafening shout of applause, such as he had never before heard. The sublime work was gone through amid repeated bursts of enthusiasm from the delighted audience after each number, some of which Mendelssohn was compelled to repeat.

Madame Caradori Allen (soprano), Miss Hawes (contralto, Mr. Lockey (tenor), and Staudigl (bass), were the chief artists; but, excepting Staudigl, with his genuine bass voice, the composer laboured under a disadvantage in this respect upon this important occasion. However, "the orchestra," writes a reliable critic, "was throughout zealous and attentive to Mendelssohn's direction, and the chorus was upon the whole excellent; the freshness of the female voices especially telling to the utmost advantage in the grand and thrilling finale of the first part, 'Thanks be to God—He laveth the thirsty land,' one of the most marvellously characteristic specimens of descriptive writing that was ever imagined and worked out."

No sooner was the "Elijah" performed than the freshness and originality of its grand descriptive music, so religious in sentiment, laid hold of its audience, and ever since has continued to increase in popularity, till now it is second only to the "Messiah" in this respect.

It is so well known, that any mention of its merits seems superfluous: yet one is loth to pass from so grand a creation without some eulogy. All its choruses are superb and masterly in the extreme, eminently displaying the learning, the vast imagination, and characteristics of this mighty genius. What could be more impressive and more characteristic than the appeal of the

Baal-worshippers in those three splendid choruses, commencing, "Baal, we cry to thee?" There are others equally masterly, especially "Be not afraid," and the majestic one which concludes the oratorio, "Then shall your light." The whole part of Elijah, which is allotted to a bass voice, is exquisitely written, and notably so the energetic aria, "Is not his word," and Elijah's impressive request that he might die, contained in the fine adagio movement, "It is enough, O Lord; now take away my life." The two airs, "If with all your hearts," and "Then shall the righteous," have become universal favourites among tenor singers; while that pure melody, "O rest in the Lord," for contralto, is equally well known and admired. There is yet another number that must not be passed over, the terzetto, "Lift thine eyes," the song of the three angels who appeared to Elijah under the juniper-tree in the wilderness; and surely, for sweetness, grace, and beauty of expression, this exquisite trio is matchless. From beginning to end this oratorio is a succession of gems, while the immense power and imagination wherewith the mighty genius has grasped the scene on Mount Carmel, will ensure a hearing for this wonderful oratorio as long as music has a place assigned to her among the arts.

At its performance by the Sacred Harmonic Society, on the 23rd April, 1847, Exeter Hall was crammed by a most enthusiastic audience. Her Majesty the Queen and His Royal Highness the late Prince Consort were present, and the impression it made upon them is best told by the few words inscribed in the book of the oratorio which the prince used, and which he sent to Mendelssohn on the following day as a token of remembrance :—

"To the noble artist, who, surrounded by the Baal-worship of corrupted art, has been able by his genius and science to preserve faithfully, like another Elijah, the worship of true Art, and once more to accustom our ear, lost in the whirl of an empty play of sounds, to the pure notes of expressive composition and legitimate harmony; to the great master, who makes us conscious of the unity of his conception through the whole maze of his creation, from the soft whispering to the mighty raging of the elements— written in token of grateful remembrance, by
"ALBERT.
"Buckingham Palace,
"April 24th, 1847."

On the 8th May following, the great musician turned his steps towards Frankfort. This last visit to London had quite overpowered him. He had tried his strength too much. At Frankfort he was once more surrounded by his happy family; but no sooner had he arrived than there came the terrible news of the sudden death of his sister Fanny. With a fearful cry, Mendelssohn fell to the ground, nor did he ever quite recover from the dreadful shock this irretrievable loss caused him. His kind wife took him to Switzerland, and amid this pure air he seemed improved both in health and spirits. Yet he would not entirely give up work, for the sudden death of his father and mother, and now of his beloved Fanny, had possessed him with the presentiment that death was hanging over him. Alas! he did not see that year out.

He applied himself to composing with more activity than ever. Two great works were commenced—an oratorio, entitled "Christus," and the opera "Loreley," but they were destined never to be finished. What there is of the oratorio points to the belief that it would have been a most important conception of this great subject. "There shall be a star," and "Crucify Him," are glorious examples of what the choruses of this work would probably have been; also, there is sufficient of "Loreley" to prove how successful Mendelssohn would have been in this form of composition. Its "Ave Maria," the jovial "Vintage Song," and the spirited chorus of the finale to the first act, would alone insure its keeping the stage.

In September Mendelssohn returned to Leipzig, where he continued to work upon the "Christus," "Loreley," and some smaller pieces. Among these latter was the "Nachtlied" ("Night Song"); and on the 9th October he bore this to the house of Frau Frege, a distinguished amateur singer, who was generally the first interpreter of his inspirations. While accompanying her, a delirium came over him, and soon he was insensible. Deadly pale, and as cold as ice, poor Mendelssohn was borne to his home in the König-Strasse. Here he lay for some days, till about the 18th he was sufficiently restored to discourse upon his future plans. A second attack occurred soon after this, but he struggled over it, till about the 30th October he was seized for the last time. He remained unconscious up to the 3rd November, when he spoke a little. "Tired, very tired," he answered to Cécile's anxious inquiry as to how he felt. The next day convinced all that he could last but a short time longer. Surrounded by his wife and children, and a few of his most intimate friends, he passed peacefully away at nine o'clock in the evening.

The body was placed in a costly coffin, surrounded with tall shrubs and flowers, awaiting the day of the funeral. Then, amid thousands and thousands of spectators, the grand funeral procession passed through Leipzig to the church of the University, where an impressive service was performed. That same night his remains were carried to the family grave at Berlin, and, with the early morning sun shining over the coffin, it was lowered out of sight and sound. Side by side with his beloved sister Fanny, the thoughtful mourners placed Mendelssohn, and the earth closed over one of her fairest and most beloved children. Can we ever forget him?

PRINCIPAL INCIDENTS IN THE LIFE OF MENDELSSOHN.

Born at Hamburg on 3rd February	1809
Placed under Zelter for Theory	1819
Introduced to (Sir) Jules Benedict	1821
First Compositions	1821
C minor Symphony composed	1824
Taken to Paris to see Cherubini	1825
The "Wedding of Camacho" produced . . .	1825
The "Midsummer Night's Dream" Overture written	1827
The "Calm Sea" Overture composed . . .	1828
Bach's "Matthew-Passion" performed under Mendelssohn's Direction	1829
First Visit to England	1829
Visit to Italy	1830
The "Walpurgis Night" music composed . .	1830
Second Visit to England	1831
G minor Concerto produced	1831
Appointed Director at Düsseldorf	1833
Conductor of the Gewandhaus Concerts . . .	1835
"St. Paul" first performed at Düsseldorf . .	1836
"Lobgesang" first performed at Leipzig . .	1840
The Leipzig Conservatoire opened	1843
The Last Visit to England	1846
The "Elijah" performed at Birmingham . .	1846
Death of Mendelssohn	1847

Schumann.

ERE Mendelssohn had left his mother's arms, was born one who was destined for the same glorious calling as awaited that lovable child. Schumann was not so successful as young Mendelssohn; yet he followed his calling quite as nobly. The two chose different roads for the one great end: one achieved all in his lifetime, short though it was; the other, and his music, are only now receiving that recognition they so richly deserve. The "Music of the Future" had one of its founders and first exponents in Schumann, and in this school we may safely class most that he composed, for there is a romanticism about it, which, whatever may be said and written to the contrary, undeniably heralds a new era in art.

Only now is this music—this "work of art of the future"—beginning to assert itself, at any rate in England, and it has yet to become popular. Schumann's music certainly has not had its day. Will it ever become as universally known as it undoubtedly should? Will the strange characteristics of his style get to be understood and accepted—the wild beauty; the startling modulations he revels in; the eccentric changes of time and tone; the fantastic flights; the restless imagination pervading his works—in short, his whole nature exemplified in his works; will all this ever become clearer, better understood, and loved?

It was on the 8th June, 1810, that Robert Schumann surprised a quiet home, in the obscure town of Zwickau, in Saxony, where his father, August Schumann, was in business as a bookseller.

As soon as possible Robert was put to school, but he made no great impression as a scholar. In the playground, however, he was the favourite, and took the lead in all the boyish games and adventures.

Thanks to the education system in Germany, among his other studies was included music, and, when at the early age of eight or nine years, he received his first music-lessons from Kunsch, his wonderful aptitude for the art became known; they made a great impression on his excitable mind, and even at this age he attempted to put his ideas upon paper. Soon he got to be exceedingly clever on the piano. He could extemporize well, and was very happy at portraying scenes and characters through music, so that it was no uncommon thing to find him seated at the piano, and surrounded by schoolfellows bursting with laughter at the accurate manner in which he produced their portraits. But, in spite of all this, his parents had no great idea of making a musician of Robert; in fact, his mother was strongly opposed to it; her "star of hope," as she called him, was to be something better than a *virtuoso*.

With school studies still going on, with the burning love for music growing with him, Robert entered his seventeenth year. Then his father died.

Robert loved his mother, and she had unbounded influence over him. What wonder then that in 1829 he obeyed her wish, and entered the university at Leipzig as a student of law. But law to a born musician was dry work, and Robert soon felt this. To wit, there are his own words which he wrote to his guardian: "I have decided upon law as my profession, and will work at it industriously, however cold and dry the beginning may be."

The language of jurisprudence, however, was not to be understood like the language of music, and Schumann as good as told the learned Thibaut so, when, after one of the lectures, he went to his piano, and taking up Weber's "Invitation to the Waltz," played it, here and there remarking, "Now she speaks—that's the love prattle;" "Now he speaks—that's the man's earnest voice;" and further on, "Now both the lovers speak together," concluding with the remark, "Isn't all that far better than anything jurisprudence can utter?"

At length came the vacation weeks at the university, and these were to be occupied with a journey to Italy. The Italian language was rubbed up, and nothing hindered young Schumann from starting but money, which old Rudel, the guardian, seems to have parted with very sparingly. No doubt there was a cause. A most woful letter was written, which had the desired effect. The money came, and the trip was commenced. That he enjoyed the little excursion, his letters home plainly testify, There was only one drawback, and that concerned the finances, which Schumann never could manage, his ever-recurring thought being, "I shan't have enough, and shall have to pawn or sell my watch."

In November, 1829, he had returned. If music had been dear to him before, it was a thousand times dearer to him now. More than ever he devoted himself to his piano, and to the study of musical works, and soon Heidelberg began to talk of Schumann. But, just as he was in the ascendant, came a freak of his strange nature. A most successful *début* had been made, invitations were flowing in from all directions, when of a sudden the fellow drew himself aloof, refused to accept any of them, and would play nowhere but in the circle of his most intimate friends. Sullen and determined beyond measure was he in this.

Things went on till the beginning of 1830. The studies that he had been sent to Leipzig and Heidelberg for, had not been pursued, and but little progress was made in anything but music. What would be his mother's feelings on hearing this? Only a few months more, too, and the confession must be made.

At last it came—a loving letter to his mother—confessing and breathing all the struggle between music and law; full of his ardent love for music; assurances of success, and betraying the excited youth—with his strange uncertain nature just verging into manhood—waiting eagerly for that word of permission, ere he plunges into the fray to win for himself a place in art.

The answer. What was it? Consent? Yes! but not until the distressed parent had applied to Wieck for his opinion. Happily this was favourable to music. It was communicated to Robert, who, intoxicated with joy, at once wrote off to Wieck. "Take me as I am," the letter runs, "and above all things bear with me. No blame shall depress me; no praise shall make me idle. Pails upon pails of very cold theory cannot hurt me, and I will work at it without the least murmur."

No time was lost. Preparations were begun, and by Michaelmas of this eventful year, young Schumann was in lodgings in the same house that Wieck occupied, 36, Grimmisch Street, Leipzig.

A more anxious student never breathed. The zeal with which he pursued the studies his teacher gave him was astonishing. Alas! he was far too ardent. To make a short cut to perfection of execution, he, aided or unaided, invented a machine and used it so incessantly that he crippled his hand for life. How sad a sight! Schumann, with this great gulf betwixt him and his highest hope. Shall *we* lament this?

Now all his darling aspirations as a pianist must be banished. What should he go to? Still did the young fellow cling to his beloved art. To be a composer was now his hope, and at the age of twenty he made the first steps on this long and difficult road.

His first master in theory was one Kupsch, but shortly afterwards he gave place to Heinrich Dorn, under whom great progress was made.

Passing on to 1833, for there is little that needs to be mentioned in the interim, a sad incident has to be told. This alas! is nothing less than the first outbreak of that mortal disease which terminated so terribly. A sister-in-law died late in the year, and this greatly affected Schumann. One night he could not be left alone. An old friend was sent for to stay up with him, and it is said that he attempted to throw himself from his window on this occasion. Before long the symptoms disappeared, but never again would the poor fellow live on an upper floor, and the terror of that night, "the dreadful night of the 17th October," was never forgotten. Alas! this was the beginning of the end!

The year 1834 Schumann says "was the most remarkable of his life," and no doubt it was. Then the "Neue Zeitschrift für Musik" was inaugurated—the journal which was to pave the way for his ideal music, and to be the organ for disseminating the views of a party of enthusiastic art-students bent on a reform in art, and of lifting it to the poetical and the ideal. Among its earliest contributors were Wieck, Schunke, Knorr, Banck, and Schumann, the latter writing under the pseudonyms of Florestan or Eusebius. This journal flourished wondrously and gave Schumann plenty to do for a long while after its starting.

There was a love affair also, this year. In Wieck's house he came across Ernestine von Fricken, for whom he conceived a most passionate love. But this did not last long: it cooled down, and two years afterwards a parting was mutually agreed upon.

His next love was Clara Wieck. She was in her

ninth year when Schumann first met her in her father's house, and his admiration of her then had grown with him. Now (1836) she had reached the years of womanhood, and as he puts it, "loves and is loved." But papa Wieck was strongly opposed to this, and forbade all intercourse. Moreover, he took Clara on a journey, and Schumann was left to pine for his love. In time matters became more pleasant for Schumann, for the once angry objections dwindled down to one of waiting till they could earn more money, so as to live comfortably.

No doubt it was this that spurred our young artist on to make the effort he did, to establish himself and his journal in Vienna. Despite all exertion, however, the change did not prove a success; and after a trial of eighteen months or so, Schumann in 1839 returned to Leipzig, a wiser if not a happier man.

Here ends his first period, the "storm-period" as he was wont to call these years of preparation and transition, and here perhaps is as fitting a place as any, to glance at the creative side of these earliest years of his artist life—that is, the works they gave birth to.

These are neither numerous nor valuable, if we except the "Fantasias," the "Scenes of Childhood," the "Etudes Symphoniques," and the "Kreisleriana,"—works breathing all his ideal originality and characteristics, abounding in strange and fanciful beauties, uncertain figures and modulations, but nevertheless evidently well under the firm and strong sway of Heinrich Dorn's tuition. In these works the impulsive Schumann is seen like an unbroken steed, full of valuable qualities, but unruled, now revelling in wild freaks and movements, now submissive and quiet.

This, however, was the transition from disorder to order. Hitherto his music had been composed at the piano-forte regardless of the theory and rules of composition; and this erring path he trod till it could carry him no farther. Now came a new order of things. The straight but only sure road to the desired goal had been made under Dorn's supervision, treatises which should have been mastered in boyhood were pored over; and at the age of thirty years he completed studies which should have formed the occupation of his youth. Robert Schumann, however, was a rare and original genius, determined and persevering in character, and prolific in mind, hence he was enabled to gain the position in art that he now holds.

The remaining compositions of this first period are the "Abegg variations:" "The Papillons;" the "Paganini Capricios;" "The Carnival;" two sonatas, in F sharp minor and G minor,—the former, a work stamped with genius of the highest order, and of sublime beauty in many parts; some fughettas, and other small pieces.

The year 1840 marks the beginning of a second period—one which we may term as *classical*. It was brief, certainly not extending beyond 1846, but it was very productive of works, and these evince remarkable improvement in every way; brought about no doubt by some of those events which the continuation of his biography will make us familiar with.

Early this year the University of Jena conferred the degree of Doctor of Philosophy upon Schumann—an honour which he had long coveted, though he belonged to many other learned Societies at this time. But an event greater than this occurred.

On the 12th September the long looked for marriage with Clara Wieck took place at a little country church near Leipzig. Won she was, after sore troubles and long waiting. What happiness this union brought him has frequently been the subject of his own pen and lips, and the world knows how she, the mother of his children, has battled for her husband's inspirations, how she understands them better than any living being, and how she has striven to this very day to make them more and more known.

After his marriage, Schumann sank into the retirement of his home, and worked incessantly. The joy and happiness of so bright a year found vent chiefly in song. Nothing short of the human voice could suffice to express the agitated joy he was in, and for this most divine instrument there gushed from his soul a stream of rich lyric melody which has never been approached except by Beethoven and Schubert. Well may this be called the "year of song;" for, ere it waned nearly one hundred and fifty of these inspirations saw the light. They are full of pathos and breathe all the higher emotions and lofty aspirations the soul is heir to. His favourite poet was Heine, and so often has he drawn upon this *repertoire*, and so congenial a rendering of the poet's sentiments has he embodied in his music, that he has got to be known as Heine's musical exponent.

Following these lyric compositions he essayed a yet higher stage of artistic form. He turned to the orchestra: and ere he left it, succeeded in rendering it so subservient to his immense imagination as to unquestionably entitle his works to a place among the most gigantic efforts contributed to this phase of art. True it is that in these more perfect of Schumann's productions, we occasionally come across vague passages, crudities, and novelty giving place to beauty. But may we not rather regard such specks on the ocean as resulting more from his magnified idea of art, of his belief in the illimitable sphere and capability of music to express anything poor human nature could conceive, than from any premeditated desire to upset old, or to invent new, theories of music? This certainly was never Schumann's desire after his youthful excitement had cooled down. It might have been so before, while his contempt for rules existed; but, when this sort of theory could carry him no farther, when he found that a technical basis must be laid, that rules must be learnt and observed, and more than ever when all this drudgery had been overcome, a more zealous advocate for the observance and veneration of rules could not be found. Besides, did he not take his earlier works and remove from them all the eccentricities of his youthful enthusiasm for the poetical and ideal?

Nevertheless, the Futurists have this satisfaction. Whatever Robert Schumann's opinions may, or may not have been, his music from first to last undeniably belongs to that school which now has Richard Wagner at its head. It *does* overstep the generally accepted boundary, and to them it matters not whether this is with its composer's will or not. Schumann in the period from 1840 may not have intended this, nay, he may have been strongly opposed to it, but as to this affecting the Futurists' claim to him as a champion of their school it certainly does not.

Of all composers he certainly is the most advanced, the most difficult to understand, the most daring in flight, the one most clearly betraying the mental excitement that attended upon work, and which no doubt frequently lifted him to regions where had he been less susceptible he could never have soared to.

The symphony in B flat, op., 38, was the first contribution to this new form. It is one of four great orchestral works which are universally accepted as masterpieces. Written soon after his marriage, it teems with vivacity and joy, happiness is reflected on every page; notably, for instance, is this the case, in the *allegro molto vivace* movement. Following this comes the *larghetto*, brimful of the most impassioned melody, and abounding in the fanciful individualities of its composer. The remaining movements are strikingly beautiful, and exceedingly rich in those little inventions and deviations which Schumann has made so completely his own. Compared with his other symphonies this one is unquestionably the least original, the most restrained and free from peculiarities, and the most popular of the set.

It was first performed at one of the Gewandhaus concerts at Leipzig on 6th December, 1841.

Between this and the second symphony, the "Overture, Scherzo and Finale "—a kind of symphony without a slow movement—came to light. This is a most pleasing work of art, fanciful, and rich in grace and spirit.

The one in D minor should really be recognized as the second of the symphonies; for though it was not completed till 1851, yet it was fully planned and sketched ten years earlier. Looking at it as a whole, it is the least interesting of the four, partly from the unhappy nature of some of the subjects treated, as well as from a seeming longing and striving for originality and effect, and from an evident want of fixed conception in his work. Nevertheless, it contains indescribable beauties. Take for instance the Romanze in A minor immediately succeeding the Allegro. What could be more beautiful than this movement? It is the most delightful one in the composition, and with its various elegant episodes, so artistically treated, never fails to please all hearers.

In the first sketch of the work there was a guitar employed in this movement, but Schumann discarded it in his revised score. Some of the effects produced, too, are very striking. One of the most noticeable is that which occurs about half-way through the trio in B flat, where there is a wavering and gradual dying away of the parts, to a seeming standstill; till suddenly the *tempi* is resumed with the wind instruments and goes on as if nothing in the least out of the ordinary had happened. But many other equally good points do not atone for the general character of the composition.

The other important works composed about this time were the three beautiful quartets, so greatly esteemed by all lovers of chamber music; that most perfect composition, taking it all in all, that ever flowed from Schumann's pen, the piano quintet in E flat major; and a piano quartet, little below the quintet in lofty expression and freshness, and in the exquisite finish which pervades it.

Lastly, there was the so-called profane oratorio, "Paradise and the Peri." This came to light under the following circumstances.

One of his schoolmates had still retained the love for translating poetry which he and Schumann used to practise together. The latest effort was this selection from Moore's "Lalla Rookh," which Schumann was to set to music. It was completed: but critics are far from agreeing that Schumann has left a perfect work. In spite of the warm and appropriate colouring which pervades the whole, the beautiful passages and the rich flow of melody, the want of dramatic conception is painfully apparent. Moreover, the voice parts are not always happy, and the orchestration is frequently too thick and heavy. It was first performed at Leipzig under its composer's direction on the 4th December, 1843, when Frau Frege created the "Peri" *rôle*.

The year 1844 brought Schumann out of his shell. A journey to Russia had been agreed upon by the artist couple, and now he did not care to move. "Forgive me," runs a letter to a friend, "if I forbear telling you of my unwillingness to leave my quiet home." At length, however, the two set out, and arrived at St. Petersburgh safely. A most pleasant reception awaited them. The emperor and empress frequently had them at the Winter Palace, and were very enthusiastic about Madame Schumann's piano-forte playing. Concerts were given, and all the musicians were most friendly to them.

On the return from this journey in the summer, a plan conceived while he was away was actually executed by Schumann. This was nothing less than the giving up of all connection with the "Journal for Music."

A severe return of ill-health was the cause of this retirement from literary work; but, alas! this step did not stay the disease. The alarming symptoms increased, and ere the year was out, Leipzig was changed for Dresden as a residence. A close application to work at this time did not improve his condition, but no other subject than music would do for his artist mind. His doctor advised diversionary studies; but, no, these gave way in every instance to composition. The absorbing work of interest was nothing less than the music to the epilogue of Göthe's "Faust." He was in a miserable condition when he completed this, and suffering from all the premonitory symptoms of his terrible malady.

The next year was productive of little, save some studies in fugue and counterpoint, and, excepting the C major symphony, the following one (1846) was equally as uninteresting.

This last-mentioned work is the third of the symphonies. It was written in the early part of 1846, when its composer was suffering severe physical pain. "Through it," he says, "I sought to contend against my disease." Nevertheless, it must not be supposed that in the least this had influenced the work. It is a colossal musical structure, and quite worthy the great name that has reared it. A special feature of it is its somewhat profound allegro movement, so grandly energetic in its first part, but in its second far more diffuse, rugged, and restless. What shall be said, too, of the composer's contrapuntal powers as exhibited in this movement? The scherzo comes next, and a most interesting and lively movement it is, revealing a wealth of ingenious invention, a rare and prolific gift of rich melody, and a command and knowledge of the orchestra as masterly as the music is sublime. Yet, to our mind, the adagio, in C minor, is the gem of the work. Occurring immediately after the sprightly scherzo, its dreamy and expressive tones contrast boldly with those of the preceding movement. From beginning to end it is full of the most tender and beautiful music, enriched with numerous little forms and effects, thoroughly Schumannish.

A romanticism, too, pervades it, which, while easily perceptible, does not approach to mysticism. Its closing bars are quite original, and contain some pleasing and very striking harmonies. A well-developed *finale*, bold and vigorous in character, closes the work.

We reach Schumann's third period, and find it bearing no little resemblance to the first, displaying, as it does, all that romanticism, that disregard of keeping within bounds, that fantastic and restless fervency, which characterize his earliest works.

"Genevieve" should come first in the new category.

After a deal of indecision, this subject was chosen for an opera. It was in 1847 that Schumann set to work upon his score, and it took eighteen months to complete.

Not long after this, it was brought out at Leipzig, under the composer's direction, and was a complete failure. Time has not altered this decision, and probably never will; for, notwithstanding the sublimity of some of the music, it lacks qualities absolutely essential for a successful opera. There is too much detail, and a want of that broad dramatic treatment of the whole, which is a *sine quâ non*. Besides, the old fault in writing for voices is also to be met with here; so that altogether Schumann's first and last opera incontestably proves his incapacity in this sphere, and that he really has little claim to rank in it.

Many other works were produced during this year (1848), but the "Manfred" music is all that can be touched upon here.

Unfortunately, this music has not yet been given in its entirety in England; but, thanks to Mr. Manns, three or four numbers of it were produced at the Crystal Palace afternoon concert of April 25th, 1874. Then the "Invocation of the Alpine Witch," the hymn, "Hail to our Master," sung by the attendant spirits of Arimanes, and the passage in the course of which Manfred addresses his beloved Astarte, were heard for the first time by an English audience, and notwithstanding that on this occasion Schumann's music lacked the advantage of scenic surroundings, the great beauty and dramatic power of these pieces seemed apparent to all.

If, therefore, the remaining numbers—for there are

fifteen—are of the same quality as those performed at this concert, it becomes more than ever difficult to conceive how Schumann could have so signally failed in his first attempt at dramatic composition. Possibly "Genevieve" may not have interested its composer so much as Byron's powerful subject did, and if so, all who are acquainted with the setting of words, will understand the probable effect this would have. "Manfred" was a very congenial subject. The wild, restless, and distracted hero, Schumann could follow in all his wanderings, and, with the affinity which one cannot help noticing between the two natures, would be sure to be led away in the awful tragic flights the self-tormenting hero takes. Such, indeed, was the case. Schumann was alarmingly affected while engaged upon this subject, and on one occasion it is said that he was reading the poem aloud to two friends in Düsseldorf, when of a sudden his voice faltered, he burst into tears, and was so overcome that he could read no farther.

The next year was a prolific one. Work after work followed each other, till the list grew long with books of songs, marches, pieces for the piano, numerous compositions for solo and combined instruments, small vaudevilles, and part of the "Faust" music. To dwell upon each of these is impossible. With a sincere wish that many, or all of them, will ere long be heard, and become known in England, they must for the present be left to that people amongst whom they were inspired and written.

It was May, 1850, before the "Faust" music received its final touches, and even then the overture added in 1853 was wanting. All writers—except, perhaps, the late Mr. Chorley, who never would look over Schumann's mannerisms—agree as to the extreme beauty of this music to Göthe's immortal scenes. Many go still further, and aver that Schumann's music has enabled them for the first time to fathom the poet's intentions. The first performance of it in its entirety took place at Cologne, on the 14th January, 1862.

Before the year 1850 had gone by, Schumann was offered the post of director of music, which Ferdinand Hiller had vacated, at the Institute of Düsseldorf. He accepted it, but, alas! it was a fatal step. The correspondence between himself and Hiller betrays the sad state of his health, and the ever-present fear of his impending fate. Thus the presence of a lunatic asylum in Düsseldorf caused him great distress of mind, and was one of his objections to taking the new post. A passage from a letter shows how it troubled him. "I was looking recently in an old guide-book for information about Düsseldorf, and, among other buildings, found three nunneries and a lunatic asylum. To the first I am indifferent, but the last causes me great uneasiness."

Nor was his health alone against him. He lacked qualities which a successful conductor must possess. He was too reserved, silent, and moody, so that frequently he was misunderstood by those about him. Disorder appeared in the chorus and orchestra, as, consequent upon the progress of the nervous hypochondria, the leader gradually grew inattentive to his duties. Then the Committee offered a temporary rest to Schumann, which, however, was misunderstood. At the following rehearsal he did not appear, and so closed his connexion with a post he had occupied three years, and which his fame and great creative powers alone entitled him to thus long.

"We must work while the daylight lasts," wrote Schumann a few years before his death, and this feeling seems to have prompted him during his first years at Düsseldorf, so numerous are the compositions of that time.

First in importance is the E flat symphony, op. 97, the last of the four, known also as "the Rhenish," from Schumann's habit of saying that it was suggested by the sight of the Cologne Cathedral, and by a grand and impressive ceremony he witnessed within its walls. Strange to say, it contains five movements, and further differs from its predecessors by having no introduction before its first movement. This, however, is not to be regretted, for nothing could be more grandly noble and impressive than the manner in which the first vivace of this symphony enters upon its subject, with the full power of the band. As it proceeds, a sublime tone-painting is unfolded. The second subject is heralded in due course by the wind instruments, and a most charming and melodious theme it is. Page after page of what is known as the "free fantasia" then follows, and the whole of this remarkably beautiful movement closes with a vigorous coda. The scherzo follows, but, instead of at once partaking of the vivacity common to it, it leads off with a dreamy and most enchanting melody, marked *molto moderato*. It grows more playful, however, as it progresses. The clever imitations, the piquant staccato passages, the fanciful touches the composer has given to this movement, all tend to gain for it new admirers whenever it is performed, and seldom does this occur without an enthusiastic *encore* being the inevitable result.

The third movement of this symphony is in the relative key of A flat, and is of the most unpretending character. It consists of three chaste and beautiful subjects, delicately treated for a light orchestra, but its peaceful and somewhat sad character causes an impression which happily does not vanish with the last notes of the delightful music.

The "Feierlich"—the fourth movement—opens in a slow and religious manner, and, as a whole, is intended to portray the impression its composer received on witnessing the enthronement of Archbishop Geissel to the rank of cardinal. It is grandiose, very impressive, and bears an antique ecclesiastical character. The resources of fugue and counterpoint are appealed to, as being fitted, by their severity, for the solemn occasion treated of. How successful Schumann has been it is hard to decide. The writer has thrice heard the movement in question, and still thinks, with a high authority, that "it is one requiring considerable familiarity before a definite opinion can be given on it."

The concluding movement of this fine tone-work is exactly opposite in character to that which precedes it. The listener is carried, as it were, outside the great Cologne edifice. The crowd of holiday folks are jostling by, and the merry dance-like character of the music leaves no doubt as to their general feelings. All is bright and enticing, and Schumann, for one, cannot be said to have missed the spirit of the gay and lively scene around him. A short but very animated stretto closes the symphony in a very effective style.

It was first performed at a Düsseldorf subscription concert, on 6th February, 1851.

The "Julius Cæsar" overture, op. 128, belongs to 1851, a very productive year. It is a grand and majestic composition, martial in character, and depending upon broad effects for its success, rather than upon the great beauty of its melodies. The tromboni and corni. have some very effective passages assigned to them, which tell out wonderfully fine as the time gradually quickens and concludes the overture in a brilliant and masterly manner.

Other works of this and the following year were the "Pilgrimage of the Rose"; the "King's Son"; the setting of Uhland's "Minstrel's Curse"; the "Bride of Messina," and "Hermann and Dorothea" overtures; the playful "Children's Ball" pieces; some Latin church music; and many more, too numerous to mention.

Little more remains to be told. There were a few works in 1853, alas! the last flow of melody from this precious fount. Schumann could work no longer. Slowly, but most surely, had the terrible disease crept upon him. It was soon to overpower its victim. This year the symptoms increased alarmingly. The poor fellow could not hear music performed without feeling that the time was too fast, and, when conducting, insisted upon his painful error being observed. This was not all. A continual drone of the note A pursued him wherever he went. He spent much time in table-tapping, which excited him to the highest pitch of frenzy. He imagined spirits conversing with him day and night, and on one occasion rose from his bed to write out a theme the departed Schubert and Mendelssohn had sent him! To friends he behaved with great apathy, and sometimes failed to recognize those most intimate with him. Who then will wonder or blame the immortal master, for seeking to drown his miseries from one of the Rhine bridges?

Such was the case, but he was saved; and the townsfolk saw an affecting sight on that spring morning of 1854. There was the world-famed Schumann, who in health, had been so calm and dignified in his bearing, being borne along, saved from a watery grave. Yet, for what? At Endenich, near Bonn, there was a private mad-house, and there he was sent.

For a while he corresponded with his wife, but this soon ceased, together with visits from his friends, so excited and worse did they make the master. A piano-forte often occupied his attention, but the playing was strange and unintelligible, and no music came from a soul which once had been so rich in harmony.

On the 29th July, 1856, a summons came from above. At four o'clock in the afternoon, in the presence of his wife, his spirit parted from its weary frame, for that peaceful and eternal home, where it can ever rest.

Schumann.

Principal Incidents in the Life of Schumann.

Born at Zwickau, 8th June	1810
First Lessons from Kunsch	1818
Designed for a Lawyer	1829
Adopted Music as a Profession	1830
The "Neue Zeitschrift für Musik" started	1834
Made a Doctor of Philosophy	1840
The B flat Symphony composed	1841
"Paradise and the Peri" first performed	1843
The C major Symphony composed	1846
"Geneviéve" written and first performed	1848
The "Manfred" Music composed	1848
The "Faust" Music composed	1850
Director of the Düsseldorf Concerts	1850
The E flat Symphony completed	1851
Placed in the Endenich Asylum	1853
Died, 29th July	1856

THE END.

www.ingramcontent.com/pod-product-compliance
Lightning Source LLC
Chambersburg PA
CBHW022333230426
43664CB00040B/476